SEX AND THE COLLEGE GIRL

Also by Gael Greene

DON'T COME BACK WITHOUT IT

SEX AND THE COLLEGE GIRL

BY *GAEL GREENE*

A DELACORTE PRESS BOOK

The Dial Press / New York

1964

This book is dedicated to . . .

DON CONGDON, as generous, intelligent and demanding as an editor should be.

and to . . .

DON FORST, lover, keeper, buffer, playmate, healer, magician and champion.

CONTENTS

Introduction by Max Lerner   9

The Colleges   13

Author's Note: Kid Gloves and Confessions   17

The Questions   27

1   Even Nice Girls   33

2   College: Challenge to Chastity   49

    I LOVE YOU FOR EXPERIMENTAL REASONS   68

3   Geography of the Sex Revolution   77

    MARSHMALLOW HUNG-UP ON A HOT

    VOLCANO   100

4   To Each Her Own Morality   107

    COME LIVE WITH ME AND BE MY LOVE   124

5   A New Style of Chastity   130

    SNOW MEN, YOU'RE MELTING ME   144

6   Sex as Hobby, Obsession, Part-time Profession   150

    "ARE YOU A VIRGIN?" "NOT YET"   159

7   The Men—and Boys—in Her Life   165

    AND THEN HE BLUSHED   184

8   Birth Control: The Numbers Game   188

    I MYSELF GET KIND OF SAD   202

CONTENTS

9   *Babies and Abortions*   206

     A VISIT TO A SHY ABORTIONIST   222

10   *Now, What Were You Saying, Miss Sarah*
    Blanding?   229

     BIBLIOGRAPHY   247

     RELATED FICTION   255

INTRODUCTION

If you are a college male or female, a teacher or school administrator, a parent, a social scientist, a moralist or a novelist —or if you just want to know about the new generation of American *jeunes filles* for the Hell of it—then this is your book. I don't commend it to any of tender age, or to any of mature age who have tender minds and sensitivities. For Miss Greene has a fine ear for the argot of campus sex talk and at times it is rough going. But having taught at a half-dozen of the colleges covered by the author's interviews, and lectured at all but a handful, I must say that the sexual profile she draws of the college girl today strikes me as authentic.

It is of a new type of adolescent, no longer girl, not yet woman, never lady, but by every sign a revolutionary. The old codes will not do for her: in fact, she has largely broken communications with her parents, who in turn present her neither with credible codes nor credible examples of a working model of love and sex. She must experiment for herself, spurred and supported by her fellows—"the club," "the gang" —as her prod and prop. She is riddled with anxieties, determined to belong, fearful of being left behind—by the boys, by the rival girls, by fun, by popularity, by experience, by marriage, by life. She plays it cool, yet is boastful of her sexual drive and hedonism. She has discarded the traditional moral absolutes, living in a world of relativism that at once frees her from the old restraints yet leaves her pathetically floundering with little sense of limits. When she tries to apply "wait until marriage" as her frame of limits, the boys mock her and she panics at the fear of being outdistanced in the competition. When she tries to apply the "everything but—" standard, either through parental teaching or through fear of pregnancy, she is cursed as a teaser or ends in a tangle of contradictions, missing expressiveness and morality at once.

Her world is that of motels, parked cars, drive-in movies, fraternity houses, dormitory rooms during "parietal" hours, apartments loaned for the weekend. It is a world of interminable talk that wears away the edge of pleasure as well as of resistance, of continuing self-analysis, of "all the decisions, the decisions." It is a world of buzzing booming internal confusion, of sex without bed, of bed without love, of hedonism without joy. It is a world where the knowing often have little true knowledge, a twilight world of psychological counseling that comes too late, of pregnancies that are meant either as marriage-snare or self-punishment, of collection parties to pay for the abortion, of breakdowns and even of suicides.

Amidst it all the girl is often left hungry: she has sex but she is hungry for affection. Sometimes this is an improvement on her mother at college, who didn't have either. College girls once traded the promise of sex for a promise of marriage: they now trade the currency of sex for some modicum of affection, college status, security. The trading mentality persists.

Miss Greene sorts out the welter of evidence, draws the picture. She does not pretend to give answers. That must be left to the culture, in the way it shapes the totality of its life-purposes and communicates them to its best young people. My own hope is that they will continue to be revolutionaries, but in a more satisfying way: that they will have less anxiety and more uniqueness of expression, less calculation and more sense of their own personal frame of limits and commitment, less cool hedonism and more joyousness.

Toward such a goal I bid this book Godspeed.

—Max Lerner

THE COLLEGES

Alabama, University of (*University, Ala.*)
American University, The (*Washington, D.C.*)
Amherst College (*Amherst, Mass.*)
Antioch College (*Yellow Springs, Ohio*)
Bard College (*Annandale-on-Hudson, N.Y.*)
Barnard College (*New York City*)
Bennington College (*Bennington, Vt.*)
Boston University (*Boston, Mass.*)
Bowdoin College (*Brunswick, Me.*)
Brandeis University (*Waltham, Mass.*)
Brooklyn College (*New York City*)
Brown University (*Providence, R.I.*)
Bryn Mawr College (*Bryn Mawr, Pa.*)
California, University of (*Berkeley, Cal.*)

/ 13

California, University of (*Los Angeles, Cal.*)
California, University of (*Santa Barbara, Cal.*)
Chicago, University of (*Chicago, Ill.*)
City College of New York (*New York City*)
Colby College (*Waterville, Me.*)
Colorado, University of (*Boulder, Col.*)
Columbia University (*New York City*)
Connecticut College for Women (*New London, Conn.*)
Connecticut, University of (*Storrs, Conn.*)
Cooper Union (*New York City*)
Cornell University (*Ithaca, N.Y.*)
Dartmouth College (*Hanover, N.H.*)
Delaware, University of (*Newark, Del.*)
Denison University (*Granville, Ohio*)
DePauw University (*Greencastle, Ind.*)
Eastern Michigan University (*Ypsilanti, Mich.*)
Elmira College (*Elmira, N.Y.*)
Endicott Junior College (*Beverly, Mass.*)
Florida, University of (*Gainesville, Fla.*)
George Washington University (*Washington, D.C.*)
Goucher College (*Towson, Md.*)
Harvard University (*Cambridge, Mass.*)
Hofstra College (*Hempstead, N.Y.*)
Hollins College (*Hollins College, Va.*)
Hunter College (*New York City*)
Illinois, University of (*Urbana, Ill.*)
Indiana University (*Bloomington, Ind.*)
Iowa State University (*Iowa City*)
Kalamazoo College (*Kalamazoo, Mich.*)
Kent State University (*Kent, Ohio*)
Long Island University (*Brooklyn and Nassau County, N.Y.*)
Louisiana State University (*Baton Rouge, La.*)
Mary Baldwin College (*Staunton, Va.*)
Marygrove College (*Detroit, Mich.*)
Maryland, University of (*College Park, Md.*)

Marymount College (*Tarrytown, N.Y.*)
Miami, University of (*Coral Gables, Fla.*)
Michigan State University (*East Lansing, Mich.*)
Michigan, University of (*Ann Arbor, Mich.*)
Middlebury College (*Middlebury, Vt.*)
Mills College (*Oakland, Cal.*)
Minnesota, University of (*Minneapolis, Minn.*)
Mississippi, University of (*University, Miss.*)
Mount Holyoke College (*South Hadley, Mass.*)
New York University (*New York City*)
Northwestern University (*Evanston, Ill.*)
Oberlin College (*Oberlin, Ohio*)
Ohio State University (*Columbus, Ohio*)
Ohio University (*Athens, Ohio*)
Oregon State University (*Corvallis, Ore.*)
Pembroke College (*Providence, R.I.*)
Pennsylvania State University (*University Park, Pa.*)
Pennsylvania, University of (*Philadelphia, Pa.*)
Pittsburgh, University of (*Pittsburgh, Pa.*)
Princeton University (*Princeton, N.J.*)
Purdue University (*Lafayette, Ind.*)
Queens College (*New York City*)
Radcliffe College (*Cambridge, Mass.*)
Reed College (*Portland, Ore.*)
Rochester, University of (*Rochester, N.Y.*)
Rollins College (*Winter Park, Fla.*)
Rutgers, The State University (*New Brunswick, N.J.*)
San Diego State College (*San Diego, Cal.*)
Sarah Lawrence College (*Bronxville, N.Y.*)
Shimer College (*Mt. Carroll, Ill.*)
Simmons College (*Boston, Mass.*)
Skidmore College (*Saratoga Springs, N.Y.*)
Smith College (*Northampton, Mass.*)
Southern California, University of (*Los Angeles, Cal.*)
Stanford University (*Palo Alto, Cal.*)

Swarthmore College (*Swarthmore, Pa.*)

Sweet Briar College (*Sweet Briar, Va.*)

Syracuse, University of (*Syracuse, N.Y.*)

Temple University (*Philadelphia, Pa.*)

Texas, University of (*Austin, Tex.*)

Texas Women's University (*Denton, Tex.*)

Trinity College (*Washington, D.C.*)

Vanderbilt University (*Nashville, Tenn.*)

Vassar College (*Poughkeepsie, N.Y.*)

Vermont, University of (*Burlington, Vt.*)

Wayne University (*Detroit, Mich.*)

Wellesley College (*Wellesley, Mass.*)

Wesleyan University (*Middletown, Conn.*)

Western Reserve University (*Cleveland, Ohio*)

Wheelock College (*Boston, Mass.*)

Williams College (*Williamstown, Mass.*)

Wisconsin, University of (*Madison, Wis.*)

Yale University (*New Haven, Conn.*)

AUTHOR'S NOTE:
Kid Gloves and Confessions

This book is a prologue to a study that has not yet been under-
taken—a study of the sexual attitudes and sexual behavior of
the American college girl. This book is not science. It is not
sociology. It is not statistical analysis. It is a journalistic report
on love and sex as the college girl sees it, and as she revealed
it, in word and without word, in group interviews and after-
curfew dormitory gab sessions, in campus coffee shops and
outside university libraries, in sorority house recreation rooms
(over the turmoil of homecoming weekend display construction), in between dates or lack of dates during Christmas
vacation, over hamburgers, cider, and potato chips in the living room of my premedical-student brother's off-campus
apartment in Ann Arbor, Michigan, in the wood and stone
Gothic of a main floor lounge in Wellesley's Beebe Hall and in

a secluded corner at a University of California (Berkeley) professor's Sunday evening "at home."

Six hundred and fourteen students from 102 colleges and universities throughout the country were interviewed: 418 girls in small groups, another 53 individually, and 76 college men. I began the interviewing in New York, traveled extensively in the East with its heavy concentration of colleges and universities and then made a series of one- and two-day stops at campuses in the Middle West, Far West, South and Atlantic seaboard states. Student interviewers, working with a list of suggested questions (see p. 27), interviewed another 67 girls on 18 campuses, submitting typed or tape-recorded reports.

There are statistics here but none is culled from this research. The behavorial scientists, the professional computers of opinion and the orgasm counters, the guilt-measurers and those trained to translate potential for falsehood into algebraic formulae, are quoted here and possibly I would have been more willing to accept all their findings and interpretations without some question if I had not talked to today's college girls myself.

What do their statistical curves mean anyway? What, if anything, does a graph profile of sexual *attitudes* tell us about actual *behavior?* After the impact of the Kinsey reports, what validity can we expect to find in Kinsey's figures? There have been many attempts since the Kinsey study of the American female (published in 1953) to survey sex activity—some of them focused on the college student. But sampling is usually limited to a single campus, possibly two. None has been conducted on a national scale. Yet it seems clear from my own research that geography (California hedonism, Southern fundamentalism, Texas automobilism), location (how far to the nearest metropolis, the most accessible boys college, the quickest source of alcohol) and type of institution (Big Ten, country club, church-run, Brahmin deb, community college) does influence the sexual climate, the atmosphere of freedom or repression, and the pressures under which sexual decisions are made.

The impact of regional mores and the eccentricities of a

particular campus have been ignored in most polling efforts, though it is clear that behavior guaranteed to offend 53% of the coeds questioned at Purdue might well be *de rigeur* to 53% of the young ladies no one bothered to ask at Bennington. Assuming, that is, one could begin to weed out the lies, the exaggeration, and the meaningful memory lapses a researcher would have to expect in soliciting opinions, much less confessions, on so loaded-with-*angst* a subject as sex.

Candor itself is going to vary sharply from one campus to the next and within various crowds on a single campus. It might take thumbscrews to pry loose from a Michigan State University sophomore the same confidences an Antioch coed would divulge with pride before the sugar had time to dissolve in her coffee. A Trinity College (Washington, D.C.) freshman's concept of her schoolmates' sexual behavior would probably bear no resemblance at all to that of the Trinity senior. The Sarah Lawrence girl, imbued with the cult of individuality, confides in a whisper that she would die, "literally die," rather than appear anything but devastatingly knowledgeable about sexual matters before her schoolmates— even if her own particular individuality happened to include chastity.

Girls do not necessarily speak the same language. I asked a pert, subtly made-up, chic little sophomore from Wheelock College about the level of sexual sophistication among her friends. There was silence and a blank stare. "Are girls at school apt to be involved in affairs?" I asked. There was another silence and then she launched into an aside on the Boston rape-strangler and exhibitionists apprehended on the Wheelock campus. When I asked a pert, shiny-faced Barnard blonde the same question, she replied with a wacky, lewd, and delicately pornographic account of how she seduced one of America's most celebrated playwrights. There's not a pertinent statistic in either reply but there is much more, truths, if not necessarily *the* truth.

At first I was uncertain how to get at this truth—what sort of language to use with teenage girls who showed up in response to an unexpected phone call from "A Miss So-and-So who says she's writing a book"—how to phrase the most loaded questions—how to avoid an atmosphere that would embarrass or provoke anger and a refusal to cooperate. My approach was kid-gloved. It seemed important to me to make certain the girls realized nothing anyone said or did could shock me, offend me, or elicit my disapproval. The first questions were the least loaded. I asked about campus rules, sign-out procedures, dating traditions, the importance of sororities and fraternities, bed checks, drinking regulations, automobile restrictions. Often by mid-interview the gloves were torn to shreds, four-letter words were flying freely, stitches dropping wildly. (Some girls knit while they talk and one informed me you could judge how good a girl's sex life was by how much knitting she got done each semester. "It took me two years to finish this sweater," she added proudly.) Often one or more girls would linger afterward to pour out sad, funny, hysterical, and/or erotically exuberant tales of sexual adventure and social dilemma. They answered my questions freely, with sometimes painful frankness, but they asked questions too: "Do you think my father is right when he says this boy would lose respect for me if I did go to bed with him?" a University of Maryland senior wanted to know. "Where can I go to be fitted for a diaphragm without having to lie about being married?" a Queens College sophomore asked. "Was I wrong?" "Do you think it's right?"—this last query, over and over again.

Some group sessions were awkward, tense, and constricted. Others were far more candid and intimate than I had imagined possible. Girls might be close-mouthed before friends and dormmates with whom they had not previously shared confidences, yet were astonishingly candid in a circle of total strangers (to whom they had been introduced by first name only, and sometimes not introduced at all). With roommates who already knew the most intimate and clinical details of each other's private lives, the cross comment, the teasing, the "hey, who're you trying to fool—why, just last week you were saying. . . ." was, I suspect, almost as effective as a lie detector. My constant interruptions were meant to be both encouragement and goad. Actually it is inaccurate to call these "interviews." They were conversations, debate; for some girls, it seemed to me, a wanted, needed chance to pour out doubt, confusion, and half-formed philosophies—as though a girl wanted not merely to say it, but also to *hear* what she herself had to say.

With the promise of anonymity—all names used in these chapters are fictitious—and in this permissive, often highly casual atmosphere, these girls offered not merely chitchat, pose, and dormitory myth, but the most painful confidences. Many of them refused to be content with their own first automatic response to a specific question. They would insist upon digging deeper, trying to sort out rationalization and pose. They would tear into each other, pleading with a perfect stranger across the room, as one Oberlin girl did: "Can't we stop playing on the surface and get a little deeper into this thing?"

There was one glaring exception to the rule of candor. The topic of discussion was sex, yet not one of the girls interviewed ever brought up the subject of homosexuality. Often a plot complication of the college novel and a behavior found constant over four decades, by Kinsey, homosexuality appears to be a subject the college girl of the sixties finds difficult or impossible to discuss. Although no one *volunteered* comment on the subject, a few had observations to make when the questioner brought it up. Most of the comments were vague, mostly hearsay and gossip, and not enough was learned to justify a discussion of homosexual behavior in this book.

Statistics are also revealing. Obviously, many came from studies that were of great value to this book. But when the college girl herself talked to me about love and campus sexual activity, she made most available statistics sound as dated as whalebone corseting. "What percentage of girls would you guess graduate from this school still virgins?" I asked both coed and college boys. Although I never for a moment expected to get reliable estimates, I was fascinated by the repeated pattern of response. A group of University of Michigan boys estimated "about 50 percent" of Michigan girls would be sexually inexperienced at graduation. Several Michigan coeds put the figure at only 15 percent, 20, and the most conservative at 30. A student leader, who said she herself was a virgin, guessed that her fellow maidens would be reduced to 10 percent by graduation. Harvard men ventured that 40 to 50 percent of Radcliffe girls would have sexual experience by graduation. The girls themselves, again, saw greater odds against such survival—their figures ranged from 10 to 40, and the inexperienced gave as pessimistic a prognosis for chastity as the nonvirgins. Two recent graduates of Mary Baldwin, a small Virginia school for young ladies, testified as to the "sheltered life of the small-town Southern girl" and then guessed that 75 to 85 percent of Mary Baldwin's girls were sexually experienced by graduation. The curious discrepancy in these figures suggested several possibilities: that the boys had no idea what the girls were up to; that the college girl is no judge at all of what her friends are doing behind closed doors; that girls tend to exaggerate the bustle of sexual activity (unconsciously) to justify their own activity, minimize their guilt, or, in the case of the virgin, through fear, or to demonstrate her own heroism under incredible pressure and perhaps to prepare a cushion should she ultimately fall.

It seemed important to give perspective to what often seemed like sexual anarchy by talking to the college girl's housemother, her professors, her psychiatrist, her fiance, her lovers, escorts, and would-be lovers, and by weighing the analysis of deans, anthropologists, and marriage and family experts. Especially helpful, generous with time, bibliography, and advice were: Prof. Robert V. Bell of Temple University's Sociology department, who loaned me an advance manuscript of his new text and a file drawer-load of research materials; Prof. George W. Goethals of Harvard's Social Relations department; Prof. Thomas R. Arp of the University of California (Berkeley) English Department; Dr. Abraham Weinberg, psychiatrist and member of the Society for Clinical and Experimental Hypnosis; Psychoanalyst Harold Greenwald, author of *The Call Girl* and coauthor of *Emotional Maturity in Love and Marriage;* and Virginia Voss, college editor of

Mademoiselle magazine. But even with this more subjective perspective, the statistics still seemed dated and almost naive.

When the first chapters were completed, those who read them were shocked and bluntly skeptical. They found it difficult to believe that college girls used the kind of language I quoted, felt that a sameness of slang and the repetition of phrase suggested bias or inaccuracy, were appalled by the flip and sometimes icy comments. "Even your virgins are too hip and tough about it," one editor complained. Those who did not question my accuracy as a reporter wanted to know what I could have done to encourage the candor and intimacy of these confidences and how I had separated truth from exaggeration and falsehood.

Undoubtedly there *were* girls who lied or exaggerated and managed to fool me. Possibly they manage even to fool themselves. But much of the exaggeration was quite blatant, more a style of speaking than an attempt to mislead, and some of the falsehood was almost as obvious. A City College of New York freshman chattered away for nearly two hours about her erotic adventures before something she said struck a false note and I prodded her into confessing what was, to her, apparently a disgraceful admission: that she was actually a virgin.

But at no other time did I ever ask the question outright: "Are you a virgin?" or "What is your favorite coital position?" or "Have you ever been pregnant?" Girls were able to be frank and vivid and explicit because I did not ask them to account for themselves but rather to talk about the attitudes and behavior of their schoolmates. Questions began, "What do your friends say about—" or "Would your dormmates be likely to—." From dissecting the activities of their friends, many girls moved easily to a most merciless and frank examination of their own sexual behavior.

Certain words and phrases *do* keep cropping up in their comments—even with 3,000 miles between conversations. The phenomenon known as the "teen culture" does not end at the campus boundary line. In the college girls' conversation you hear jazz and J. D. Salinger, echoes of introductory psychology courses and David Riesman, debts to Lawrence Durrell, D. H. Lawrence, the Beats, Federico Fellini and the local rock 'n' roll disc jockey. The seeming uniformity of tone—flip and coolly sophisticated—indicated to me not that college girls are uniformly flip, but that many of them feel the need to assume that pose. Those who could not believe that "nice" girls "talk like that" listened to a tape recording of a session conducted by a California state college coed interviewer. The doubt was then withdrawn.

What did I do to inspire from so many of these girls a quality of candor so startling that brave men of the publishing world questioned it? This afternoon I phoned a Boston University coed and asked her to describe her impressions of our interview session. "Well, it was in your living room for one thing," she said, "and you were wearing tights and pigtails and there was not the slightest hint of condescension or judgment in your manner. Nobody knew anyone else—you didn't even know some of the girls' names. It was absolute anonymity. You never asked a personal question but you made it all so personal by telling us how you felt in college and your reactions and your doubts. You said 'I' so many times attached to such personal remarks, everyone else sort of just fell into it."

Was the atmosphere possibly too permissive? Was it the kind of conversation, that might intimidate a virgin into silence for fear of exposing herself as incurably old-fashioned? It is true that some girls who were asked to join an interview session refused and others failed to show up and some pleaded exams or term papers. Several girls showed up uninvited and most of them turned out to be sexual vagrants with a need for confession or a tendency toward exhibitionism. But the shy virgins came too and the staunch supporters of chastity spoke out. Many girls participated eagerly because sex is a subject about which they have much to say, about which they are often defensive, and about which some burn with all the fire of the first-year missionary.

It was essential never to accept any observation at face value because it seemed pleasingly logical or added support to a pet theory. Judging long distance—as with the California college tape mentioned above—was difficult. Without holding the reins of the conversation, I had only the taped voices to go on. I had invited a Columbia University law student to listen to the tape and comment on it in terms of his own experience with the college girl. The tape opened with giggles and much fussing about with a microphone. At first the responses to questions were cautious. Then the voices relaxed, the language became more explicit, the comments more cynical, the observations more personal and probing. By the end of the tape, the conversation had grown raucous, heated, and lewd. "That was quite a transition," I remarked. "They sounded like four innocents at the beginning and by the end it finally came out there was only one virgin in the crew." "You're kidding," the young man said. "I'm sure there were at least three virgins there. Only one actually came right out and said she's slept with a man. You mustn't confuse sophistication with experience," he warned me. Was I sliding into the very weakness I'd braced myself to avoid? I wrote to the student interviewer. She replied: "You were right. Only one of the four girls is a virgin. In fact, I've learned since that one of the four was pregnant the night we made the tape."

The comments of several girls had offered such detailed and revealing insight into stages of sexual development common to many of the coeds interviewed, it was decided to include excerpts of their dialogue in the first person. They are arranged as abbreviated case histories following the chapter they seem to clarify or illustrate. If the stream of dialogue seems occasionally disjointed, it is because a number of these sections are transcribed entirely from tape recordings. If it seems contradictory, it is because the female *is* contradictory, especially on the subject of sex. In several of these case histories, I have withheld the name of the college to further shield the girl's identity.

What these girls had to say may not be what their parents or educators or religious leaders would like to hear. There are ways to ask questions that might guarantee prettier, less discomforting answers. It was my feeling that I had found a way to permit the college girl to look at herself without the mask and artifice of the skilled actress society forces her to be.

—GAEL GREENE
New York City

THE QUESTIONS

After the first few sessions had provided an indication of directions questioning might take and the variety of reactions I might expect from the girls interviewed, I prepared a question sheet to guide subsequent sessions. Actual questions asked at any one session would, of course, depend upon the quality of rapport and the girls' sophistication. A remark or incident related by a girl might suggest a new line of questions. But unless some unusual resistance was encountered, the dialogue followed this outline:

THE CAMPUS

Where is your college located? What is the town like? How much influence does the town have over university regulations? What is the enrollment? The ratio of men to women students? If yours is a girls' school, where do your dates come from? What are the favorite hangouts? What are the big weekends? Where do people go to neck? What are the regulations on social conduct? Curfews? Automobile regulations? Rules about drinking, leaving the campus weekends, fraternity house conduct, chaperones, etc? A dating activity unique to your area?

Is there some sort of statue or landmark on campus that's alleged to react when a virgin walks by? Any interesting campus myths or legends pertaining to chastity, virginity, being pinned, becoming engaged? Is there much agitation on campus to change any of the rules governing social conduct? Has the student paper been editorializing on any social issue? Do you feel rules should be stricter, more liberal, are best as they are? Is it easy to break rules? If a girl climbs down the sorority house fire escape to spend a few hours with her boyfriend, would girls tend to protect her, ignore her, turn her in? If you knew a girl had signed out for a weekend at home and went to her steady's apartment instead, would you feel obliged to report her, protect her? Does it ever seem some girls break rules just to break rules? What happens when someone gets caught? What kind of rule infraction might mean suspension?

SEX AS CONVERSATION

Is there much conversation about sex? Mostly in small groups? With best friends? In large after-hours bull sessions? With dates? Does conversation about sex tend to be theoretical, clinical, personal? Do some girls seem upset by the candor of conversation? Do some girls seem overinfluenced by what they hear? Do you think a lot of the talk is exaggerated? Do many girls seem to talk a more or less sophisticated sexual game then you believe they play? What are your friends or dormmates talking about, worrying about, debating? Would a girl who has fallen in love and is considering sleeping with a boy for the first time be likely to seek support from a friend whose judgment she valued? Would you be aware if your closest friends, less intimate friends, were having an affair? Is there much speculation? Gossip? Is it vicious, just curious?

NECKING, PETTING, EVERYTHING BUT—

Do girls seem more or less emancipated and casual about sex than you expected? What about petting? How do most girls feel about mild petting—with dates, with steadies? Does "everything but—" appear to be a common practice? Is it likely to be condoned, approved, disapproved? Do girls seem concerned about the heaviest petting? Are girls often accused of being a tease? Is this another "line" boys use, or is it sometimes justified?

VIRGINITY, PREMARITAL INTERCOURSE, PROMISCUITY

Are sexual activities handled quite openly? With great secrecy? Do girls seem to be, or pretend to be, bored with the subject of dating, men, sex? Is there an atmosphere of approval or disapproval of premarital relations? Are there situations where it might be approved among girls who otherwise disapprove? What do girls have to say about the wisdom or desirability of sleeping with a fiancee? steady? the man you love? What sort of pro's and con's does a girl weigh in considering a response to the pressures of a boy who is trying to get her into his bed? What about going to bed just because a girl is in the mood—would this be approved, disapproved? Is the girl who goes to bed rather casually or with many boys likely to be admired, ostracized, pitied, or not particularly noticed?

At some schools a virgin will feign great experience and sophistication in order to appear hip—how does this strike you? Is it usually just the opposite—an experienced girl pretending to be inexperienced? What effect do you think premarital intercourse has on future marriage?

Why do girls have premarital intercourse? Why don't they? Women tell me they have lost, surrendered, traded, gambled, gloriously consumed (depending upon the attitude) their virginity for a great variety of reasons, in a wide variety of situations. What reasons, rationalizations, situations have you heard about?

A recent article in *Esquire* suggests that birth control pills and wide dissemination of contraceptive information have removed the last real reason that college girls might hesitate to have an affair—i.e., pregnancy. Do you agree? What do you think are the most compelling reasons? What reasons seem to you rationalizations?

Is the word "promiscuous" or "promiscuity" used? What does it mean to you? To your parents?

MEN AND BOYS

Is there a status date on your campus? Among your friends? Is there dating of professors? What about the visiting poet, novelist, actor as a date? Why do you think an affair with a faculty man would appeal to some girls? What about a married man? A younger man? Fraternity *vs.* independent? European men? Foreign students? How do the boys you date feel about chastity in the female? The double standard? Do they expect to marry virgins? What are the lines or arguments they use in trying to get a girl to bed? What does promiscuity mean to a boy? Do the boys you know often seem more or less emancipated about sex than the girls? More or less narrow-minded? Do boys' attitudes seem to change over the four college years? Do boys ever convey the impression they are testing a girl to see how far she will go? Do girls use sex to hold on to a boy or is it more likely they permit intimacies because they themselves enjoy the physical act? Do boys have a stronger sex drive than girls? How do female motivations seem to differ from male?

PREGNANCY

Is there much contraceptive information passed around the dorm or between friends? Much misinformation? Do you know anyone who has taken or is taking Enovid? On some campuses the diaphragm is a status symbol, on others a girl would never let anyone know if she had one. How do your friends feel? Do many girls seem to leave the contraceptive problem up to the boy? How much do boys know? Do many girls prefer to leave the whole contraceptive question to fate? Why? Do some girls seem to have the feeling about pregnancy that "it can't happen to me?" What happens when it does occur? Can you recall specific pregnancy cases, reaction of the girl, boy, parents, college administration, other girls—and the ultimate outcome? How do you think a girl feels about having a child and then surrendering it for adoption? About abortion? About the forced or hastened marriage? What is the campus reaction?

PARENTS

How much do parents know about what is going on sexually? What sort of advice, help, nagging, encouragement, information, or misinformation do parents give? What kind of information should parents be expected to give? What sort of sexual guidance would you want to give your children? What parental advice or approach have you heard about that particularly impressed you? Appalled you? Is there ever a feeling that parents should be protected from the truth?

AND

How might Junior Year Abroad affect sexual attitudes and behavior? What is social life like abroad? What are the reactions of the continental male to American dating customs? What about Spring Vacation, Rose Bowl weekends, the Fort Lauderdale, Nassau, Bermuda, Aspen-Stowe, Palm Springs, Mardi Gras jaunts? What about homosexuality? Is there much dormitory or house gossip, speculation? Any incidents of lesbianism that you can recall? What about dating the male homosexual?

EVOLUTION

How do attitudes and behavior evolve for the college girl in her undergraduate years?

After half the interviews were completed, these questions were condensed and mailed to professors, journalism departments, campus news service offices, friends and college girls at 52 schools with a covering letter requesting assistance. Girls were asked to conduct interviews or find a friend who would. The others were asked if they would pass along the assignment to a girl student they considered competent and willing. Thirty-six girls mailed back return postcards accepting the assignment: eighteen eventually filled it and dispatched reports.

I

Even Nice Girls

The name of the game is Cool.

And she *can* be cool, the American coed. Cool in the hipster sense. She can be calmly, casually, matter-of-factly, coolly erotic.

The rules of the game are: there are no rules. But there is a firm understanding: ostentatious display of virginity is strictly uncool. Among the coolest, the diaphragm is a status symbol; as a cool Cornell sophomore remarked with almost angry impatience—"Well really, what does morality have to do with it?"

The voice of the cool coed is speaking out at colleges and universities across the country, sounding the slogans, the boasts, and the doubts of a new sex freedom. Although definitely a minority voice, the cool coed, as champion of the new sex ethic, makes a loud, impressive, and persuasive noise. The more conservative college girl echoes the cool coed's slogans —often in the same hip language—although she would not dream of emulating her sexual behavior.

It is startling to hear the idiom of the junky or the argument of the existentialist coming from a primly dressed Wisconsin University farm girl or in the soft drawl of a Mississippi deb at the University of Maryland. Even if she has yet to pick up the idiom—even if she is too naive to recognize the genesis of the argument, the college girl reflects fragments of the new ethic in what she says about sex.

The fact is morality has a great deal to do with sex on the American campus, but the word "morality" is avoided. Hours are consumed in sober, painfully candid, and sometimes desperate search for answers, *the* answer, for values, for a reasonable code of behavior—over tap-water tea and pretzels in dormitory ironing rooms or a sorority house lounge. But girls do not like to call it a moral dilemma because morality is an absolute, and absolutes are constantly under fire as part of the education process.

Most college girls would consider it sophomoric to judge in terms of Good and Evil what goes on in the cemetery across from the University of Michigan's Stockwell Hall or on a sticky leather sofa in the blackness of a Dartmouth fraternity's TV room.

Sex to these girls is healthy or unhealthy. It is wise or foolish. It is glorious or wasted. It is repressed, childish, neurotic, or mature, meaningful, wholesome. It is "whatever I can get away with and still be a 'nice girl,' " a Swarthmore junior said. "It is whatever I do as long as no one is hurt and I can live with it," a Mt. Holyoke senior said. "It is nobody's business but mine," volunteered a slim 17-year-old Queens College freshman who recently "celebrated my first anniversary of freedom from virginity" on a ski weekend at Stowe "with my deliverer, of course." It is "something each girl must decide for herself," suggested a tall, suntanned Stanford University education major who is, she confesses with an apologetic shrug, a virgin but does not feel compromised if she spends weekends with her steady, skiing at Aspen, where "we sleep together, shower together, admire each other, and play wild, mad games."

Virgin and nonvirgin, sexually emancipated and romantically, stubbornly, or fearfully chaste, with few exceptions college girls agree: Sexual behavior is something you have to decide for yourself. Rarely do they condemn another for behavior they might regard as personally unwise; although in certain sexually sophisticated circles a virgin might find herself an object of derision. Discretion is essential to survival on some campuses; candor to the point of sexual boasting is a must on others.

Petting is increasingly widespread, increasingly intimate, involving, according to Temple University sociologist Robert Bell, far more incidence of oral-genital stimulation than most behaviorists would concede. "The meaning of the word virginity has been grossly perverted," a Pembroke junior observed, and her comment was echoed by at least a dozen coeds.

There are no comprehensive, recent statistics on campus premarital intercourse, but recognized authorities in the field —Oregon State University's Lester A. Kirkendall for one— are convinced that it is increasing. Engagement, not marriage, is regarded as license to enjoy complete sexual intimacy by most college girls, and some stretch that license to being pinned, lavaliered, going steady, or—simply—in love. Though college girls invoke the name of love as though it were a magic wand with the power to transform brass into wedding-ring gold, love is but one of many forces that ultimately pushes—or leads—a girl to the prenuptial bed. They talk about themselves as if they were idealists and romantics with iron wills. But their actions often are those of moths or wind-up dolls.

It is not the drastic revolution wrought by two world wars —female suffrage, the automobile, Freud, and the shedding of Victorian repressions—that are reflected so vividly in the sexual climate of the sixties. It is far subtler, a nuance of evolution in just seven years since I was last on the campus of the University of Michigan.

"Playing house" or "going all the way" (two euphemisms current where girls can't quite get themselves to call it an affair) is no longer universally regarded as cheap, desperate, promiscuous, loose, or "strictly for girls who can't get a man any other way."

Girls who signed out for home Saturday night and went to motels with young men did not advertise it then. And I was rather shocked to learn that some of the most sheltered and coddled offspring of proper bourgeois Baltimore made little or no pretense about where they were going when they left their University of Maryland sorority house with toothbrush and a change of underwear in a shoebox to return the following morning at 11:30 A.M.—motel check-out time.* But even the motel-goers maintain an apple-cheeked innocence. "We don't have affairs," a pretty junior corrected me when I used the term. "An affair is something for Liz and Richard Burton. We have relations," she exclaimed. But spending the night in a motel with a young man does not mean "relations" can be taken for granted. "You never know what goes on behind locked doors, do you?" a second junior suggested.

This, then, is the new style in sex ethics. Mama, the Church, Baltimore (and Springfield and Three Rivers), and the Dean of Women may pledge allegiance to the traditional standards of chastity and worship at the altar of purity in soul and reputation, but the accepted, vigorously voiced public moral codes are practically meaningless to young women of today. This does not mean, however, that they are unaware or able to ignore their existence.

"Most of us start out with the basic freshman orientation," a shiny-faced, delicate-featured Radcliffe junior began. "I mean we all get sort of the same 'nice girls don't' routine at

* Restrictions on overnight absences designed to halt the motel traffic were announced by Maryland's Dean of Women, Helen E. Clark, October 31, 1963.

home. Well, I for one really believed it. There just wasn't any doubt in my mind that I would be a virgin when I got married. But then I came up here and there they were—all those nice girls, much nicer than I if you talk about family and background—and they were doing it. I felt betrayed. Maybe all I had holding my determination together was just that one idea: 'nice girls don't.' My virginity lasted exactly four months. Not that I gave in without an utterly unsophisticated struggle. But frankly, my heart probably wasn't in protecting it any longer. The truth is, nice girls do."

"Nice girls don't"—"your reputation will be ruined"—"no man will ever marry you"—"pregnancy is unavoidable." These are the threats girls hear from those who urge her to "stay out of trouble." When they discover how little wallop these traditional threats seem to pack, some girls react as though they have indeed been betrayed. Their intelligence has been insulted. In fury at being so unfairly misled, they may seek revenge—a very complicated revenge—in bed. Or they may simply be left with no particular justification for refraining from the siren call to sensuous ecstasy or instant intimacy or the bed of a particular young man.

"I used to think it would show on your face," said a Marygrove sophomore, "or you could always tell a girl who went to bed with a boy by her mascara or a skintight sweater. That's ridiculous," she said with a giggle, tugging at her own outsize Shetland. And it is *not* the girl in the skintight sweater. It's the president of the snootiest sorority on campus and the frumpy Phi Beta Kappa with the contact lenses. It's the marriage-minded mama's girl and the marriage-panicked maiden who plays little Miss Chastity with dates who might be marital potentials and then sneaks quietly off to a young teaching fellow's apartment Sunday afternoon and begs him to relieve her of her maidenhood.

Hearing what these girls have to say, sitting in on their spirited and challenging after-hours bull sessions, eavesdropping on an after-the-big-weekend-date train and at countless plastic-and-vinyl-and-incandescent-bright student unions, I was

/ 37

struck both by what has not changed at all and how much has happened in the past decade to provide an atmosphere in which sexual freedom—and sexual panic—can flourish.

"Sex," suggests critic and English professor David Boroff, "is the politics of the sixties—the last arena of adventure in the quasi-welfare state in which we now live." Sex, says David Riesman "provides a kind of defense against the threat of total apathy. . . . [The other-directed person] looks to it for reassurance that he is alive." Riesman obviously knows his confused and threatened other-directed American college girl. But then the other-directed college girl often knows her Riesman. His analysis may become her rationalization. "I suppose I slip into bed too easily," said a UCLA coed. "And often with the wrong guy and for the wrong reasons. But most of the time I'm nothing. A cipher. A vegetable. In bed, at least, I'm alive." Is she that perceptive? you wonder. Or is such neat analysis designed to distract you and the girl herself from deep motivations? What came first: Riesman, the bed, or the zero of her ego?

The college girl, it is true, had Riesman a decade ago, and we had witnessed, as Boroff describes it, the sexualization of our culture in our heroes, the ingenuous virility of the late Clark Gable giving way to the inarticulate Brando "whose arrogant sexuality clearly announces his intentions." *

But we had not yet witnessed Hollywood's curiously belated coming of age. Three-times married Doris Day was still a virgin. Movie stars married their lovers or at least made a pretense of wholesomely continent courtship if they knew what was good for their box office. A newly grown-up child star did not celebrate the shedding of her husband by cooly and openly voyaging around the world with Warren Beatty. An Elsa Martinelli would not have welcomed an inquiring journalist from *Esquire* into her Manhattan hotel suite to meet her suite-mate lover and hear all about "Accommodation— Italian Style." ** Elizabeth Taylor Hilton Wilding was still

* "Sex: The Quiet Revolution," by David Boroff. *Esquire Magazine,* July, 1962.

** "Accommodation—Italian Style," by Gay Talese. *Esquire Magazine,* February, 1963. Talese opens with a quote from Elsa:

paying lip service to her fan magazine image and it would be two husbands and one Richard Burton later before Max Lerner would be inspired to comment on ". . . the dawning recognition that even a movie goddess has the right to her frailties and pleasures and joys, and that the kind of morality she practices has little to do with the kind of job she does as an actress." * "What are you trying to do now?" an interviewer for *Look* magazine asked Miss Taylor and she answered: "I try not to live a lie." It is an answer with a persuasive appeal for the college girl. Idealistic and essentially conservative, the college girl might be appalled by the imperiousness and self-centeredness of the *Cleopatra* affair, but her sympathies are likely to be stirred by that cry against the life of hypocrisy. And she cannot help but notice that, so far at least, as Lerner points out, Elizabeth Taylor seems to be getting away with it.

Sex in the past decade has become more explicit, rawer, as well as more public. We gulp our sex straight. Language that would once have prompted a lady to burst into tears or leave the room now punctuates cocktail-party chatter. Eavesdrop on an after-hours gossip session in a college dorm with your eyes closed and pick up all the old four-letter Anglo-Saxons plus a few you might not yet have heard. You might think you had walked into an army barracks, were it not for the sweet soprano trills and the soft scent of Blue Grass. "There are a certain number of short Anglo-Saxon words for bodily functions that were regarded as a secret language for men," critic Malcolm Cowley testified in a requiem for gentler days at the Post Office Department hearings on *Lady Chatterley's Lover*.

" 'Willy and I started living together in Tanganyika,' she said.

" 'No,' Willy corrected. 'St. Tropez.'

" 'Oh yes,' she said, after a pause, wondering how she could have forgotten. 'St. Tropez.'

"Elsa Martinelli was sitting next to her lover, Willy Rizzo, the photographer, on a white damask sofa in an elegant hotel overlooking Central Park. It was like so many other hotels that they had chosen since their love began in the spring of 1960; it was a big, expensive, No-Questions-Asked hotel, and its room clerks were among the most sophisticated men in the world. . . ."

* "Gilded Rebel," by Max Lerner. *The New York Post*, April 20, 1963.

". . . No woman was supposed to know them unless she was an utterly degraded women . . . [but] there is no more secret language for males. That has been abolished." "Of all the roles imaginable for the Supreme Court of the United States," writes *The New York Times* high-court reporter, Anthony Lewis, "liberating this country from puritanism might seem the least likely. . . . The United States has moved from one of the most timid countries in dealing with sex in the arts to what many believe is now by far the most liberated in the Western world. The nine no-longer-so-old men are responsible." *

It has been quite a leap from the morality and romanticism of Hemingway, whose illicit lovers have to be punished by ("It's just a dirty trick") death in the rain, to the matter-of-fact sex of fiction today. A big fat romantic Hemingway-type death would seem almost merciful to contemporary literature's unpunished illicit lovers forced to sprawl about brooding while passion dies of sheer boredom.

Can it be less than a decade since *Marjorie Morningstar* (now regarded by most college girls as "a kind of humorless *Much Ado About Nothing* in modern dress," suggests writer Gloria Steinem) ** was taken seriously enough to precipitate outbreaks of sexual panic? "I suspect Herman Wouk would be somewhat upset if he realized how many nice middle-class Jewish girls lost their virginity because of him," a self-described "ex-nice" Hunter College graduate told me. "Silly as it sounds, I know for sure at least three girls who gave up the good fight just to prove they weren't Marjories."

There are, of course, legions of diehard Marjories on the campus today, but many of them seem pressured and torn by the challenge of the campus counterpart to Marjorie's younger sister, Merrit, well-stacked heroine of Glendon Swarthout's *Where the Boys Are,* a saga of the adolescent lemmings who descend on Fort Lauderdale for Spring Vacation suntans and sex. "In my opinion," says Merrit, "it's ridiculous and picky

* "Sex . . . And The Supreme Court," by Anthony Lewis. *Esquire Magazine,* June, 1963.

** "The Moral Disarmament of Betty Coed," by Gloria Steinem. *Esquire Magazine,* September, 1962.

of society to turn it [virginity] into an *institution*. The whole deal is simply not that *monumental*. And I am not merely a poor loser either. . . . What with pimples and puberty boys have enough to endure without being terrorized about the sanctity of every so-called vestal in his neighborhood nor do I think a girl's misplacing it somewhere as catastrophic as The Decline and Fall of the Roman Empire."

Where do wholesome Middle-Western teenagers like Merrit pick up this brash confidence? From each other, of course. From the "strong youth 'subculture,'" which is confident, vocal, and self-conscious," * spawned by the increasing complexities of contemporary life and alienation within the family. Adolescents don't really speak to adults, don't actually expect to be understood, may even disdain adult approval of their heroes. Adolescence is not envious of adult standing. Adolescence is seen as a golden time of sanity before the inevitable acceptance of adult world hypocrisy. The move is too fast for Holden Caulfield and his admirers.

Life has indeed been sharply accelerated sexually.** The drama of gender begins early.*** Never did it begin earlier

* "The Role of the Counselor in Sex Behavior and Standards," by Kate Hevner Mueller. *Journal of the National Association of Womens Deans and Counselors,* January, 1963.

** It has speeded up biologically too. Dr. Thomas E. Cone Jr. of the U.S. Naval Hospital in Bethesda, Md., reported to the recent International Congress on Pediatrics that in 1900, American girls first menstruated at the average age of 14. The average has dropped to 13—a statistic duly noted by one sanitary-napkin firm that recently featured a pigtailed child in their magazine ads. She might have been 13—she might have been 10.

*** Sex-directed education, often neglecting allover female potential to concentrate on educating girls for their sexual function—marriage and motherhood—takes over where popularity-panicked parents leave off. Betty Friedan, author of *The Feminine Mystique,* describes a lesson plan for a junior high life adjustment course: "Entitled *The Slick Chick,* it gives functional 'do's and don't's for dating' to girls of 11, 12, 13—a kind of early or forced recognition of their sexual function. . . . Though many have nothing yet to fill a brassiere, they are told archly not a wear a sweater without one, and to be sure to wear slips so boys can't see through their skirts. It is hardly surprising that by the sophomore year, many bright girls are more than conscious of their sexual function. . . . One cannot help wondering (especially when some of these girls get pregnant as high school sophomores and marry at 15 or 16) if they have not been educated for their sexual function too soon. . . ."

than for the child now or soon to be a college girl of the sixties, born in the decade when Middle-Class Mamas, terrorized into raising baby by the book, moved from the rigidity of the Toilet-Training Thirties to the permissiveness, even anarchy, of the forties and fifties. The college girl of today probably played post office at mixed parties by the age of nine, began dating for the afternoon movies at ten, has her hair done once a week at a neighborhood beauty parlor by twelve, has gone steady at least once by thirteen, suffered from a broken heart or a slight fissure by 13¼.

With a buying power that packs an impressive wallop, the teenager is the pet of manufacturers, who woo her with sex and encourage her to spend $25 million a year on deodorants, $20 million on lipstick, $9 million on home permanents. In her 30AA bra and Jackie Kennedy hairdo, she is a living, fire-breathing *femme fatale* at 14. There is no time to be a child. She is quickly an adolescent and a teenager, a strange interim plateau that is fraught with paradox and goes on forever. "In the first decade of life the boy and girl learn that love is good and sex is evil," as Morton Hunt notes in *The Natural History of Love;* "in the second decade that love is still better, while sex has been slightly upgraded to the status of a forbidden fruit; and in the third decade that love is better than ever, while sex has suddenly become normal and healthful and is, in fact, a major means of expressing one's higher sentiments." *

While young people cope with this unsatisfactory and bewildering inheritance, time presses from another direction. War. Not a new specter, war has been haunting college students since 1914. Peace marches and bomb-banning demonstrations are not new. But only within the last decade has the total annihilation of the Earth become another dimension of everyday existence. "Today every inhabitant of this planet must contemplate the day when this planet may no longer be habitable," the late President Kennedy said; and in psychiatric sessions as well as school essays, young people reveal how vividly they have indeed contemplated the threat. "They are

* N.Y.: Alfred A. Knopf, Inc., 1959.

not primarily afraid of hardships. Rather it is the thought that there may not be continuity and sense in the life that lies ahead." * They react "live now." They react "how dare you tell me what to do—you who made the world what it is." They react "I won't think about it." "I woke up one night and I thought, 'I am going to die a virgin,' " a Stanford coed recalled. "I decided it was time to do something about it." "During the Cuban crisis my best friend got on the phone with the boy she'd been dating," a Berkeley junior said. "She told him, 'Listen, I'm ready to get laid.' " "We were sitting around," a Barnard senior said, "and we were telling each other how if this is really the end of the world coming, what would we do. It was the morning when no one knew what Russia would do about the Cuban blockade. We decided we'd run to the nearest frat house and grab the first available man." "We had just seen 'On the Beach' again," a Hollins senior said, "and I was thinking 'If I'm not married by the time I'm 21, I *will* have an affair.' " "I don't expect to live out the second half of my life," a City College of New York sophomore said. And a pretty, sensitive, not too happily promiscuous Barnard senior, commenting on a plea for chastity by her college's former president, Millicent McIntosh, remarked: "I agree with Mrs. McIntosh that sexual freedom is not easy to handle. She says, 'Wait.' But she's a Quaker, you know, and an optimist. Maybe I could go along with her if I had faith in the sanity of the world. But I don't."

Sex on the campus reflects all the factors contributing to teenage marriage—the search for emotional security, the need for a deep emotional attachment, fear, alienation, ego deficiencies, hedonism, the big sell on togetherness, constant sexual stimulation, love as a panacea, the idea of love as instant medium for gender identification and release from the tensions of home—where parents seem to alternate between overprotectiveness, apology, and unjustified demands. A girl tends to seek a sympathetic, understanding stand-in parent.

* "Children and the Threat of Nuclear War," by Sibylle Escalona. A Child Study Association Publication with the National Institute of Mental Health.

Her steady becomes, as William Graham Cole suggests, "parent, comfort, confessor and arbiter" of sexual codes.* The monogamy of most collegiate lovers is positively tame. Except in the South, stag lines have just about disappeared. Couples become each other's property, sticking together through bliss and boredom in an imitation of married life that often leads to married life ** (witness the blossoming of campus housing for newlyweds), both with and without benefit of shotgun.

It was one thing to give women the right to vote. It is quite another to make such a noisy fuss about her right to an orgasm. It is a fuss that dates back to the twenties but has taken its time to filter through to the most conservative quarters of the middle class. Colleges had a less complicated task keeping nubile young women out of the prenuptial bed in the days when sex was an unpleasant duty, possibly vile and disgusting, endured for the sake of a husband's animal desires. But the day the word started getting around that sex was the great ecstasy of woman's existence linked to the edict that it must be foresworn until marriage, the task became Herculean. "Have you noticed?" asked a recent graduate of Smith, "how even the sex manuals reflect the change. Not so long ago the best seller was *Love without Fear*. Today it's *Sex without Guilt*. And even the 'guilt' tends to sound a little old-fashioned."

Is it any wonder that educators look back to the mid-1950's nostalgically as "the good old days of sexual innocence?" The Kinsey works themselves took a toll of this innocence. "In the years that have elapsed since their publication," medical sociologist Dr. Celia S. Deschin of the Adelphi Graduate School of Social Work, writes, "Kinsey's findings have become a new kind of social norm. . . . I find those favoring higher moral standards are often reluctant to express their opinions too openly—so widespread is the notion that to be normal is to

* "Early Marriage," by William Graham Cole. *The Nation Magazine,* February 8, 1958.

** Population Reference Bureau (1961) statistics show that 12 percent or 162,000 college women were married; 77,000 high school girls had husbands.

have a lot of sexual involvements." "Gradually . . . one after another of the 'old-fashioned' standards have been questioned and put aside. . . ." Barnard President Millicent McIntosh lamented in a recent plea for chastity.* And it was an ultimatum on the subject, from Vassar's Sarah Gibson Blanding, that became the campus *cause célèbre* in spring of 1962. Her highly publicized pronouncement that premarital sex relations constitute "offensive and vulgar behavior" and her suggestion that Vassarites who disagreed should resign aroused a storm of outrage on campuses across the nation, not the mildest of which echoed through the vestal halls of Vassar. "If Vassar is to become the Poughkeepsie Victorian Seminary for Young Virgins, then the change of policy had better be made explicit in admissions catalogues," a cynical Vassarite was quoted. Some equally cynical Yale lads predicted "a mass exodus from Poughkeepsie of indignant Vassar women wearing their diaphragms as badges of courage." Such an exodus failed to materialize. A survey by the *Vassar Miscellany News* indicated only two students planned to resign. None has to date.**

How shall the colleges be involved in the debate over sex ethics and sex behavior? "How much authority must still be

* "Out of a Morals Revolution: A Moral Revelation," by Millicent McIntosh. *Glamour Magazine*, January, 1963.

** The Vassar Questionnaire was answered by 1,040 students and the results were printed in the April 11, 1962, issue of the *Vassar Miscellany News:*

Question 1. Do you agree with the position taken by Miss Blanding in her speech Wednesday night?

52 percent—Yes   40 percent—No   Rest—Undecided

Question 2. Do you believe that social morals are a personal matter that should be of concern to the college only when they bring the name of Vassar into public disrepute.?

81 percent—Yes   15 percent—No   Rest—Undecided

Question 3. Do you think that the purpose of Miss Blanding's speech was to determine your personal moral standards and the moral standards of every Vassar student?

32 percent—Yes   65 percent—No   Rest—Undecided

Question 4. Do you think that the speech reflected a change in the administration's attitude toward its students' moral standards?

29 percent—Yes   62 percent—No   Rest—Undecided

Question 5. Do you take the suggestion of withdrawal for the reasons suggested in the speech seriously.

28 percent—Yes   65 percent—No   Rest—Undecided

invoked in order to keep human error at a safe minimum for inexperienced youth? At what age in any one individual's development do we withdraw authority and fear, and allow rational and social sanctions to take over?" Educators were asked these questions and collegiate sex made predictable headlines when the Association of Womens Deans and Counselors devoted its entire January, 1963, issue to "Student Sex Standards and Behavior." The gist of its several articles, by some of the most respected authorities in the field: student sex behavior and sex ethics have become national problems, "unacknowledged, unsavory and unsolved"; youth, alienated from adult contact and influence, makes its own sexual decisions; the power of such traditional fear-evoking threats as pregnancy, venereal disease, and community disapproval is decreasing; neither parents nor teachers have been facing the problem with honesty, courage, or adequate insight.

But the point that didn't make headlines was a suggestion many student counselors and advisers dare not utter aloud: that sex on the campus is more an adult problem than it is a youth problem; that, as Lester Kirkendall has stated over and over again in his 30 years of working with youth, young people are not sex obsessed. "They are more moral, more straight forward, more honest than most adults when it comes to thinking about and searching for meaningful answers to the sexual dilemma." Adults, Kirkendall writes, are crippled by fear . . . fear "which pervades our whole society, makes both teachers and administrators evasive and dishonest when issues arise involving sex."

When Vassar's Miss Blanding spoke of the indecency of premarital sex, editors and headline writers spread the word about the "ban against free love" and sober articles appeared applauding the stand against promiscuity. But premarital intercourse is neither free love nor promiscuity.

Cool is rarely as cool as it looks. Young people today are so very vulnerable and alone they could scarcely bear exposure to the scorns of contemporary existence without borrowing the pose of blasé disdain from the Beats. The first beatitude of the cool is simply: no sweat. An Eastern women's college dean, obviously taken in by the pose, is quoted as saying: "It isn't that they're preoccupied with sex. It's that they accept it so easily and then turn to you and say, 'And now what?' " Most of the college girls I interviewed *are* preoccupied with sex. They do care. They do not accept it so easily, they confess privately, as they pretend publicly. They do not all have the courage of their free-love convictions. Even those who embrace the "sweet" life often discover they have more courage than conviction.

The college girl *has* sexual problems: misunderstanding and abuse of sex freedom, guilt and self-recrimination, the burden of constantly reevaluating her own inner convictions to form and reform the sexual code she must author herself, and, I suspect, far more incidence of pregnancy than has yet been documented.

But it is a mistake to lump all premarital sexual acts into such categories as "scandalous," "unsavory" and "disaster." Dr. Walter Stokes, the psychiatrist, told the 34 educators who recently assembled behind closed doors at a Columbia Teachers Conference on sex behavior: "Anything that promotes successful interpersonal relations is moral." Stated more cautiously, this has been Kirkendall's thesis. "Sex that builds and does not hurt is good," an earnest Antioch junior put it. "There is good love and bad love and just because you happen to be married is no guarantee of either," a Wisconsin University sophomore suggested.

Men and women at all levels of society are questioning sexual codes; values are changing. College students are not a separate population; they are a vocal, intelligent, and intellectually curious segment of our society. They have every right to question too.

The dilemma "created by an uneasy equilibrium between two contradictory values," as sociologist Winston Ehrmann has written,* has created the unique patterns of American courtship and dating. The conflict between sex as sin, and sex

* "The Variety and Meaning of Premarital Heterosexual Experience for the College Student," by Winston W. Ehrmann. *Journal of the National Association of Womens Deans and Counselors,* January, 1963.

as the ultimate expression of romantic love has led youth, on its own, to "invent" new social devices—dating, petting, going steady, and intercourse under an elaborate code of what is considered proper.

How these "inventions" work and how they fail is the subject of this book. Some readers will be shocked, alarmed, and offended by what these college girls had to say and how they said it; but with wisdom, charity, patience, and the courage to rise above one's own personal anxieties, they may grasp an essential message: that the love-making of young people is, as Ehrmann notes, not merely exploitive, animal, selfish, or "a single set of mechanical acts in which young people engage solely to have 'fun.'" It is also affection, chivalry, romantic, idealistic, fulfilling, and "a way of reaching identity and growing up." Educators can have little hope of ever influencing the values on which youth base their codes of sexual behavior without at least this much faith.

2

College:
Challenge to Chastity

Campus folklore promises that DePauw University's iron owl will hoot whenever a virgin walks by; that the two stone lions flanking the University of Michigan library are poised to roar should a maiden cross the mall; that University of Mississippi virgins may expect a salute from the campus monument to the Confederate hero; that Abe Lincoln, seated in sculpted repose on the University of Wisconsin campus, rises in the presence of chaste femininity.

At Penn State there is a "giant phallic symbol that's supposed to crumble or shower pebbles when a virgin passes," a recent alumna reported. "Girls have been known to walk by crying, 'Fall, damn you.' And once someone hung up a sign lettered 'out-of-order.'"

But the owl has yet to hoot, the stone lions have not sounded even a tentative purr, Confederate heroes have not saluted, and Abe is thus far unmoved, a phenomenon noted as follows by a Wisconsin lad in the letters column of the student paper, *The Cardinal:*

"We are now engaged in a great moral war to see whether our women or any women can long endure pure. For many years I have watched an unnecessary factor usurp the morals from the feminine sector of our campus. It is an utter disgrace and a sterling example of the immorality sweeping this University. I propose to elevate Abe Lincoln so that he may ever stand before the young ladies. It hurts us all to see a female pass before Abe on the hill, see him remain seated and then give him reason to remain seated so he shouldn't have sat for naught. Abe Lincoln is no reason for any maiden to lose her head."

Is it possible that any college girl—even the impressionable freshman—could conceivably be pressured into an untimely deflowering simply because a lion refused to roar, snicker, even yawn? Possibly not. Not in the strictest sense of cause-and-effect. But some reasonably bright and apparently not at all superstitious coeds do brood over the insensitivity of such inanimate objects. A recent Michigan State graduate told of experiencing great anger and genuine alarm when the campus monument to a sinewy Spartan failed to wave, drop, or tip his hat in tribute to her virginity, as an upperclassman escort assured her it would. Not that she literally expected "Sparty" to react. But when her date pointed next to the top of the Carillon Tower where one of the four projections was missing its finial and assured her it had fallen eons ago, the last time a virgin passed, she grew panicky. "I was terrified . . . I figured I'd definitely come to the wrong school—this place was going to be much too fast for me. How would I ever keep up?" And a San Diego State coed underlined how campus virginity myths take on a literal reality. "I used to think nobody had affairs except the very *risqué* and the slobs," she said, "so I'm really surprised at girls' attitudes about sex. And all in the last couple of months. You know that big black statue of Montezuma that's supposed to turn white when a virgin walks by. Well, I know now that it's never going to."

COLLEGE: CHALLENGE TO CHASTITY

Mute and inanimate, the owl, the lions, Abe, and Montezuma are symbolic, a constant reminder to the coed of a world that doesn't know a virgin when it sees one and seems to value little the state of chastity. Nobody gives me any credit, the college virgin often mutters. Not even Montezuma. But isn't paranoia almost an occupational disease of the teens? Some college girls howl in outrage at unjust accusations and become even stauncher advocates of chastity. Some do not. "My parents accused me of all sorts of wild things long before I ever did anything," a Northwestern sophomore said. "It made me feel like I ought to do something to justify the accusations."

The incidence of persecution complex among virgins on the American campus is growing. This does not necessarily mean that the primrose path is about to become a teeming thruway. "We have very anxious virgins and very relaxed virgins," Harvard's Dr. George W. Goethals notes. But there is the suggestion from anthropologist Ashley Montagu * that the torrent of public discussion among college students—in which chastity emerges as an unwholesome state—threatens the right of a girl to say "no."

As professor and prolific profiler of American colleges, David Boroff, notes: "The loss of chastity is no longer the fall from innocence; it is the fall upwards, so to speak, to maturity and self-fulfillment." Young ladies, on and off campus, go through intensive analysis to unblock sexual timidity. A sociologist and his wife confided to me that they are worried because their coed daughter is still a virgin. "Our dorm has a reputation for being fast and we're proud of it," a University of Indiana maiden boasted. A Stanford graduate student quieted a senior who was spreading unkind rumors about him by threatening to tell all her friends she was merely posing as a *femme fatale* but was, in fact, a virgin. She shut up. Obviously the sexually inexperienced college girl is very much on the defensive. You hear it echoing in all that she has to say about sex ethics and sexual behavior. She is apt to be

* "Has Chastity a Chance at College?" by Ashley Montagu. *McCalls Magazine*, September, 1963.

apologetic as was the Brooklyn College freshman who said, "I am ready to give from the head and the heart but I'm not so sure I'm ready to give from the womb. I'm still a virgin, but I'm only 17—do you think there's hope for me?" A girl can't even wear a plain gold circle pin on some campuses without inspiring snickers and wisecracks about what has become the costume-jewelry symbol of chastity. Many a young Hester of today would find it easier to adjust to a scarlet "A" than the stigma of a solid gold "V."

Away from home (possibly for the first time), in some cases overwhelmed by too sudden or too much independence (her first checking account, her first charge account, her first chance to slop through the snow *without* galoshes and without an argument), treading water in a sea of anonymity ("My dear, I am the sum total of my I.D. number, my room number, my phone number, and my gym locker number," a Minnesota University freshman said), a new girl on campus sniffs the air. Rebellion, she soon discovers, is the prevailing climate. College is the time for challenging all that till now seemed unchallengeable. Old villains are found not to be so villainous after all. The new villains become hypocrisy, dogma, absolutes, provincialisms. "I don't believe in anything," a UCLA sophomore said with a studied weariness. "But I believe *against* a lot of things." To distrust authority and question conventional morality becomes a part of the college experience. All taken-for-granted values are slated for examination and, inevitably, merciless attack. Sexual values are not exempt. Chastity as an absolute is a clay pigeon. "What could be phonier than hanging on to it simply because Mama said to?" a sleekly dressed and apple-cheeked Smith senior asked. "It's just as phony to run out and do it for no other reason than everyone else is," a schoolmate retorted. "Chastity for the sake of chastity is meaningless," an Oberlin sophomore said. "It's like what happens to a lot of kids with religion," a Bard sophomore said. "You come here blindly believing— in your family's religion and your family's sexual code—but after a semester or two, you find yourself agnostic—and a sexual agnostic." "Sex and God. Sex and God. That's all we ever talk about," a San Diego State sophomore said. "You can start talking about George Washington and next thing you know, someone is saying how Martha was pregnant before they got married."

Many college nonconformists are quasi rebels to be sure, characterized by comedian Mort Sahl: "May I have the car? I want to run away." But linked to the revolt against the values of society is the genuine respect for scientific inquiry that is academic bedrock yet uncomfortably precarious, for bedrock. Journalist Martin Mayer was talking about Harvard but pointed to the universality of his remarks when he wrote: "What Harvard teaches—what any faculty teaches, taking all together—is the complexity and uncertainty of human knowledge. The lesson goes out to students at an age of what looks like irrevocable decision, when it seems to make so much difference whether one knows or one doesn't know. Students and younger faculty alike have been chosen because of someone's belief that they will, each in his own way, increase the prospects of human understanding—yet they are constantly confronted, both in their work and in their private life, with evidence of the limits of the understanding they have achieved. They cry out like Job for release, for the power to control the reality they perceive, for certainty of their own superior consciousness." *

Influential in the campus climate too is the stress on individuality. In their critique of American education, Prof. Solon T. Kimball, of Columbia University Teachers College, and Prof. James E. McClellan, Jr., of Temple, blame "cult of self" for the loneliness afflicting contemporary man. "What struck us so intensely," the professors write, "are the desperate efforts all around us to escape this loneliness, efforts which seem to lack any sense of the source of the difficulty, any rational

* "Getting Alienated with the Right Crowd at Harvard," by Martin Mayer. *Esquire Magazine*, September, 1963. Mayer was suggesting that Harvard "by its most admirable qualities" was "less well protected than most institutions against onslaught by an intellectual fanaticism," in this case, the experiments with the psychotomimetic drugs—mescaline, psilocybin and LSD-25—that led to the spring, 1963, firing of two Harvard research psychologists.

basis by which individuals can free themselves from the unseen pressures and strains that make them move like leaves in a windstorm." * Sexually, the cult of the individual—and to Hell with society—seems to cast man off on his own fenced-in island where nothing matters but his own ego and libido. Certainly there are echoes of this loneliness described in the coed tales of sexual behavior that follow.

On some campuses these forces—the fiber of Academia in the mid-sixties—will be heady and overwhelming; on others, less discernible. And much depends upon the girl herself.

It is impossible to describe The College Girl. She is a brainy, socially retarded 16-year-old from Gary, Indiana, arriving at Shimer College in Illinois, escorted by a frightened mother and a taciturn father. She is a 20-year-old Swedish princess registering at Radcliffe. She is the 18-year-old daughter of one of America's 25 most powerful industrialists, already the veteran of one marriage, annulled, and one abortion. She is a not-too-ambitious and amiable Flint, Michigan, girl who couldn't get into Michigan State and has settled for a year or two at Flint Community Junior College.

The range is infinite as will be the range of what college means to her: learning, fun, a teaching certificate, a happy hunting ground, getting into Theta, postponement of responsibility. She may never in her life have been alone with a boy —she may be, at the moment she signs up for orientation, already pregnant. She may come from a small town where youngsters are sheltered and unworldly. She may commute from a middle-income housing project to both after school job and a tuition-free city college. She may arrive exhausted from a debut in the affluent upper-strata of Tuxedo Park or Southampton.** Or she may come fresh from Darien, Con-

* *Education and the New America,* by James E. McClennan, Jr. and Solon T. Kimball. N.Y.: Random House, 1963.

** The riotous aftermath of a Southampton coming-out party in which young men sequestered for the night in a rented mansion went on a destruction rampage, with damage estimated at between $3,000 to $10,000, prompted *New York Times* reporter Fred M. Hechinger to describe "a pattern of destructiveness among affluent youth." In a column of news analysis, headlined "Affluent Delinquency" (*N.Y. Times,* September 5, 1963), Hechinger linked the Southampton, Long Island, incident to teen-age riots

necticut, where a parents group recently published a report documenting "alarming number of pregnancies in high school . . . our greatest problem is shoplifting . . . unbelievable necking and petting at the theater on Friday night . . . accepting a date to the drive-in is like accepting a date for sex relations."

How has high school affected her? What do the headlines about pregnancy drop-outs and shoplifting clubs and upper crust free-for-alls tell us about the American college girl of 1960's? At least 20 coeds remarked that high school sex was wilder, more wanton, more blatant, with generally more public disasters (college pregnancies are more likely to be handled quietly). "Think of it this way," a Cornell freshman suggested with a grin. "We're the high school girls who *didn't* get pregnant. Now the question is," she added, "are we the ones who were too smart to let accidents happen—or too bookish to have the opportunity?" More likely the latter.*

---

at Hampton Beach, N.H., Ocean City, Md., Lake George, N.Y., and a racetrack near Indianapolis, all during the Labor Day weekend, as well as a rash of attempted burglaries by teenagers of a country club golf shop in a well-to-do Connecticut community, and "the habit of party-crashing" which has "increasingly terrified suburban parents." What are the causes of such rowdyism? Hechinger asks. His answer: 1) Drinking (he quotes Dr. Frederick Hudson, of San Francisco's Presbyterian Medical Center, as confirming "that alcohol had become a trap for the very young, beginning at the age of 11."); 2) Abdication of adult responsibility . . . "leading to a lack of discipline."; 3) Fewer useful outlets for today's youngsters; 4) Affluence itself . . . "giving . . . children too much, too soon." Hechinger concluded: "Teen-agers know that, in an air of easy affluence, money will take care of all consequences."

* "At the time of marriage more of the girls who had gone to college had experienced coitus than girls who had not had any college life. The reason behind this finding is that females in the lower educational levels marry at an earlier age, and the sexually most active period of the single female is the one or two years prior to marriage. Consequently girls in the lower levels are sexually more active at an earlier age and those in the higher levels at a later age. Eventually, therefore, the collegiate females equal, then surpass, the noncollegiate female in the proportion who had premarital coitus." Excerpt from "The Variety and Meaning of Premarital Heterosexual Experiences for the College Student," by Winston Ehrmann.

Dr. Herbert H. Herskovitz, a Philadelphia Main Line psychoanalyst "with an extensive practice among collegians," estimated that 80 percent of the girls at big coed colleges and "sophisticated women's colleges with 'brother

The girl who knows a high school diploma signals the end of formal education and the beginning of a hunt for a job—unless marriage takes her off employment rolls—tends to date more and become more intimately involved than the girl who is intent upon scoring an all "A" average in order to win a scholarship to Ohio State or make the grade at Bryn Mawr.

But now she is here. Chances are she will be thrown into social activities a week before she even sees the inside of a classroom. There are mixers and Jolly-ups and horrendous get-acquainted rituals. There is a roommate and a bedspread with the price tag still on it, the photo of the boy back home to be placed lovingly on top of the bureau (inside of which it may disappear as soon as she finds a campus replacement). Someone shows her how to put a bottle top on the room buzzer so she'll know if she had a call while she was out. There are batteries of tests, including one wild questionnaire asking: Does your soul sometimes leave your body? Is your sex life satisfactory? Is the top of your head tender? There are catalogues and maps and chili con carne after lockout and catastrophes and homesick long-distance phone calls. And then classes.

She may have been valedictorian of her class. Now she is a Radcliffe girl sitting in Harvard classrooms surrounded by valedictorians. She may have come from a town where everyone knew everyone; now she finds herself dating strangers. Not just freshman boys, but lordly seniors and graduate students swarm around. From a graduation class of 45, she may enter a freshman class of 1,000. She may never have seen an Indian before or sat next to a Negro.

In anthropology she is exposed to *Coming of Age in Samoa*. In sociology she learns to sneer at the other-directed. In social psychology or social relations, she studies the genesis of prejudice and the mechanics of attitude change. Her English teacher's rapier cynicism may be unleashed in antireligious asides for which she can suddenly find no rebuttal. Her phi-

colleges' close by, have had sex relations by the time they have completed their college careers." Quote from "Campus Romance: A Degree in Divorce" by Martin Abramson, *Cosmopolitan Magazine,* September, 1963.

losophy instructor is so intent upon neutrality, he may dispose of all proofs of the existence of God as casually as he dispenses with Bishop Berkeley and that infamous tree in the Quad.* At the International House, she is exposed to foreign observations on the American female and learns about cultures and sexual codes someone else obviously regards as far superior to her own.

And there are dates. There are coffee dates, movie dates, cocktail dates, theater dates, lecture series dates, library dates, exam cram dates, dates for the hockey games, and double dates for bridge. There are folk sing dates, let's-explore-the-countryside dates, let's-explore-each-other dates. (To combine the latter two, a Santa Barbara duo toured the countryside weekends in his stationwagon—completely outfitted with bed and housekeeping equipment.)

There are beer busts, the University of Colorado's "Woodsy's," fraternity pledge formals, open houses, Fiji Island Night, pajama parties, Halloween Frolics, the Anti-Military Ball at Wisconsin, Kakewalk at the University of Vermont, Rebellee at Mississippi, Paddy Murphy Day at the University of Miami, thousands of Homecoming Weekends, Dartmouth's Winter Carnival, the annual Humphrey Bogart film festival in Cambridge, Mass. There are Scavenger Hunts, Hillel Mixers, boozy evenings at Rahar's, Cronin's, The P-Bell, The Brick, The Can, Pete's on the Drag, The Rathskeller, Doc Connel's, The Riv, The Oasis, Rossotti's.

There are blind dates, dates that get stood up and dates who stand you up, dates that end early with a headache, late dates, overnight dates and weekends at Carmel, Stowe, and

* In *God on the Secular Campus*, (Doubleday & Company, Inc., 1963), Father Richard Butler, Newman Club chaplain at the University of New Mexico, finds "most abhorrent, and all too prevalent on the college campus today" is "the teacher who delights in the destruction of traditional ideas and values, without any balanced appraisal in the beginning or replacement of intellectual security at the end of this devastating process." These, he writes, "are what I call the scholastic perverts, guilty of contributing to the mental delinquency of the minors before them. And the corruption of the mind, in extent of damage, is far more pernicious than the corruption of morals; for the mind motivates the will in its determination of human behavior. . . . The professor presumes to be a devil's advocate!"

the Waldorf. A date may be as casual as an ice cream cone after an intellectual pickup at Harvard's Widener Library, or as carefully planned as that of the Ohio State youth and the Miami University (Oxford, Ohio) coed who carried on a correspondence all winter, agreeing each to furnish three friends of their gender and share a suite in Ft. Lauderdale during the annual rites of spring. "Fun and companionship for all," a campus correspondent reported.

"Dinkie," the Toonerville Trolley from Princeton Junction, pulls into Princeton proper. Car pools crisscross the Ivy League circuit. A Dartmouth boy hitches 140 miles to take her for a walk and a cheeseburger at Wellesley's Howard Johnson's. He stands there at the Greyhound Terminal in East Lansing. She is summoned to the lobby of Briggs Hall by the girl on phones. Is this the boy she flipped for on the Ryndam coming home from Europe this summer? A phone rings at the University of Pennsylvania's new women's residence, the late Eero Saarinen's five-story dorm with glass-roofed court. "We need 20 beautiful girls for a champagne party—who's home?" says the boy at the other end. It is 7:30 Friday night. The call rings out: "ANYBODY FOR A PARTY?" She goes. It is beer, not champagne, but she meets the darlingest new boy.

She may discover that an invitation to a tea party does not necessarily require white gloves. She may discover that tea is pot and pot is marijuana. "I always say 'no thank you,'" a Queens College freshman said. "I don't even know how to inhale an ordinary cigarette." Her date is smashed and he stalks around the Deke house at Williams announcing, "Vice is nice, but incest is best." The absolutely first thing that happens to her at her first Dartmouth weekend is she gets pinched by a boy she hasn't even been introduced to. Fraternity weekends on a nearby "animal" (male) campus are a special trauma. And the big weekends are fraught with potential for disaster. Relationships that took months to nurture fall apart overnight. Everyone tries desperately to make it New Year's Eve. "All those hours of enforced togetherness," a Wellesley girl recalled. "He asks you two months ahead of time. He gives you a tour of the house. He throws open the door of a great big black room with nothing but mattresses on the floor. 'What's that?' you ask. 'The pit,' he says. There's an awful glee club concert, inevitably, and then you go to see his laboratory experiment. Necking, at least, helps make the hours pass."

Wherever chaperones are required, she discovers, they seem to be chosen for their hearing infirmities, myopia, sensitivity to liquor or as advocates of free love. It certainly seems that way. She learns that "nice" girls at the University of Maryland don't go on a fraternity ski weekend—unless they are pinned or going steady. At Carmel, stuffing bodies in a phone booth is *passé* for the weekending lads of Berkeley and their dates. It's how many slippery souls can be crowded into a single shower stall.

She worries about etiquette. A DePauw University freshman, who had visited Indiana University for spring weekend, told of sharing her motel quarters with another girl. When her date dropped her off, she discovered her motel-mate had male company in the other bed. Next morning she heard two voices singing in the shower. "I wondered how I was supposed to behave," she said. "But they just came out, yelled good morning and left."

Usually when she doesn't know what to do, she asks. And debate on social proprieties waxes on into the night. More experienced upperclassman can be maternally protective of freshman innocence. True, there will be an exhibitionist in every dorm—the girl who boasts of sexual debauchery, exhibits "his teethmarks" on her back to the terror of the more vulnerable. But I watched juniors and seniors grinning at the stern idealism of a freshman dormmate, refusing to utter a word in her presence that might stir up any doubts. Fresh from European fields of conquest, a klatch of Radcliffe seniors trading concessions of summertime adventure, remember to close the door. "No point shattering the new girls," one explains. And a sorority rushing chairman doesn't bother to mention her own sexual intimacies with her fiance when she lectures rushees sternly on the importance of chastity. "They'll learn the exceptions to the rules later," this University of Texas coed explains.

She does learn. She learns there is no single collegiate standard of sexual behavior. There are dozens of codes, some of them rigid and spelled out, some of them blurred, obscure, many of them in a state of constant reassessment, advance, retreat, and realignment. A girl may march into the groves of Academe wrapped in shining idealism. By the time the groves shed a bit for fall, she may be swathed in less shining cynicism, or she may emerge glowing with a revised idealism. The chameleon quality of her own sex codes may be quite a burden for the college girl. "It was so much easier when the taboos were rigid and unchallengeable," a Sarah Lawrence girl remarked. "Life is so simple when you can say to yourself, 'I am a virgin, I don't sleep with boys ever' " a Cornell sophomore said, adding, "The minute you say, 'I am a virgin but I will have intimate relations when and if . . .' then each new man in your life is a brand new decision. You drive yourself nuts with all those decisions."

Her dates are persuasive. "There are 9,000 variations on maybe 12 basic lines," a UCLA sophomore said, "and eventually you hear them all." He may try the scientific approach as one Amherst lad did with an indignant Smith girl I interviewed. "We were petting and I said, 'Stop, I'm afraid,' so he got up and filled a condom with water from the tap and said, 'See, nothing to be afraid of—it works,' I must admit I was impressed with the demonstration but he sort of ruined my mood for him—for life." If she is one Texas Women's University coed interviewed, she will be amused and secretly appalled when the girl down the halls floats in two minutes after curfew on a breath of bourbony air with a length of red fabric trailing behind, and bubbling: "What red thing?—Well, what do you know? I got a necktie caught in my panty girdle." If she is a chunky, brusque George Washington University coed with opaline blue eyes, sharing a Washington, D.C., apartment with two sexually emancipated schoolmates, she may be offended, and tense too about her own chastity, when she comes home to find two bodies asleep on the living room couch and "two not asleep in the only bedroom. The first time I nearly got pneumonia walking in the rain," she told me. "The next time I tried sleeping in the bathtub."

She sits in on the endless dissections of men, boys, dating, chastity, and virtue, with unread Tillich or Twain or Toynbee on her lap and hamburger grease on her fingers. "But there is no Right or Wrong," a dark-haired, determinedly virginal senior announces flatly. "What's right is what's right for you," this University of Michigan coed says. "Coming to the bridal bed *intacta* is not a virtue in itself," argues a slender blonde deb at Goucher. "I know a woman, a virgin," says a San Diego College freshman, "and she always tells herself, 'Virginity is like fruitcake—the longer she keeps it, the better it gets.'" She giggles. "She's 65 years old, of course." "Well," a schoolmate responds, not giggling, "You could also say, what is it they say about precious pearls—the more you use them, the lovelier they get." "But nice boys want to marry virgins," a Wellesley freshman points out. "Who wants to marry 'nice boys?'" someone snaps back. "And how do men know, anyway?" asks a curly-haired Brandeis senior. "If they find out on the wedding night—what do they say? 'Sorry, honey, it's all off?'" "You don't have to tell boys *everything,*" suggests a gamin-faced Radcliffe girl to the Briggs Hall Cliffies assembled around a dining room table. "Yes," another picks it up, "like that you wear contact lenses."

After the first dizzy whirl of freshman mixers and ardent courtship from upperclassmen eligibles, there comes a pause in life's occupation known as sophomore slump. Instead of being dated up six weeks in advance, the college girl may find herself unhappily accepting a blind date at 6 o'clock Saturday night. She may or may not have made the sorority she had her heart set on. She may be snowing her professors or pulling "D's" and "C's" or may, indeed, have become so enmeshed in the literary magazine or student government or lab work, she rarely has time to notice the social lull. But if she is the typical college girl, she notices. She daydreams, sleeps through morning classes now and then, comforts herself with calories, finds it impossible to get term papers in on time. As her self-esteem plummets, she may somehow become convinced that sexual abandon—or even one boy's welcoming mattress—could be the path to renewed popularity. Instead of a highspirited fraternity cut-up who regards her as a sweet, presentable date, she may now find herself attracted to the kind of boy who does not easily take "no" for an answer.

"The books say you're supposed to dangle yourself as a lure, leading the guy on indefinitely till he pops the question from sheer frustration," a Goucher junior complained. "That's not my idea of the cornerstone for marriage." "You find yourself involved increasingly with guys who can't imagine a meaningful relationship that doesn't include sex," a Sarah Lawrence sophomore remarked, "and you just have to question all your old stock responses—all your little-girl-from-school procrastinations." "You start seeing it as the intellectual thing," a Brooklyn College sophomore said.

By the time she is a junior, the college girl has heard every nuance of every argument for and against sexual intimacy before marriage. Indeed, she may have heard much more than she has wanted to hear. "This pathological exchanging of confidence," an outraged Texas Women's University maiden described it. "They talk so much about it because they want to annihilate the act." "Do what you must," a Smith bluestocking cried, 'but for heaven's sake, spare me the grisly details."

What used to be theoretical discussion of sex ethics is now painfully personal confession and trading of technical know-how: How to seem poised at a motel, how to pinpoint your ovulation date, which local doctor will answer her birth control questions without asking any questions. Torn between the idea that erotic sex is sin, her inherited image of virtue, and the lure of sex as an expression of romantic love, she is able to reject the concept of sin and succumb to the wonders of love. Sin is so old-fashioned. Love (as *Vogue* might say of a gown by Mainbocher) is so utterly timeless. Tristan and Iseult. Goya and the Duchess of Alba. Lady Chatterley and what's his name. The college girl can become quite caught up in Simone de Beauvoir, D. H. Lawrence, Henry Miller, Lawrence Durrell. "We all got terribly excited about *Clea,*" a recent Shimer graduate recalled, "and the idea that once you get virginity out of the way, you can get on with your creative and intellectual growth." She pulled *Clea* out of the bookcase and it fell open to the page with Clea's speech: "You know it is a terrible business to be a virgin . . . You long to be delivered from it yet . . . at the same time this valuable experience should be with someone you care for, otherwise it will be without value to your inside self . . . I decided—guess what? To offer myself grimly to the only artist I knew I could trust, to put me out of my misery . . . At last I burst in on him like a fireman into a burning building, startling him, and said with trembling lips, 'I have come to ask you to *depuceler* me, please, because I cannot get any further with my work unless you do.' I said it in French. It would have sounded dirty in English." * A recent Radcliffe graduate told how her roommate had read a *New Yorker* story about an affair between a Harvard boy and a Cliffie, and decided to go to bed. "She was the last of our crowd to go," the girl recalled. And a UCLA junior said Bertrand Russell's *Marriage and Morals* was "more or less my undoing." The would-be seducer had given her Russell's book to read and two days later "settled the virginity matter more or less forcibly in the back seat of his car," she said. "But I must give him credit for preparing me intellectually at least."

Though the printed word has its special powers of persuasion for citizens of the academic community, the appropriateness of sex as a prenuptial expression of love, lust, or just a pleasurable way to pass a lazy afternoon is still not a simple matter, even with paperbound Simone de Beauvoir offering encouragement in the pocket of her duffle coat. There is more talk, endless, searching verbal dissection of meaning and motivation. She talks to her roommate, her best friend from back home. She might even discuss it with her favorite professor, her older brother, the campus psychological counselor. She talks to him . . . I mustn't . . . I couldn't . . . I'm afraid . . .

---

* *Clea,* by Lawrence Durrell. N.Y.: E. P. Dutton & Co., 1960.

I shouldn't . . . I want to . . . do we really . . . well we . . . but where . . . Over a hundred cups of overcooked black coffee in thick white cups, they debate. He reasons. She implores. He begs. He curses. She curses back. She soothes. He cajoles. By the time their conversation ultimately takes them to bed, they may be so exhausted and unnerved by the debate that their love-making may be doomed to joyless anticlimax.

She hates it. She loves it. She is disappointed, unmoved, unleashed, unhinged, uncertain. She now feels "in." As a Northwestern coed recalled, "You just assume everyone is a virgin when you are, and after, you discover how many aren't." "It's like they welcome you," a Stanford sophomore said, "to the club, I mean." A Radcliffe girl told how a dorm-mate came in one evening after a weekend off-campus and announced, "Well, I'm one of the club, girls. Now we can really talk it up." And a University of Vermont coed, who came back to her room on the night of nights, closed the door and began to cry, reported that "one by one, all the nonvirgins trooped in to comfort me. How did they know? They just knew."

She discovers the subtleties of love in the afternoon, any afternoon, starting at 4 P.M. when Harvard house suites are open to the ladies.* Love makes Monday seem less dreary. If she lives at home in Philadelphia, attends classes at Temple,

* A belated discovery of the national press, marked by a flood of head-lines in late October, 1963, when a controversy over visiting hours blos-somed into a wordy debate over the undergraduate's "inalienable right" to sexual privacy. The conflict went unnoticed as long as the issue was docu-mented by *The Crimson* under the heading, "parietals." To most of the "outside world," parietals "probably meant something to do with pariah," a Collegiate Press Service Bulletin explained rather arrogantly. When it became clear that parietals referred to college rules and rules to S-E-X, the story made the national wires as a nation rejoiced that its intellectual elite had proved to be basically human. But Harvard professor-on-leave John Kenneth Galbraith found the revival of the parietal debate "depressing." He wrote in a letter to *The Crimson*: "No effort need be made or should be made to protect individuals from the consequences of their own errors, indiscretions or passions. Parents of Harvard and Radcliffe applicants should, no doubt, be put firmly on notice, so that they may send them elsewhere."

and Mom does volunteer work at the hospital Thursday afternoon—Thursday is The Day. If the young man who has
loaned her the key to his apartment lives down the street from
the nursing college dorm, and he and she just happen to have
11 o'clock free each morning, well, that's fine too. And, of
course, there is the weekend when love may or may not be
widely, devoutly, deliriously celebrated. She loves to play
house. If "he" happens to share an apartment with four other
boys, she may find herself Friday night cooking dinner for
eight, washing dishes in the bathtub under the shower spray.

She wants to be in love. She thrives on commitment. She is
emotionally involved (though the involvement may be, as
Harvard psychiatrist Carl A. L. Binger feels, "as a fly is involved with a piece of flypaper"). Maybe it lasts. Maybe it
doesn't. Maybe it was love. Maybe it was a mistake. Maybe
by the time she has convinced herself it was right, he has
convinced himself it is over and is backing out of the relationship. As a Sarah Lawrence girl put it, "Premarital intercourse may be one great romance with the man you later
marry, or it may be a series of little growing affairs."

Saturday, she discovers—usually to her dismay—is also a
night to study in, a time to clean bureau drawers, give a home
permanent to a friend. From the second floor of the Tri Delt
house at The University of Miami to Peabody Hall at Temple
and Rockefeller House at Bryn Mawr, the air may still be
moist from dozens of showers, heady with the mingled scent
of talcum, hair spray, fluoridated toothpaste, posy-young
colognes, the musk of reputedly aphrodisiac perfume.

Now added to it, the perfume of orange peels, browning
apple cores, contraband beer, coffee, thousands of pizzas or-
dered to cheer the keepers of the weekend wake: the dateless.
Some by choice, of course. Some like to think it's by choice.
Some prefer to avoid men and boys. Some feel physics or
poetry are far more important than collegiate dating. There
are girls who have sacrificed a fraternity party to do a term
paper, girls with fiances on other campuses, girls with fictitious
fiances, girls who were stood up. And thousands who just
didn't get asked.

They bowl, play bridge, study, read, groan, go to a movie, sleep, eat, masturbate, write a sonnet, crash a party, have an hysterical fit, call a boy they swore never to call again, commit suicide,* and, maybe, turn off the lights in the third floor study hall so they can see "who's making out" on the front steps. " 'Do you think so-and-so is sleeping with him?' is a big topic of conversation," a Smith junior said. "And 'How do you keep from becoming promiscuous?' is something we're always asking each other," an Oberlin senior reported. "We *do* talk about other subjects now and then," a second Oberlin girl pointed out. "But not often," the first said wearily. "We're making too much of sex," a Northwestern senior protested. "If we weren't so hung-up on the subject, blowing it up all out of proportion, people wouldn't marry for love and then discover it wasn't love at all, just sex," a Brooklyn College sophomore observed. "Well, don't you feel yourself sort of losing all control?" a UCLA junior wanted to know. "Promiscuity is—" a Wellesley girl groped for the proper word, "—insensitive."

At curfew, the girls trudge in. The girl down the hall was pinned tonight. She can hear the squeals. Her own roommate is AWOL because she suddenly decided to elope. As senior year approaches, the sparkle of diamond chips in the dining room—modest though it might seem to Harry Winston—is more dazzling than she can bear. In a letter from home, Mother wants to know whatever happened to that nice Milwaukee boy she used to see so much. Suddenly "career" is an ugly word. That job in San Francisco waiting after graduation has lost its appeal. Another thick ivory wedding announcement in the mail this morning. And that makes three baby gifts this semester to offspring of her class' early brides.

* Nationally, suicide is the sixth most common cause of death among young people of college age, according to Morton M. Hunt and Rena Corman. In "The Tormented Generation" (*The Saturday Evening Post,* October 12, 1963), they report: "A recent study shows suicide to be the second most common cause of student deaths at Yale, after accidents." They blame several causes, including the pressures of college-conscious society and hard-driving parents determined their child must enter a particular school (he may not need or desire) and achieve academic honor and excellence (of which he may be far from capable).

How real is the pressure? So real that the grades of Swarthmore girls—higher than those of Swarthmore boys until the junior year—decline as the marriage panic heightens.* So real that, in the post-Sputnik concern about lack of interest in science majors, the National Education Association was told: "Once the child gets the point that one who takes science is more likely to get married . . . then you are in business as far as the sell is concerned." ** So real and so disturbing that the college girl who is still a virgin when the pair-off pace quickens may decide that chastity was her mistake—or she may decide nothing at all—-and hurdle off aimlessly in a number of directions, bed being but one of them.

What happens to the college girl's ideas about herself and sex over the four undergraduate years seems, to Boroff, relatively predictable. Describing what he calls "the pilgrim's progress on the road to sex freedom," he divides it: "Freshman year, girls tends to be idealistic and to believe in premarital chastity. Sophomore year is the season to go steady, and sexual urgencies increase. Junior year is often the time when the breakout from the cage of virginity is likely to take place. . . ." From what the coeds interviewed here said, Boroff's timetable would seem to be typical, although it is doubtful that it leads to "sex freedom." "If only it were really freedom," an Oberlin junior remarked, "but for most of us it's merely a relaxation, nothing as deliciously wanton as 'freedom' implies."

Except for pockets of orgiastic sensuality, "in sheer wildness," as the Harvard *Crimson* put it, "today's college students do not compare with their fabled predecessors." Sexual involvement tends to be intense, sober, rigidly idealistic, monogamous. Promiscuity, which most college girls flatly condemn (even though some of them aren't too sure what the word means) calls for, at the least, a special drive and stamina. On the other hand, should that one great romantic involvement fail the college girl, she may find the only way to patch together the pieces of her self-esteem is to pursue that same

* *Campus U.S.A.*, by David Boroff. Harper & Brothers, 1961.
** "Kalamazoo College," by Virginia Voss. *Mademoiselle Magazine*, February, 1959.

intense monogamy in another bed. What may sometimes look like an erotic free-for-all is not to be confused with "free love" if free means no strings attached. The college girl *does* attach strings to her sexual favors—and the boy who thought he was picking up a notoriously "easy make" may discover she is thinking about the Military Ball three months away, Europe together this summer, making slip covers for his day-bed—and always, marriage.

"You like to think you can be casual about sex," a University of Delaware senior said. "You say, okay, I'll go to bed with him because he's cute—or he sort of likes me—or it's such a lovely night. Next thing you know you're hung-up emotionally. Maybe we do it because, as emancipated and intellectual as we like to think we are, deep down we don't fancy ourselves girls who go to bed without love."

The dedicated scholar or ambitious would-be career girl may grind away through four or eight years of college and graduate school, without ever getting around to sexual awakening. And many college girls, it must be pointed out, have no desire to rebel or question. Some are totally deaf to the rumblings of dissent and anger about them. Mama said nice girls wear socks with their sneakers and this type of coed will wear socks with her sneakers when more rebellious coeds are tramping the campus barefoot. But just because she wears socks with her sneakers, it does not follow that she is chaste. Campus sex is compounded not only of rebellion, permissiveness, and the passion for scientific inquiry, but also loneliness, idealism, the need for security, the desire to be popular, the time and place for privacy, and the din of the drums that never cease to remind her that she must not fail in achieving her destiny of domesticity.

I Love You for Experimental Reasons

"No, I never paid any particular attention to her. She was just another bright, quick mind, another nubile creature in a class of bright-eyed maidens. Her term paper was brilliantly handled but the thesis was nonsense and I knew the grade would upset her. It was in my office and I was hunting for the paper when she leaned forward and plopped two plump little tits smack down on top of my desk. Two fat little apples for teacher—wrapped in some sort of flesh-colored sweater, cashmere, no doubt. On top of a pile of books—atop a copy of Donne's *Love Poems,* appropriately enough.

"Unflusterable I am not. But she just looked me in the eye as though it were nothing unusual at all and said how she wished we might have time to talk—to *really* talk and how she might as well be just a bug crawling out of the woodwork in time for classes—and then she said, let me quote verbatim, 'Mr. McEwen, I could be the living reincarnation of Edna St. Vincent Millay and I doubt if anyone would . . .' the dear child had the grace to stammer here . . . 'would even light one of my candles.' "

He teaches English at the University of Michigan. We were close friends during my undergraduate years there. The affair he described seemed to be a classic illustration of what I had come to think of as the cross-cultural sex underground: Unwilling or unable to throw off traditional moral restraints within her own circle of escorts and possible marriage prospects, a girl slips off to another dimension for "just a taste" of sexual experience. When I realized the girl was still on campus, I arranged that she be invited to one of my interview sessions. Her responses supported freedom of sex decision— "It's up to the individual . . ." She complained, "Even the girl who is intellectually and emotionally capable of a premarital relationship is held back by her awareness of society's disapproval . . . you can't talk about what you would do if you were transported for one day to another universe . . . the point is, you're here. You can't act in a vacuum." She gave an impression of a girl who might like to but would not permit herself to have an affair. When I asked how girls felt about dating faculty men, she smiled and said nothing. When I asked what effect Junior Year Abroad had on sexual mores—was it likely some girls felt freer sexually in a situation "where no one back home ever has to know?"—she said nothing. She lingered afterward, returning to that last idea—"No one back home has to know." "I was intrigued with that concept," she said, "and I thought I'd tell you about an experience of the girl who lives across the corridor from me." After a few minutes she said: "You must know the friend I'm talking about is myself, of course." "I was beginning to wonder," I said. Whether she would have given quite the same account of her affair had she known of my knowledge, I cannot say.

"It's really a crime wasting brains on a female. I have exactly one semester left to get engaged, and at this moment, it certainly doesn't look like I'm going to make it under the wire. No one has to tell me how I've messed up. You see, I never have exactly made up my mind what I was doing in college. Freshman year, I knew everything. Sophomore year I let a doubt or two creep in. By my junior year I finally realized what a dunce I was—what a zero—the literary genius of Mumford High and the literary nothing as far as the rest of the world was concerned. I had such big plans. A master's. A Fulbright and a year overseas. Then a Ph.D. But now when I think of even lasting through a master's I get panicky. It turns out, you see, that I'm as middle-class as the next girl. I really just want to get married like everyone else seems to be doing—to someone special of course—special—that is to say, a specialist would be nice, the ambition of every nice middle-class Jewish girl—or certainly, of every nice middle-class Jewish girl's mother.

"This teacher I mentioned earlier had been flirting with me in a way the whole semester. I'd look up in class and he'd be staring at me—at my sweater more likely. But I imagine he might have been intimidated about asking out one of his own students. He needed a bit of encouragement. It was part of my plan. You see, I have every intention of being a virgin on my wedding night. In my family, girls just are. Period. But by junior year I was aching to go to bed with a man. Curiosity? I don't know. I just had to—wanted to. It seemed to me if it were someone like Mr. McEwen—absolutely unrelated to anything that would ever touch the world of Northwest Detroit and related suburbs, I could still be a virgin on my wedding night. No one would ever, ever know. It wouldn't really count."

"That's what she told me, that she was curious. Felt it was time she had the experience. Once my ego had returned to its normal miniscule size, I realized why she had picked me of all people. Not for my obvious virility and classic Greek profile. But simply because I was there. A good safe, young, unmarried Mt. Everest, glamorous by virtue of the podium, but hardly more glorified than the beanery waitress a college boy might release his passion on if his virtuous girl friend said 'hands-off.' She could as safely have flung herself at some international commuter, one of the foreign students here today, the Philippines and no recriminations tomorrow. Or some good-looking colored kid from out of state—a lot of girls can't resist the ultimate rebellion. Or just some local construction worker who caught her eye. But I offered an extra dividend—100 extra Green Stamps, as it were—the status of academe. And, of course, most important of all, I wasn't kosher. It *had* to be someone gentile, a citizen of another dimension as far from her tight little world as possible and with a definite guarantee not to overlap back home."

"As soon as I made up my mind, I got very shaky. I started thinking of all sorts of extraneous and ridiculous reasons why not to. It would hurt. I'd never be able to fake it on my wedding night. Or once I did it, I'd never be able to control myself. I'd become insatiable. Or I'd be graceless and clumsy and he would hate my body. It was much too squashy for him and my great marshmallow thighs. Ugh! Oh, it wasn't his type of body at all. Let's see—I think I had about 27 other doubts on my mind besides. As far as pregnancy was concerned— I don't know, I guess I thought I'd just let him worry about that. He had more to lose than I if something happened. Then I got to thinking, where will it happen? I didn't want it to be in the backseat of a car on a road somewhere. His address in the faculty directory sounded sort of shabby and not too promising. A slum street in downtown Ann Arbor. Even a car on a country road would be better than bugs and mildew. But I'm not the kind of girl that does things in the back seat of cars. I had to laugh at that. I *am* that kind—in fact this particular thing was just about the only sexual experiment I hadn't attempted in an automobile. But this had to be special. I had in mind a bed—clean, cool sheets, champagne, a lacy white nightgown . . ."

"Much as I hate to be accused of gross traditionalism, I will have to confess that the official deflowering took place, alas, in our traditional flowering and deflowering spot, the Arboretum. As eager as she was, when the moment came, she took two days of gentle convincing, which is why it was the Arb and not my digs. As I told you once, I have rather a way with virgins. I never intended it that way. But young beginners seem to sniff me out and plant themselves in my path, or, as in this case, plant their bazoom on my desk and say, 'Please Mr. Mac, talk me into it.' It requires persistence, soft, gentle persistence, wooing, aimed not at a particular area between her thighs but at the particular girl—at her brain.

"You start with the brain—these are hot little intellectual hopefuls, you know. You convince the hot little brain it is the right, intelligent, emancipated, etc., etc., etc. Then you convince the hot little emotions there is no other girl existing at this moment. She is the woman—she, her face, her body— they are frightened, you know, of winding up objects under your body, as they should be because eventually most of them do. If a man cares for women at all, he will have the decency to conceal their own object-ness from them. All the while, of course, you are working on their hot little bodies. Possibly in their campus mewings and maulings with heavy-pawed but awed young men, they will have discovered lust-potential. Probably not. But, hello lust, Mac is here—the lust juices are bubbling now past their delicate little earlobes and you are breaking their breakable maternal little hearts with your cry for understanding—'I need you, baby'—only you never say baby, always her name. Let her know you know it. She's all yours. Telling it I'm flip. In truth, of course, I'm not at all. Tap the shell. Inside I'm soft boiled. Maybe they sniff that too."

"It was even worse than I thought. It didn't hurt. Are you sure you want so many details? This is embarrassing sort of. . . . No, of course I don't mind. My last gesture for science. Let's see. What I was about to say was I rather disappointed myself at being so insufferably modern and healthy, I didn't feel anything at all alarming or even unpleasant. It was just sort of nothing much at all. I kept thinking. Is this it? I kept waiting for something ecstatically divine to happen but nothing I would describe as ecstatically divine did happen. But then I cheered myself up a bit remembering it isn't something you're born knowing—it takes time to pick up all the techniques.

"At first I'd been furious because he couldn't wait for a bed and the perfect moment. My spine was sore from the ground and I almost died thinking someone would come along at any moment. But he was very sweet, very tender and loving afterwards, kissing a leaf and putting it in my pocket and I realize now, it was beautiful there in the Arb even if it was the absolute cliche place for it to happen."

"I only saw her when she called me. I never called her. If I wasn't otherwise occupied, I would see her. She came to the apartment and broiled a steak she brought along—probably cost $5, it could have fed a family of six. Once she called and announced she'd been given—she said given underlined —a pair of tickets to a concert. Afterwards, walking her up the hill, it was too late to go to my place. There were only a few minutes until lockout and I pulled her into a dark driveway between two houses across from the dorm—then I tugged off her panties and stuffed them into her purse and made love to her against the wall. She had never become so excited before. Never mind. The point is that this chaste and sheltered maiden from the smothering bosom of middle-class familial fidelity had a taste for the exotic. She kept asking 'could we do it differently, Mr. McEwen?' That was a cute touch. Mister. We tried all the positions—everything I could think of, and then she apparently dipped into some sort of marriage manual or interviewed a visiting sadist because she came up with some suggestions of her own, including one or two specialties I'd never tried because I thought they must be somewhat painful. . . ."

"He wasn't nearly as experienced as I had imagined. But he was gentle and very considerate. What kills me about all this was that no one ever dreamed—absolutely no one had the slightest idea what was going on. My roommate knew I was dating this teacher and was, needless to say, most impressed but she didn't dream what was actually going on. She just said I better not fall for him or my family would have a fit— I hadn't the slightest intention of that, though I was growing fonder of him all the time and I could see he was becoming more attached to me. But wouldn't the Phi Sigs be bowled over if they knew. This boy I used to date would have a heart attack if he even for a minute thought. Little old hands-off-me. . . . Sometimes I had the feeling I embarrassed him— the teacher, I mean. Sometimes, in fact I embarrassed myself. But he kept calling and he was always very loving, very thoughtful—lonely and, in a way, sort of helpless."

"She hadn't called for a few weeks and then one afternoon she strolled into the office just as I was about to leave. She'd been dating a new young man, it seems, a very important fraternity man from a very important family with very important ambitions to be a very important dentist. She was impressed. She was also in heat again. 'Oh, Mr. McEwen,' she said. 'Wouldn't it be fun to do it in your chair.' Can you imagine? You know how precarious these swivel chairs are at best—occupied by one sober and reasonably coordinated person. But two—going at it full speed, as was her wont. I offered her my desk. That didn't appeal to her. The floor. Too dusty. The wall. Well, all right. The wall would have to do. Broad daylight in the English department office. I must have been insane. Then to make it even more distressing she kept kicking over some Coke bottles my office mates had lined up against the wall. After the first bottle or two, though, I stopped paying much attention."

"As far as I was concerned, summer would have to end it. Mr.—I mean this teacher stayed on at school during the summer session and I went home to Detroit and took a part-time job to keep from going stir-crazy. It was grim in a way. Oh, plenty of men, lots of dates, but I was different. I just couldn't fool around with all that petting stuff anymore. It just didn't make sense anymore. If you're going to get that worked up, you really should go all the way. But I certainly wasn't going to start that stuff at home."

"Out of nowhere one Friday night she called and announced she was driving down for the weekend. I was surprised. I had the feeling when she kissed me off in June that was adieu. I'd been had. It had all happened in another dimension. She was going to erase it from the book of time and regrow a psychosomatic hymen for her betrothed—when and if she located him. The dentist, possibly. But she showed up with her genuine leather overnight case with the solid gold clasps, and I could tell she planned to spend the night. Obviously, she hadn't known what she was signing on for. I'd gotten myself involved with one of the first fraternities, you see, as a tutor of sorts for one of the more Neanderthal brothers. In exchange for room and board. Which meant I was holed up in a rather grimy den off the furnace room in the cellar.

She was brave. Determined to stick it out. Elegant to the end. She put on a lacy blue negligee, I believe you call it. Then unhappily she developed an irrepressible desire to pee. Quite a problem. The boys were playing poker in the recreation room and that meant she couldn't possibly sneak through the hall to the basement john and I would be out on my ear if it were discovered I entertained negligeed coeds in my boudoir. Nor was our modest little maiden about to pee in front of me. Not even if I turned my eyes. No. Not even in my precious coffee pot, which I so gallantly offered. There was only one solution. Little Miss Two Apples for the Teacher climbed out the window, which just happened to lead out to the sloping front lawn of the fraternity house overlooking the intersection of Fraternity Row and Sorority Lane. And peed, almost triumphantly I might say, on the front lawn. I was never prouder of her. It was a most precious exhibition of *savoir faire*."

"It was a strange relationship. At times I hated him. At times I frightened myself. But all the awful things I had thought might happen, never happened. No pregnancy. No uncontrollable lust. I became engaged to Tony that following fall. We broke up a few months ago. I can't see myself as a dentist's wife. I really can't. Which means I have exactly one semester left to find or be found by The Man."

"I had left for Oxford before she came back to school that fall and I haven't seen her again. That pleases me in a literary way. I like that last glorious memory of the wind blowing through her hair while she stood there watering the fraternity lawn. It seemed to me the grass grew greener thereafter. Well, of course, she used me. I realized what young ladies mean when they complain of a fellow's having used them. But with me, it was 'pleasantly' used. For experimental purposes, as it were. And if it shook her out of that gelatinous complacency, I think she will be better for it. That fall in Oxford I got a clipping in the mail from Ann Arbor, from her, obviously. It was an engagement notice cut out of the Detroit Free Press. No note. Just the clipping. She has another semester to go, I believe, and then I suppose she'll be off and safely married and gone chastely to her bridegroom."

3

Geography of the Sex Revolution

Nothing is static on the map of the emerging revolution in sex ethics. Its collegiate frontiers and wilderness are as yet uncharted by professional behaviorists. But I feel it is possible from the observations and confidences of the college girl herself, to describe regional sexual climates in the manner of a television weather map—the cold wave moving across Utah, some turbulence over the Great Lakes about to collide with hurricane Eros sweeping along the Atlantic Seaboard, haze obscuring the Gulf Bay. As we begin to fill in the shaded areas, we discover that the continental United States appears to be hemmed on either side by a hand of sexual sophistication with pockets of erotic permissiveness sprinkled about the map, seemingly at random.

Nature, topography, and the pleasure-bent tradition of California sets the pace for the physical exuberance and amorality of the West. In the East, warring forces—vestigial feminism and the feminine mystique—spurred by the upper-crust tradition for *avant garde* sexual nonconformity have spawned an intellectualized sexual freedom. The Midwest, long regarded as the great plateau of conservatism, has always tolerated small enclaves of Bohemian nonconformity. But now the provincialism of home-grown tradition is under attack by outside forces. Clinging bravely to the legends of Southern womanhood, the South resists some of the same attack from contemporary realities and is abetted by the rigidity of Fundamentalist religion, but the South too is responding to the new sex ethic by substituting discretion where once only chastity was tolerated. And Texas seems to combine Western hedonism and outdoor license (plus air conditioning and space, lots of space) with the South's magnolia-scented niceties of discretion, chivalry, femininity, and appreciation for romantic love.

"Free love"—sex without affection—were it to make any headway at all, would thus thrive best in the East-West bands of intellectual and physical amorality. The new single standard of "sex with affection" has increasing influence everywhere and finds modest, discreet supporters in what has always been regarded as strictly "double standard" territory.

It is revealing to consider feminine geographical stereotypes. Although the entire nation has been exposed to all the forces for change described earlier * and the communications media move influences, fads, and new idioms around faster than ever, there is still validity in stereotype. No single girl may ever match type but, depending upon the strength of her drive for conformity, the college girl demonstrates an awareness of her public image.

No female respects her own public-relation image more than the Southern Belle. If she is not soft, feminine, helpless, and innocently naive, she will fake it. "The South is the land of the nation's greatest actresses," a Mississippi coed declared. Less inhibited, not quite so sexually threatened as the Eastern

* See Chapter 1, "Even Nice Girls."

male, the Southern college boy appreciates wonmanliness.* His appreciated beauty queen and baton twirler must be chaste but she may be sexy.** Even a shedding Angora sweater is forgivable if it is worn by a Southern coed. She may be as bosomy as nature allowed and more so,*** wasp-waisted and crinolined on all occasions, while her Yankee counterpart might appear sleekly black or chicly neuter. She may wear the same back-to-school sweaters, skirts, kilts, and wash-and-wear blouses as the Big Ten coed, but either she buys them a size smaller or else her torso simply does more for them. Yet there is a ladylike restraint in her sexiness— Terry Southern compares the majorette's strut to contemporary burlesque, grind but no bump—it is never the exaggerated sequin-mascara-ed variety of high school sexiness. In this era of the Tyranny of the Hairdresser, only a Southern belle would appear in the long bob and masses of waves and curl. Hair may be long on Yankee territory, but it is straight and some-times a bit grimy.

The Southern girl's dress is homage to her stereotyped moti-vations. "She is here," a Mississippi professor comments, "to win beauty contests, learn grooming and enough culture for

* The Southern boy may be just as troubled by fears of latent homo-sexuality as the Northern and Eastern Joe College, but he is more likely to express his doubts in heightened sexual activity off-campus than is the more constricted and intellectualized Ivy Leaguer.

** If you are willing to consider panty raids as "ritual rape," you might wish to ponder the sexual symbolism of baton twirling hinted at by Terry Southern in "Twirling at Ole Miss," *Esquire Magazine,* February, 1963. "The development of American baton twirling closely parallels the history of the emancipation of our women," Southern writes. "A larger version of this same baton (metal with a knob on the end) was first used, of course, to direct military marching bands, or prior to that, drum corps— the baton being manipulated in a fairly straight forward, dum-de-dum, up-and-down manner. The idea of *twirling* it—and finally even *flinging* it— is obviously, a delightfully girlish notion." Becoming a majorette, he ob-serves, "is generally considered the smartest status a girl can achieve on the Southern campus."

*** The ice cream cone bosom has been gently rounding off in the trend toward less projection and less exaggeration of the American bosom, but brassiere manufacturers report "they still demand headlight reflector bras in the South and West and the old hit-em-in-the-eye look in Texas and the Southwest."

Browning Club participation later, and, of course, to marry the lawyers, doctors, and business executives Ole Miss graduates." Thus, she hides her brains if she has them because she knows what a liability brains can be in the hunt. (Not that the Yankee coed *doesn't* know, only that she is apt to fight it.) She would not dream of competing in class with a man. "I get all tore up the way I see you Yankee girls pouncin' on some po' Yankee boy out-articulatin' him to death," said a Southern transplant at Ohio State. A brainy girl (she could obviously out-articulate anybody to death), she had come north to escape the limitations of the magnolia mystique, only to find her Southerness too formidable a social weapon to abandon.

The Southern coed is not untouched by the academic traditions of scientific inquiry, self-determination, and the distrust of dogma that lead to the idea that each girl must create her own sex ethic. But she never loses sight of the *really* vital issue: marriage. That is why a University of Alabama coed may concede, as one luminous blonde did, "Premarital relations or promiscuity are fine for the girl who feels them to be so," adding: "but never is indiscretion permissible." "The unquestionable essence of disgrace to a Southern lady," a Mississippi coed expanded, "is the *known* loss of virtue." He wants to marry a virgin. Very well. The "world's greatest actress" will be a virgin. She will not, as a Yankee girl might, try to convince him virginity is not that important.

The "world's greatest actress" may be fooling me, too, or I may be judging the situation from distances that make other yards look greener, but it seems to me the Southern girl is far less troubled by masculine-feminine role conflicts. She seems willing, content, even proud to be what her man imagines her to be. Not that a Northern girl would necessarily envy the limitations of that role, but you have to envy the by-products. Regardless of geography, when this kind of girl goes to bed with a man, it is more likely her emotions that take her there than her intellect. Her joy in her own womanliness, and the Southern male's appreciation of that womanliness, makes her a far more gracious bed-partner.

I concede the air of calm acceptance could turn out to be a

gigantic hoax. Yet testimony from a chauvinistic but otherwise generally reliable Southern bachelor seems to confirm elements of accuracy. Asked to comment on the difference between Southern and Yankee coeds as love-partners, the young bachelor reported: "The Yankees like to get right down to it,* while the Southern ladies like to play games about it a little more, though they are just as eager. Once having committed herself, the Southern girl is more enthusiastic. Whether this is real or pretended—on either side, Yankee or Southern— I can't say. But you have the feeling of actually existing for the Southern girl. With the Yankee young ladies, you feel yourself uncomfortably like an entry in some sort of bookkeeping, whereas with the Southern girl you are given the impression that it is the first time it has really meant anything to her."

The Texas coed likes to think of herself as "delicately Southern," according to a delicate University of Texas coed, and embraces some of the same respect for chastity and, in its absence, the appearance of chastity. Love is its own morality. Western hedonism and the automobile may precipitate sexual pressures the Southern girl escapes. "Space is so vast," a University of Texas junior tried to explain it, "and you don't think twice about driving 200 miles to a barbecue. Texas and Houston men are famous for their Cadillac convertibles and sports cars—and they do 'it' in the back seat stripped down to hat and boots, foregoing the hat when it's a sports car. There is a limit to American know-how," she added with a giggle. Sex in the automobile has even bred a unique rating system, described by a Texas Women's University junior: "She's a 'nice' girl if she doesn't do it in cars, only in motels."

This feeling of being "on the move" and the exposure to the constant opportunity for sexual excitation plus privacy are persuasive forces in the sexual climate of the West. The casual, relaxed, informal, and outdoor existence of California has inspired the stereotype of a Californian coed: leggy, bronzed, healthy, athletic, in white buck shoes, pale cashmeres, and the

* It is likely, as he admits, that his own Southernness was "very much in favor with the Yankee young ladies."

inevitable mackintosh. Basking in the lush foliage and mild climate, the Westerner never knows constriction. The flowers (girls) on the beach at Carmel wear polka-dot bikinis, don rubber suits to brave the icy surf, mouse (neck) in the sun, inhaling hedonism with every breath. "The outdoors all year around offers opportunity that is only seasonal back East," a Stanford instructor theorized. "The beaches, the mountain cabins, the fraternity weekends where the chaperones are as likely to get laid as anyone else—if they manage to stay sufficiently sober." Californian "cool" is more physical exuberance than intellectual. "Nobody's supposed to be inhibited," as Mort Sahl put it. "Nobody's shy and sex is the least a girl can give of herself."

But climate and foliage cannot fully explain the pleasure bent of the Californian. California is vastly rich and big, peopled by new citizens who come, as a California church leader suggested, because "San Francisco just sounds like more fun than Ohio." The vastness and wealth of its educational system breeds what one Berkeley faculty man describes as a pervasive irresponsibility, an intellectual amorality that may easily lead to a general amorality. It is all there, spread before the Californian college student. "Call it the weather, call it the closing of the frontier, call it the Failure of Eden," writes novelist and Californian Joan Didion, "the fact remains that Californians are cultivating America's largest growth of passive nihilism right along with their bougainvillaea." *

To be one small digit of the 57,000 students in the scattered ant hills that make up the University of California complex is a threat to identity. It is so easy to feel lost, insignificant. Sex may be seen as a path to Instant Identity, a way of belonging. At the same time the ant-hill anonymity provides protective camouflage.

This anonymity is very much a factor in the sexual climate of the Midwest's Big Ten universities. The big state schools are growing in all directions, gobbling up countryside, spawning monster dormitories. Several midwestern coeds described

* "Berkeley's Giant: The University of California," by Joan Didion. *Mademoiselle Magazine*, January, 1960.

a feeling that no one person matters that much, that no one really notices what one person is doing in the midst of so many. "I was pleased to come to the University," a junior from a wealthy Detroit suburb said: "It was so big and no one was going to know me or what I'm like or what to expect of me—I could start from scratch and be whatever I wanted to be. And I am."

By far the most striking evolution in sexual climate has hit the Midwestern heartland of conservatism: anonymity makes it possible. But the persuasiveness of the single standard—sex with affection—is again, here as elsewhere throughout the country, increasingly significant because of the average coed's often monomaniacal pursuit of matrimony. The campus as a marriage mart is the prime consideration for most American coeds, but the Midwestern coed may be a bit more candid (or more certain) about her motivation than, for example, the Ivy League college girl. Seventy percent of freshman women at one Midwestern university responded to "What do you hope to get out of college?" with variations of the theme "the man for me." *

In the Midwest, the hope for a firm matrimonial commitment by Commencement Day was less likely to permit premarital intercourse in the early fifties. The University of Michigan, when I was a student sheltered in the maternalistic arms of Stockwell Hall, was not exactly a fortress of chastity but it liked to present that image to the world, especially to the rural-dominated State Legislature at appropriation time; and the Michigan coed herself played along. All "nice" girls may not have been virgins but they certainly pretended to be to all but their closest intimates, and huge after-hours seminars on sex were inclined to be strictly theoretical rather than the *en masse* confessional of today.

"Nice" girls did it and "nice" girls survived, unless the word got around and they discovered they weren't "nice" girls anymore. Today "nice" girls *do* talk about going to bed with boys, or planning to—"Next year," as a serious, intense, essentially

* "Motivational Factors in College Entrance," by Elizabeth Douvan and Carol Kaye. *The American College,* Nevitt Sanford, ed., N.Y.: Wiley, 1962.

conservative Michigan freshman informed me, "because you feel more sure of yourself by the time you're a sophomore." And she said so many coeds were missing and unaccounted for during a recent after-curfew fire drill at the new women's dorm that it was decided not to make an issue of it, "for fear of undesirable publicity."

Such *laissez faire* was as great a discovery to me as the news that senior women were now exempt from curfew restrictions —and were actually trusted to carry keys to dormitory and sorority house doors. Many girls had campaigned for exactly such relaxing of University maternalism. Dean of Women Deborah Bacon had convinced them it could never be— Regents, alumni, parents, the Legislature would never permit it. And, in fact, the liberalization of social restrictions had come only after the resignation of Miss Bacon, a colorful and outspoken proponent of old-fashioned decorum* "I personally am not in tune with some of the changes which seem inevitable in the years ahead," Miss Bacon said with her characteristic blunt candor and a touch of irony.

The Midwestern mood of inquiry and ferment is no longer simmering underground or confined to wild-eyed student revolutionaries. It is gaining official administration recognition, at Michigan and elsewhere, opening the doors to a freedom that may prove a burden to the Midwestern coed: that wholesome, well-manner, never too spectacularly dazzling Pi Phi or Tri-Delt who looks in stereotype, as if she might be the earnest younger brother of the Southern coed. Yes, brother. Her hair is cropped short or possibly smoothed into a modest pageboy, and her wardrobe is a steal from the proper schoolboy, with modest bosom lost in the vastness of a Shetland sweater, further masked by the blouse beneath it, with only the skirt —plaid or grey flannel—to confirm her gender. Perhaps I am unduly bitter because I failed so miserably to conform with the little-boy look requirements in my Ann Arbor days. But I am convinced that a kind of genderless street urchin is about all the womanliness the average Midwest Joe College cares

* And lovable too. As fiercely as I disagreed with her during my undergraduate days, I could never think of her without respect and affection.

to handle. It is doubtful that the coed deliberately chooses to play down her womanliness because she senses it is a threat to the male. But the little-boy look is a campus tradition, dating back to 1837 when Oberlin opened its doors to the first coed, who probably showed up for classes in a tailored white shirtwaist and severe black necktie, a costume contrived to make her presence as little disruptive as possible.

Possibly the genderless costume—it crops up in a grimier, unpressed state on the Eastern college girl—reflects the disturbing contraditions of coeducation. Very early she learns she is not a little boy. But then for 15 years or more she is thrown into competition with boys. She attends the same classes, fulfills the same requirements for the same academic degrees. True, she is given a bonus in protective custody on the residential campus: curfew, sign-out slips, weekend regulations. But she is challenged to equal his mind, his accomplishments, his ambition. There is no escaping, though, the subversive reminders, to quote psychoanalyst Bruno Bettelheim, that "males are *more* equal"—and "that she must undergo the same training only because she may need it if she is a failure—an unfortunate who somehow cannot gain admission to the haven of marriage and motherhood where she properly belongs." * Many girls accept this absurdity calmly. Others resent it and some fight out their resentment in bed. "We have been lulled into thinking there is no difference [between male and female]," an angry young woman at Brandeis said of the conflict. "We're bred to be breeders—but we're educated to be anything else," she said. "Then we're sent off to breed. We're always being told that the essential nature of woman demands security, emotional commitment; that the female can't enjoy love-making otherwise. But we're too busy proving we're as equal as we've been told we are—in bed."

The prenuptial bed as a proving ground, an experimental laboratory, and a stage for acting out emotional conflict is a recurring theme in the sex histories of the American coed, and at times it drowns out all other themes in the sex life of the

* "Growing up Female," by Bruno Bettelheim. *Harper's Magazine,* October, 1962.

Eastern college girl. Now we move into the territory of the legendary cool college girls, who burned their candles at both ends with Edna St. Vincent Millay (Vassar, '17) or braved Marx, Freud, and a visit to a doctor colleague of Margaret Sanger in the days of Mary McCarthy (Vassar, '33). Today she alternates betwen her on-campus "total sartorial collapse," * if there are no boys around, and a wise, wistful, intense, and semi-groomed worldliness complete with stringy lanks of not too recently washed hair and a Brooks Brothers coat that looks as though it had been somehow strangled. She meets young men under hotel clocks on weekends and other young men on Rome's Spanish Steps in July. In black sheath and the inevitable strand of cultured pearls, she listens raptly or talks, I mean really talks, to the tweedy young man across the table in one of Manhattan's little French restaurants where the food isn't the greatest but it's cheap. And she conveys a blasé, almost jaded acceptance of sexual freedom that has culminated in what a dissenting Wellesley girl described as "the have-diaphragm-will-travel crowd."

It is not only the coeducated college girl who is torn by the conflict over woman's role. Any college girl who has ever contemplated achieving an identity beyond her procreative and domestic potential is at least aware of the popular faith that fulfillment away from home is unfeminine. The bookish, high-power I.Q.'s who pilgrimage to the bastions of old feminist tradition for a classic (female *more* equal than male) education are especially sensitive to the buffeting of opposing forces. The early crusading feminist made a public issue of her erotic emancipation. Today's committed feminist may do the same. Going to bed with a man may assure her of her own feminity or may seem "the only rational behavior when marriage is years away," as was suggested by a Radcliffe senior with her goal a Ph.D. in anthropology. Going to bed may be an exercise in intellectualization, a matter of principle, a shelter from too many pressures, a kind of nervous reflex, an offering from a

---

* *Campus U.S.A.*, by David Boroff. Harper & Brothers, 1961, originally appeared as "Smith: a College for ARG's (All-Round Girls) with High I.Q.'s." *Mademoiselle Magazine*, March, 1961.

not too pretty scholar who believes sex is all she has to offer, something to do when rapport breaks down. It may be hostility to men or to herself. It may be opportuniy to play the aggressor, the female *more* equal. It may also be real, unforced, unrationalized love.

To interview Eastern college girls exclusively—"I don't know any virgins in my milieu" or "Everyone I know has been pregnant at least once and nobody gets too psyched up about it"—and to accept their comments uncritically would provide impressive evidence that sexual vagrancy has become the collegiate way of life. And, in fact, several commentators on campus courtship have recently fallen into the Cool trap. There *are* spirited Eastern enclaves of the *Dolce Vita*. There *are* sexual intellects who have already graduated from mere sex and are asking, "What next?" They are a powerful force in the sexual climate of the East, where chastity, and certainly boasting of chastity, is considered hopelessly gauche. But statistically, they remain a minority.

One should not be fooled by the deep-sigh school of sophistication, as author and magazine reporter, Dan Wakefield, admits he was by one Buffie Z, "a Bennington junior who looked as if she had been born beneath the clock at the Biltmore but had given up idle collegiate concerns for the life of a *femme fatale*. Her eyes dropped knowingly," Wakefield recalls, "beneath well-applied mascara. Her mouth—thin, without lipstick—pouted in a way that would have done credit to Brigitte Bardot. The smoke from her cigarette clouded her pale, wan face in a faintly mysterious haze of dissipation. Early in the course of our conversation, she made a casual reference to her 'lovers.' I did not know whether the plural implied a succession of them, or a current stable, and, beginning to feel like a Boy Scout patrol leader confronted by Zsa Zsa Gabor, I was too embarrassed to betray my ignorance by asking. Then, after the third Martini, she happened to mention that she didn't believe in premarital intercourse. I swallowed my olive and said, 'But I thought you said something about your *lovers*.' She looked at me a bit puzzled, then explained, 'Sure—my lovers—those are the boys I date.' " *

So much for Buffie Z. She bowls over the popular stereotype of the wanly dissipated Bennington Bohemian in her black tights and horse-blanket poncho. Why bother with stereotype then? Because many girls make their college choices with little more than a stereotype in mind. College catalogues can convey little of the spirit and atmosphere of an institution and certainly none of the ingredients in its sexual climate.**
A girl has heard about the scholarly austerity of Bryn Mawr or that a Smith girl is "an organization woman in training" and Sarah Lawrence girls are "busy fulfilling themselves as individuals." By favoring the school with the image that matches her own image, she perpetuates the campus stereotype. And the administration may serve the same stereotype by looking among the applications for "the Smith girl" or "good Byrn Mawr material."

To see how the popular image of a school can have as much significance as the kind of school it actually is in affecting sexual behavior, we have only to focus on the Boston area in the very heart of the Eastern college belt.

I am indebted to the Harvard graduate who, while waiting in a Wellesley parlor for his newly ringed fiancee, offered this definitive dissertation on the comparative virtues (virtue?) of the Boston area's college girls. "If you want a show date," he said, "someone to look good, be socially acceptable in just about any situation, not the utmost in thrills," he raised one

* "Dan Wakefield's Sophisticated Lady," by Dan Wakefield. *Esquire Magazine,* July, 1962.

** As David Boroff observes in his introduction to *Campus U.S.A.,* "the institution personality may not be identical with the official philosophy of a college; it may even run counter to it." The college novel may provide some insight into the personality of a particular campus—but for some reason, most of the novels with an identifiable background are set in the East, most often Harvard. Boroff's book, portraits of nine colleges and the Claremont College complex in California, provides the kind of information catalogues do not offer. Another excellent source of information is *Mademoiselle Magazine's* continuing series of college profiles. The magazine makes reprints available through the Alumnae Advisory Center, Inc., 541 Madison Avenue, New York 22, N.Y.

eyebrow to denote that sexual thrills were what he had in mind, "and not the most sparkling conversation—you go to Wellesley. If you want conversation, intellectual stimulation, sometimes too stimulating in fact, and greater romantic potential—ahem, you would call the Cliff. The Radcliffe girl," he went on, "is as intelligent as the most intelligent at Harvard—she has that incredible intensity." He sighed. "She fights for causes, marches on Washington, you know. The Brandeis girl has the same intensity. Then we have the junior colleges," he went on, "two extremes: the finishing schools and the un-finishing. Endicott, for example, for rich little girls. Their families ship them here to meet Harvard men. They're the prettiest and the dumbest. Being rich tends to make a girl better looking," he added in an aside. "Now on a scale from one to seven, with one being the easiest to bed, and seven the most difficult, I would rate them La Salle 2, Garland 2, Wellesley 6, Radcliffe and Brandeis 4, Endicott divided into 3's and 5's." At this point his fiancee descended, displayed her diamond solitaire, and led him away.

Annoying though the condescension and arrogance of this arbitrary rating may be, the homogeneity of the small college is the point. Each school has its own culture, which students transmit to each other, and sexual attitudes are part of that culture. A Harvard boy dating a La Salle girl probably knows he is dating a "2" and conducts himself accordingly. She may respond as her schoolmates have led her to believe is proper, in a cycle that feeds upon itself.

Now both Wellesley and Radcliffe belong to the "heavenly seven," officially known as the Seven College Conference—a liaison of Eastern prestige women's schools. Other members: Smith, Barnard, Vassar, Mount Holyoke, and Bryn Mawr. Wellesley isn't *that* much farther away from Harvard to completely explain the distance between "4" and "6." The public image of the Wellesley girl as a wholesome, socially presentable, debby-looking girl preparing to be an educated wife is as firmly fixed and only as unprecisely true as that of the intense, brainy, dowdier Cliffie. But there must be enough truth in the sexual implications of the comparison because Boston students spread the word as though it were gospel.* As one Wellesley girl said, with pride and a trace of envy: "At the Cliff, an affair is a status symbol. Here we're discreet, that's what you expect of a lady." The sexually more conservative Wellesley girl would most likely abstain from premarital coitus until engagement. She is less of a threat to the Harvard male—academically, intellectually, and sexually. For he may be a rather anxious virgin himself. But Radcliffe has proximity. Though Harvard men may sneer at a Cliff "Jolly-up" as "an overcrowded mixer, full of sour cider and girls primed with smart repartee," he goes. She is on the spot, pedalling across the Square on her English bike, sharing classes, being reconnoitered at the Widener Library "pick-up" scene She needn't bother with the lowly freshman. She has that 4 to 1 ratio, all those graduate students to choose from, better than even odds for acquiring a Harvard husband. The Cliffie is even getting prettier. "It used to be that Radcliffe girls were 'dogs,' " a pretty blonde Cliffie reported. "But the school went out and made this big concerted effort to change our image." **

Certain colleges—many of them in the East—are hotbeds of spirited rebellion, attracting eager embryo nonconformists begging to be shaken out of their sneakers and Capezios (this year: boots). It is the progressive, experimental, and dynamically liberal institutions—Bennington, Sarah Lawrence, Brandeis in the East; Antioch, Shimer, the University of Chicago in its heyday in the Midwest; Reed out West—that encourage doubt, challenge, and rebellion. Girls come to Bennington, as Theodore Newcomb reported, hoping their attitudes will be challenged and changed, anxious to revolt

* "Smith to bed, Mt. Holyoke to wed," recited by generations of Amherst boys is testimony to the image of Holyoke girls as softer. And Holyoke girls agree. "Smithies really are sophisticated," a Holyoke girl assured me. "You should see the black dresses on weekends—I mean, and the high heels."

** There have always been beautiful Radcliffe girls but traditionally the Cliffie tended to be long on brains, short on style and looks. Beautification efforts were officially recognized when *Life* magazine (January 4, 1963) visited the campus and reported: "Look What's Going on at Radcliffe" with close-ups of the new-style Cliffie.

against the values of their parents.* Bard College, a small liberal arts school near Hyde Park, New York, was referred to affectionately by several coeds and at least four college boys as "the Whorehouse-on-the-Hudson." (But college students seem given to colorful and inaccurate exaggeration, as witness the Harvard sophomore who described Radcliffe as "our own private cathouse.") College students—male and female—seem almost as quick as tabloid headline writers to equate sexual permissiveness with free-for-all debauchery. Myth has consigned Sarah Lawrence and Bennington to erotic anarchy. And the popularity of the image may account for the too hasty acceptance of the Eastern college girl as an insatiable nymph in wrinkled raincoat.

Wandering into the suburban wilderness of unspoiled terrain and Tudor elegance that is Sarah Lawrence College, protected from the press of Westchester County apartment houses by a now-and-then fence, a visitor has his first surprise: There are not nearly so many leotards as advertised and not an unwashed mane in sight. Even its original unstructured dedication to self-expression has bowed to the demands of academic discipline. Its philosophy, to quote profiler Boroff, is "orthodox Deweyism with a heavy overlay of an older book-ish emphasis." And it turns out graduates who marry Hima-layan princes and complain because that same old United Nations crowd is coming to cocktails at Mums' tonight— "Adlai and Ralph and the rest of the crew." There are no grades, no majors, no class assignments (only contracts), no house mothers, and, as one pressured virgin reported, "no social sin you can be kicked out of school for, except possibly having relations in the middle of the campus." The 2:30 A.M. curfew (weekdays as well as weekends) is regarded as some-thing to aim for but nothing to fear. Legend has it former president Harold Taylor used to stand outside to boost late-comers over the fence. Girls receive gentlemen callers in their rooms, "only I wish they wouldn't hang around here taking showers and strolling the halls in a towel," one coed com-

* *Readings in Social Psychology*, edited by Theodore M. Newcomb, Eugene L. Hartley, and others. N.Y.: Henry Holt & Co., 1947.

plained. I gathered from her comments that being a Sarah Lawrence girl was a joy, an honor, and a bit of a burden. Sarah's girls worry about "outarticulating their dates," brood that their free-expressing libidos are too much taken for granted (often erroneously) and pine (confidentially) for summer vacation "where the best part of all was nobody had ever heard of Sarah Lawrence and I could be as silly and empty-headed as I pleased."

"We're not supposed to be anxious or enterprising about men," said a very feminine transplant from the Midwest. "Some girls act like they just couldn't care less—'Oh, you have a date, what a drag'—but Thursday night they disappear from campus and you don't even see them till Monday morning," her dormmate added. "You don't know for sure, but you can certainly imagine she's off for an absolutely glorious weekend. Unless she's your best friend, you'd never dream of asking." Privacy, as well as individualism, is sacred. It is undeniably an atmosphere where sexual freedom can—and does—flower. Theoretically, the more scholarly and professionally ambitious Sarah Lawrence girl will tell you that a love affair is far more moral and sensible than quitting school prematurely in order to marry. How well this works in practice, I cannot say. During my Bronxville visit I was introduced to one new bride, a junior, and two new diamond solitaires.

It seems clear that the personality and situation of the smaller college with its relatively homogenous population offers even more precise clues to the sexual climate. Oberlin, for instance, is only 165 miles northeast of Antioch. Both are small-town, coed, privately controlled, nonsectarian, nationally known and respected institutions. But Antioch is regarded, by its students at least, as a stronghold of sexual emancipation; Oberlin's reputation for tame fun and no privacy reflects this invitation, copied from a manuscript in the college Library:

> *"all you that want a berth*
> *to Live quite free from Sin*
> *you must go to ohio*
> *& Live in . . . oberlin."*

Each of the Oberlin women's dorms has its own personality and a coed, explaining why she was glad her house was known as "fast," said, "I'm convinced that being a 'fast' woman at Oberlin is the same as being normal everywhere else." Of Antioch, one disenchanted coed said, "If you just cross the street with a boy, everyone assumes you're sleeping together." Antioch with its unique work-and-study plan attracts a majority of students from outside Ohio (It had to be coincidence, but of the four Antioch students I spoke to, all were offspring of either psychologists or sociologists—which may somehow explain the sexual climate). Oberlin was radical enough to enroll the first woman coed in America and the first Negro student, even before the Civil War when it won for itself the name "hotbed of abolitionism." But its traditions are deeply conservative. Founded in a community of strict Congregationalism and New England Puritanism, it became known as "God's College" and the educator of missionaries, reformers, and spiritual crusaders. "The college is, or ought to be, an incubator for eggheads," Oberliners have been told when they complain of overincubation (no cars, dormitory curfews, little privacy). The atmosphere should be even "semi-monastic," it was suggested.* "And it is," an Oberlin junior admitted. "But a lot of students are just as happy and if you're really determined, you can always go away weekends."

Only limited statistics are available on how sexual behavior varies from one campus to another. But the few studies there are suggest significant variation.** The University of Connecticut in Storrs has a special situation that affects sexual behavior—the girls tend to be of higher economic class than

* "Oberlin College," by Allyn Moss. *Mademoiselle Magazine*, January, 1958.
** "The Variety and Meaning of Premarital Heterosexual Experience for the College Student," *op. cit.*, by Winston W. Erhmann. Ehrmann blames the limited evidence on "the general paucity of research into sexual behavior" and "with some notable exceptions, the extreme reluctance of investigators, largely college professors, to reveal the specific identity of the source of their sample populations because of assumed, potential, and actual threats of reprisals from administrators." Ehrmann, describing his own research sample as "students in a large Southern state university" (it

the boys, who outnumber them 2 to 1. Both factors, suggests a Connecticut faculty man, give girls the upper hand in dating situations "and they can manipulate the boys as they please."

David Boroff calls attention to the rural and urban variations of sex morality as they interact on the campus of Wisconsin University. "Generally speaking, rural girls become involved in intimate relationships because of deep and solemn love," Boroff writes. "They are often appalled at the cavalier way some of the more sophisticated girls have affairs with only a mild affection or a hazily defined intellectual compatibility as sanction."

But countless other variables influence the sexual climate of an individual campus. Is it isolated and campus-oriented? At Kalamazoo College with its enrollment of 675 students, the isolation is more psychological than physical. After all, the city itself is all around, but smallness and a kind of prep school feeling inspire girls to complain, "If you're with him once, you're set for life." And Brandeis is indeed isolated on rolling acres not far from Boston. Transportation is so spotty, students hitch rides at the foot of the road—"Small junky cars are faculty people and students," a coed reported, "and the big shiny Cadillacs are construction workers putting up the latest building." But the eye of the Brandeis coed is likely to be on Harvard and she refuses to let isolation limit her dating life— as a senior she may move into Cambridge and commute to Brandeis for classes.

In studying the profile of the asphalt campus, for example,

---

was the University of Florida), reported that 14 percent of the females had experienced coitus.

Harold T. Christensen and George A. Carpenter reported 60 percent of their female sample in a Danish university experienced premarital coitus, 21 percent at a Midwestern American campus and 9 percent at a Utah university with a high proportion of Mormons and consequently more restrictive premarital sex norms than the country as a whole.

Dorothy Dunbar Bromley and Florence Haxton Britten, in a 1938 study of 1,300 college students, reported 25 percent of the total female sample reported coitus but the figure went up to 36 percent at a woman's college with a reputation for liberal views and dropped to 18 percent at a more conservative school.

half a dozen variables may clash head on. Is the school secular or church-affiliated? Is it coed, junior college, an academy of commercial arts, a swank finishing school? Are we consider- ing the day or evening session? How homogenous is the population? Is it a residential or commuting campus? Is the student here by choice or because of family and financial pressure?

Both the University of Pennsylvania and Temple Univer- sity are within the boundaries of Philadelphia. But Penn, with its Main Line ties, its tuition of $1,600 (higher than Harvard, only $100 less than Princeton) and its Wharton School of Business (reputedly catering to the sons of company presi- dents—"just here to have a good time," according to a student critic—is 80 percent residential with a sharp cleavage between Indys (Independents) and the fraternity-affiliated. The social calendar is jammed with on-campus partying. In spring, students picnic along the Schuylkill River while the Penn crew limbers up. Smokey Joe's, the campus hangout on Walnut Street, with its long dark bar and booths of rough wood tattooed with collegiate hieroglyphics "looks like a Hollywood set for a 1930 college picture starring Nancy Carroll and Jack Oakie," wrote Penn graduate and journalist Alfred Bester.* For all the traffic fumes and urban realities of Philadelphia, Penn might just as well be set in sylvan surroundings.

Temple's fees are half as high and most of its predominantly Jewish enrollment live at home and find identity off-campus rather than on.** Among the tightly bound nationality and ethnic groups (Orthodox Jewish and Italian Catholic at Temple as at Brooklyn College, Queens, and Hunter), families are reluctant to let daughters leave home. The girl who accepts this fierce and loving protection will be less apt to rebel— sexually or otherwise—than the girl who seethes with resent- ment.

* "The University of Pennsylvania," by Alfred Bester. *Holiday Maga- zine,* November, 1962.
** "Courtship Intimacy and Religious Background," by Robert R. Bell and Leonard Blumberg. *Marriage and Family Living,* November, 1959.

For many coeds then, Temple is strictly a continuation of high school. Temple mothers want Temple daughters to marry college boys; and college boys marry college girls. Many of these dutiful daughters dress for the Hunt. When I visited Temple, the popular Hunt "look" included bouffant hairdo, smoldering eyes beneath charcoaled lids, and ample bosoms. As one Temple faculty man remarked, "At Temple, anything less than 36 C is a boy." The sexiness of dress cannot be equated with erotic permissiveness. "Quite the opposite," Temple's Dr. Robert Bell believes. As a Temple junior explained it: "It's all sexy packaging, but the rule is—no free samples."

Neighborhood culture has a strong hangover in many city schools. A City College of New York freshman complained about the sameness of the CCNY male: "They're all so Bronxy middle-class Jewish—even the Negro boys tend to be Bronxy middle-class Jewish." She accomplished her semi-rebellion by "making out till 4 A.M. on the front stoop" with a Negro schoolmate, noting, "The milkman was really pretty cool about it."

A fury of extracurricular activity, with over 300 student groups chartered by the administration, is Brooklyn College's bow to the need for social expression of its mostly home-bound students. So home-bound, reports Brooklyn alumnus Boroff, that mothers frequently call the school with "frantic advice for sons who left their lunch at home" and a father demanded the "lowdown" from one of the deans about a boy who was courting his daughter. In contrast with the customs of his day and the conflict of culture between American-born children and Yiddish- or Italian-speaking parents, Boroff today finds less distance between generations: "Jewish college students no longer define themselves through rebellion against their parents," he believes. But there was considerable rebellion expressed in the dating and sexual activity of many live-at-home college girls I interviewed. A sexually emancipated Brooklyn College graduate student told of bringing her Puerto Rican fiance home to meet her somewhat Old-World Jewish mother. "It helped, of course, that he was a law student," the girl said, "but even Mama was surprised to find she liked him. Afterwards she marvelled, 'He looks like a nice Jewish boy.' "

Living at home is only an inconvenience, not a hindrance to premarital romance. The big city is rich with young bachelors in their own apartments, older men, bachelor-hearted husbands, artists and actors, and acres of anonymity. At-home sexual hedonism may not be as aesthetically ideal as a coed romantic might like: "Sleep with boys?" said a home-bound San Diego State coed. "There's no time for anyone to sleep. With us it's all hit and run." But having defined the euphemism in its local perspective, she added, "Lots of guys have apartments and guys are always passing around the keys." And a schoolmate added, "There are communities around here where girls go and prefer not to know anyone's name and have a nice night and leave, no questions asked. Perfectly nice girls. Like Palm Springs, for instance."

Possibly the least affected by the evolution in sex ethics is Bohemia. There is nothing strikingly new about Bohemia. Most large campuses, and even many smaller schools, have always nurtured or at least tolerated, one or more pockets of nonconformity with the almost inevitable attention to sexual rebellion. During my University of Michigan days, sexual emancipation was shared by assorted splinter nonconformist groups—the theater crowd, co-op folk singers, the non-matriculating campus perennials and their entourage of coed admirers and the literary *manqué* set. At Wisconsin, the Rathskeller, known as "The Rat," is a hangout for beards, folk singers in sandals, and foreign students plus small-towners enthralled with the outlanders; and The Green Lantern, an eating co-op, is "reputed to be vaguely leftist and aggressively Bohemian," Boroff reports. In the San Francisco Bay area— Berkeley, Stanford, Mills, and San Francisco State—girls in seek of weekend Bohemias have the San Francisco Beat scene. "For the real odd-balls and the exhibitionists and the sheltered coeds who require something a bit more devastating than the usual rebellion," was how one Mills junior described it. "Just straight sex is nothing," a Stanford faculty man observed. "For real nonconformity, some of these kids have to reform a homosexual, befriend a Negro—preferably in bed—or have an hallucination. Pot (marijuana) or peyote (the hallucinogenic cactus) is the only kick left."

It is difficult to even guess how many college girls have heard—and actually followed—the Beat's Jack Kerouac in his celebration of "the unbelievable sweetness of sex love." And it is impossible to determine how many cool coeds have moved beyond mere sex to larger rebellions. But as beards and sandals, barefeet, burlap dresses, William Burroughs, uncombed hair, sexual freedom, and Charlie Mingus become more acceptable among the "squares," where else can collegiate Bohemia turn?

At the same time, as qualified sexual freedom—sex with affection—becomes increasingly accepted as the middle-class standard, the premarital affair loses its shock value and the heady scent of sin. I suppose it is an unhealthy legacy of our Puritan tradition, but I can't help wondering whether campus sex will be quite as much fun if the new permissiveness destroys the last elements of social wickedness.

Probably the most significant influence on the sexual climate is religious affiliation. The religiously devout female is likely to be among the most conservative sexually. Religious devoutness was one of the most significant influences in determining sexual behavior, according to the Kinsey findings.

Mormon society is regarded as "highly restrictive regarding premarital sex norms" compared to the moderately restrictive Midwest. And cultural comparisons by Harold T. Christensen, professor of sociology at Purdue, found Mormon attitudes and behavior reflect obedience to Mormon tradition.*

The girl who attends Trinity College in Washington, D.C., may not be more devoutly religious than her sister in a secular college. But she tends to be more conformist in Trinity's extremely homeogenous population. "The trouble with this place," a Trinity freshman said, "is that the students are all cut out by the same cooky cutter and the results are about as excit-

* "Premarital Sex Norms in America and Scandinavia," by Harold T. Christensen. *Journal of the National Association of Women Deans and Counselors,* January, 1963.

ing as a box of vanilla wafers." Obviously at a Catholic college, "faith is safer from subversion," writes Jane O'Reilly, a Radcliffe graduate who recently profiled Trinity for *Mademoiselle*. "People don't chuckle over their sins in a Catholic college as they do elsewhere," Miss O'Reilly commented. And Trinity's honor system puts a damper on exchange of confidence, cutting down the education by one's peers that eases and possibly encourages the shedding of sexual inhibition on many campuses.*

In Southern bastions of Fundamentalist religion, faith may dampen ardor and often douse it. "God, the Big Daddy in the sky, is unforgiving of sexual transgressions," a Vanderbilt faculty man observed. "With the inevitability of hellfire hanging over her, even the milder intimacies may be disturbing, and at the same time extremely arousing, to the Fundamentalist coed." Some courtships do reach the ultimate intimacy, and the pangs of suffering conscience echo, the faculty man suggested, in the coed's plaintive plea for reassurance, "It wasn't my fault, was it? I mean, not really?"

Although no recent comprehensive statistical analysis of geographical variations in sexual climate is available, a cross section of colleges in this country was covered in *What College Students Think,* a report of research conducted as part of the Cornell University Values Study.** Interestingly, what the researchers called "religiousness" parallels our map of sexual permissiveness *vs.* sexual repression. Sociologists interviewed 2,975 students at Harvard, Yale, Dartmouth, Wesleyan, Cornell, North Carolina, Texas, UCLA, Michigan, Wayne, and Fisk Universities. Highest in "religiousness" were students in the South, with Fisk, Texas, and North Carolina rated "most religious." Eastern college students ranked lowest, with Harvard and Dartmouth the least religious. UCLA student responses were closest to those of students in the East. The Midwestern students toed a middle line.***

* "A Very Attractive Cooky Cutter," by Jane O'Reilly. *Mademoiselle Magazine,* June, 1963.
** Princeton, N.J.: D. Van Nostrand Co., 1960.
*** *God on the Secular Campus,* by Richard Butler, N.Y.: Doubleday & Co., Inc., 1963. O.P.

But lack of religiousness, as we have seen, does not necessarily lead to sexual anarchy. Religious or not, there is a streak of sober seriousness in students of the mid-sixties. There are still pranks, the pushing of beds down highways and boozy costumed Saturday night free-for-alls, but campus observers find an increasing social awareness—symbolized by the sit-ins, ban-the-bomb marches, and Peace Corps enthusiasm—as well as an almost dreary concern with personal security. If this is true, it is a *national* concern, a *national* seriousness and the need it engenders in young people for early sexual togetherness is increasingly a national phenomenon that blurs, but has not obliterated, geographical distinctions.

Marshmallow Hung Up on a Hot Volcano

"Can a little girl from a small mining town in the Middle West find happiness hung up on a hot volcano?"

A recent Michigan State University graduate said it, but it was Donna Bruckner who laughed, flashing $1,900 worth of wondrously capped teeth.

"Change Middle West to the Bronx," she said, "and you're right. Having all New York City for a campus *is* like sitting on the rim of a volcano."

If true, there might be 200,000 students hugging the rim in the more than 40 colleges of the metropolitan New York volcano. But the volcano hangers-on population is cut sharply by the many student stay-at-homes, the commuters. These asphalt campus transients tend to identify more with their own home suburb or neighborhood than the city or the college. For a year, Donna was one of them.

"I wanted to go away to school but when my dad had his heart attack, I felt like the least I could do was stay home and so Hunter was it. At first I hated it so much I just didn't want anything to do with the girls or all the school things they do—the paper and the clubs—to make you feel more campusy. But it was one of the girls who got me my first modeling job —we were studying in the sun up on the roof. And then! Geez Louise. That was it. Nothing could ever be the same. I discovered the city and myself. A lot of it's in your attitude. Hunter was a subway school to me. Now it's the only school in the world on Park Avenue. I can bear it."

You have to look closely and think about it to realize that Donna is not nearly so beautiful as she seems, only skillfully exploited. As naive in many ways as a 14-year-old; by chronology, 22; by midtown Manhattan hip standards, ageless.

"But sexually a bit backward," she said with an apologetic grin.

Blue-white skin painted and pencilled with studied concentration and much forethought; long, lean, fine-boned body dressed with "arrogant elegance"; matte black hair artfully arranged for the maximum effect of nonarrangement—alive but hinting of anemia, the kind of girl people are always trying to force milk shakes on. Her first year's modelling income went to the dentist, now most of it goes to her psychoanalyst.

"I would have died a virgin at the rate I was going, if it hadn't been for Dr. Gold. New York is so enormous. This thing of not being judged, of no one really noticing what you do. Of the girls I know—I kept telling myself It couldn't be *that* painful if everyone else is doing It. But I was so goddamned scared. And shy. I know I give people the impression of being a swinger but—it was just plain fear. Not religion or morality or common sense. Fear came before that. I was so tight and paralyzed with fear, boys would think—still think—I'm detached, aloof, bored.

"This fear thing—it had to do with my room being next to my parents' room, and at night when I was little I used to hear the noise—their making love, only hearing the noise I got the idea my father was doing something to hurt my mother. I used to sing out loud so I wouldn't hear it. Then I'd cough and one of them would have to get up to bring me a glass of water and the noise would stop. What did my mother ever tell me about sex? I think I was 14—absolutely forbidden to have dates—and she said, 'Listen, if a boy ever comes near you—even near you—knee him. Like this.' She even showed me where. 'Don't ever let a boy touch you. Make sure he keeps his hands in his pockets.' It made no sense. I didn't know anything about any of that. But when I was 15, we had a maid who told me the facts of life. Oh, in just the worst possible way you can imagine. Four letter words and what a disgusting, painful thing it was—but if you were married you had to do it and she showed me with her fingers what happened.

"It became an obsession. I used to look at ladies, watching them to see how they walked—wondering how they could stand the pain and why they didn't walk bowlegged. Didn't it hurt just to sit? Isn't that crazy? There was a friend of my mother's—a tiny little woman married to a giant man. It really upset me thinking how that monster must crush her to death at night. How could women be so brave? Enduring the pain at night and pretending to be so normal in the daytime. So for all that pain hang-up, there wasn't any pain at all— when I finally got around to It. Not much pleasure either. Nothing like as great as Dr. Gold said it would be."

She had an hour before a booking for a cigarette ad and we met on the steps of Hunter and wandered into Central Park.

"Manhattan is really a tremendous campus! I mean it's strange how you want it to be collegey, so the first year you wear your little college-shop kneesocks and loafers and the Princeton striped scarf with your polo coat. I know some of the kids at Hunter do the Ivy League weekend circuit. There were a couple of blind date football weekend things—one real fiasco at Princeton where the boy got so stoned he was too sick to make the game and afterwards was so embarrassed he kept hiding from me. I suppose he was shy—but I was so petrified at the time that never occurred to me. I went out with boys I'd dated in high school—nice dull mama's boys who seem satisfied—grateful—if you kiss them goodnight and wouldn't dream of trying anything. But now I was meeting all sorts of men—not boys. Guys 26 and 30, divorced, separated, or—that's what they say—a hip East Side crowd. At Columbia the kids hang around the Lions' Den and Hunter kids—when they hang around—well, Mayhews, I guess, but P. J. Clarke's was 'our' place. Certain photographers, their representatives, a bunch of kids from Parsons* and the queers—of course, I didn't dream they were queers. I didn't even know what a homosexual was—it was the thing to make an entrance, kill time over a hamburger—people talked about who was sleeping with who—guys talked about going to bed. I had this thing like everybody was trying to throw me into bed. And I was really terrified. But the thing was I liked to be cuddly and affectionate. I loved to neck. The petting got more complicated and involved very gradually. Once I would try something, I would discover I liked it. But I was always in control. We would be petting like mad and my bra would get tossed to the floor and then there'd be a struggle over the panties. I might be incredibly hot myself but I always knew exactly whose hands were where. Something would like click in my head. I'd turn myself off. And then, oh brother—

"Usually the guy would be furious. Oh, they all had something to say. I heard more hateful, horrible parting speeches. Lots of guys never came back, the bastards. I really felt they should come back on my terms. But my terms were so awful. I realize that now. I came off very immature and any guy with any kind of intelligence would naturally object to what I was asking. When I tried to explain about how I was a virgin, nobody ever believed it. One guy, when I finally convinced him, just laughed. You sure look like a swinger, he kept saying. So for almost two years, it was blind dates—or one of these hip guys would take me out, usually once—and gay boys. Of course, I didn't know they were. They were wonderful escorts, well turned-out, clever, witty, with it. You loved making a big entrance at Clarke's surrounded by half a dozen guys. Especially if you were so naive you didn't know 'gay' was written all over them. I used them but they used me too. You know, it was fags who taught me how to dress. I had no style. Anyway it was one way of avoiding those awful scenes with guys zipping up their pants and putting you down for leading them on.

"My best friend at the place where I lived was also a staunch

* Parsons School of Design

virgin type. Oh, I forgot. I finally convinced my folks to let me move into the city. But they said 'yes' only if I'd stay at the 'Y' or something like that. So I moved into the East End Hotel for Women. Anyway, with my friend it was a question of morality, I think. I went along with her, but with me it was really fear. We wallowed in each other's stupidity. After a while you reach a point where virginity and all that fooling around—sleeping with guys and doing everything except that one final thing—isn't at all healthy. You can really get some sort of permanent hang-up Dr. Gold says. And the fag scene is too sick. Even I could see I wasn't getting anywhere. This doesn't tell you much about what girls think at Hunter, does it? It's funny how you can expose five girls to the same New York scene and you get five kinds of reactions. But I think you'd have to be really out of it not to see the sex thing. Nobody would ever dream of mentioning morality or right or wrong—I mean it's all just taken for granted. Everyone is so casual about it. Maybe if I'd stuck to the Bronx and the subway and dating sons of Mother's friends, I'd never have known about any of this. You see lots of that kind of girl at Hunter—good little mother's girls, going for a teacher's certificate just in case they have to work a few years before they get married. Hoping, praying they'll never have to use it. Maybe they don't have these hang-ups. I'm not going to go into all the details of all my hang-ups. Sex was just one thing. It was after I started with Dr. Gold that I began to spend a lot of time with this photographer and his girl who weren't exactly married. And sex was a very open thing. They seemed to be having such a goddam great time—being with them tore away a few inhibitions. Like I could even bear to hear certain four letter words without wanting to fall through a hole in the floor. I felt like I was ready. Dr. Gold thought I was too.

"There was a boy I'd known for several months. I never got the impression he was trying to make me. That would have frightened me away. But he was physically attractive. One night we slept together and it was so nice. I mean he was sweet and didn't try to rush me. And nothing happened. Then a few nights later I came over and I wanted to stay, only it was sort of with his understanding that maybe something would happen and maybe it wouldn't. I put fresh sheets on the bed—flowered print sheets I brought. And I went into the bathroom and spent about two hours getting ready—then I put on my little flowered nightie. So maybe I would blend into the sheets and he wouldn't be able to find me. Then I made him turn out the light and crawled into bed and pulled the sheet over my head.

"It was like so easy I couldn't believe it. At the same time there was no pain, there wasn't much pleasure either exactly. I always thought there would be. I didn't understand my feeling hung-up and didn't know about how I was supposed to have a climax. I was sort of disappointed. No pain. No nothing. All this great pleasure Dr. Gold had told me about, how it was so great he couldn't even put it into words. I really felt like a virgin until my third man. In fact I feel pretty virginal now. With Jeff it was like the first time and the rest had never happened. He was a marvelous lover—I guess he just knew what he was doing—he knew about women—and when it ended I tried to tell myself it was his problem and not a rejection of me. After five months of stewing over it, I was feeling more inadequate and shyer than ever.

"When Steve came alone I had to start all over again. I was as virginal as ever. Shy, unsure of myself, modest. I still can't bring myself to walk around his apartment naked. He's trying to train me. But I feel I must have my little towel even if I'm going to drop it in a minute. He's finally gotten me over that 'two hours in the bathroom' business. I honestly don't think morality was ever a problem for me. If it had been I would feel guilty now. Even Dr. Gold is amazed how with all these kind of hang-ups over my family, I seem so clear about the sex thing. I am. I wouldn't go to bed with just anyone. Maybe four men in only a year seems like a lot but—it was always a relationship. Each one was something special. I really was in love with Jeff and I hoped there might be something with Steve. I don't think I'll be promiscuous. One thing though. I really miss necking. Sex is so casual and taken for granted— I mean we go to dinner, we go home, get undressed like old married people, you know—and just go to bed. It's really like a marriage type thing. I mean I'm not saying I'd like to be raped on the living room floor exactly. But I would love to just sit around on the sofa and neck. I don't know. Maybe it's some throwback to when I wasn't allowed to neck. You know. My way of saying: 'Screw you, Mother!' Hey, did you hear that? Dr. Gold will be so proud."

4

To Each Her Own Morality

If sex is indeed the politics of the sixties. If it *is* the last frontier of other-directed man. . . .

If Freud, the mass media, and Margaret Mead have stripped away the veils, unburdened us of inhibitions, and guaranteed our inalienable right to orgasm. . . .

If the threat of man's extinction makes this coyness, lady, indeed a crime. . . .

If college is traditionally the graveyard of old idols. . . .

If a campus rule is regarded as that which is made to be broken. . . . If privacy is readily available, or not particularly essential, and virginity thus increasingly undefendable. . . .

If everybody in the dorm is doing It and talking It and egging her on. . . . Why does one girl join the dance and another decline?

In an atmosphere that would seem to encourage sexual freedom (with a wink, if not with an outright endorsement), why hasn't virginity become obsolete? * Given the permissive climate of Bennington or Antioch, why will one girl hold staunchly to virginity, another let love carry her to its ultimate intimacy, and a third leap from bed to bed with seeming abandon? In the heartland of conservatism, why does one coed nibble at forbidden fruit while her roommate devours it core and all and a third girl down the hall acts as if she doesn't even see the tree?

It is the emotional luggage a girl brings with her to college that determines how she will respond to the sexual climate of the campus: her values, her goals, her needs, her image of herself, the strength and quality of her fears. Is she aiming for a Ph.D. in nuclear physics or a plain gold band by the end of her sophomore year? Are her needs gently or pressingly neurotic? Does she identify more with Papa than with Mama? How scarred or undernourished is her ego? Does she want to be the prettiest Phi Bete on campus? The brainiest girl to bring home an all-D report card? Many of these forces will conflict, but soon the strongest will claim her attention and guide her sexual behavior in a way that no college rule book could hope to imitate.

Fear is a most powerful chastity belt; for some college girls, more powerful than devout religious faith.** Religious faith

* As Lewis M. Terman predicted—the female unmarried virgin would disappear by 1960—in his *Psychological Factors in Marital Happiness*, N.Y.: McGraw-Hill, 1938.

** Premarital intercourse is condemned by all of the major Protestant, Catholic, and Jewish groups. But many traditional sex attitudes are being reevaluated. Champions of freer sexuality feel they gain some support in the position of liberal Protestantism as expressed by Dr. Roger Shinn of Union Theological Seminary: "A good deal of the old repressiveness is gone—what we generally associate with the word Puritanism. Arising out of Biblical scholarship of the last twenty years is the recognition that the Bible's attitude toward sex is affirmative and that the repressive attitude is really a heresy. Sex is God-given, and man realizes himself through it." For more on changing church attitudes and a discussion of the liberalization of the sex attitudes of American ministers, see "What Clergymen Tell Young People About Marriage," by Terry Morris, *Redbook Magazine*, March, 1963; and "What Ministers Are Learning About Sex," by Dr.

may gird a freshman for courtship battles but can easily be rationalized into the background by the love-smitten sophomore or junior. "I don't think God cares about *that*," a San Diego State sophomore retorted when a schoolmate suggested there was a contradiction between the girl's sexual adventures and her regular churchgoing. "My church says even French kissing is wrong," said a devoutly Catholic coed at DePauw University. The first time her steady, a Jewish boy, French-kissed her, "I felt so guilty, we almost broke up." Now she rationalizes "terribly intimate petting" with the comment: "The Church's rules apply only to the nonthinking masses." "What keeps a girl from going to bed with a boy she loves?" I

Gelolo McHugh and J. Robert Moskin, *Look Magazine,* November 25, 1958.

The Kinsey reports found educational level was far more likely to affect the male's incidence of premarital coitus but that at each educational level, the religiously active, regardless of affiliation, reported lower incidence than the religiously inactive. Religious activity was a most significant factor in the premarital sexual behavior of women, the devoutly religious in each group being the least active. Among the females between the ages of 15 and 20, premarital coitus was reported as: Protestant, devout, 14%, moderate, 19%, inactive, 25%; Catholic, devout, 12%, moderate, 24%, inactive, 41%; Jewish, moderate, 11%, inactive, 27%. In females 21 to 25, the figures were: Protestant, devout, 22%, moderate, 33%, inactive, 44%; Catholic, devout, 21%, moderate (no cases), inactive, 54%; Jewish, moderate, 23%, inactive, 42%.

Eugene A. Kanin and David H. Howard found that 28% of the regular churchgoers among the married couples they studied reported premarital coitus. The figure was 48% for the couples with one regular and one non-regular churchgoer and 61% for nonattenders. "Postmarital Consequences of Premarital Sex Adjustments," *American Sociological Review,* October, 1958.

"Courtship Intimacy and Religious Background," by Temple University's Robert R. Bell and Leonard Blumberg, provides specific insight into a special collegiate situation—the large metropolitan university where 90% of the respondents lived at home and ". . . continued to be subject to filial and community controls." The fact that most students dated off-campus was regarded as indication that family and community pressures exerted stronger influence than those of the university.

The religious distribution of the respondents paralleled that of Temple University itself: 55% Jewish, 25% Protestant, 20% Catholic. Intimacy levels were compared for "dating," "going steady," and "engagement." Respondents were asked to indicate the greatest degree of intimacy he or she was ever involved in within these levels. In "dating" relationships

asked. "I can answer in three words," a Radcliffe freshman shot back, "I'm a Catholic." "Come back when she's a junior," an upperclassman whispered to me. "See if she can still put it in three words."

Fear, too, evolves from freshman to senior year. Some are more stubborn than others. These fears are myriad and not always labelled by their correct names. Asked, "What keeps a girl from going to bed with a boy she loves?" coeds answer: "Fear of pregnancy"—"fear of public opinion"—"fear of becoming promiscuous"—"fear of losing his respect"—"fear of losing my own respect"—"fear of being used—being exploited"—"fear you might not be good at it"—"fear you'll lose him because you did"—"fear of hurting my parents"—

---

among the female respondents, petting 50% and intercourse 11% was reported as the peak of intimacy by Jewish girls, 49% and 10% by Protestant girls, 42% and 10% by Catholic girls. For a "going steady" relationship, it was petting 62%, intercourse 14%, Jewish; 45% and 20% for Protestants, 55% and 14% for Catholics. The figures for engaged couples were 60% and 20% for Jewish girls, 55% and 38% for Protestant, 19% and 56% for Catholics.

To the authors this picture suggested Jewish young people date earlier and "play the field." Going steady "is perceived as further along the continuum toward engagement and marriage than it is for Protestant or Catholic young people."—"a reflection," the authors write, "of familial reputational norms which define the situation . . . between young people as either 'having a good time' or 'husband hunting.'" The Protestant pattern involves "commencement of dating at a later age" and "greater reluctance to feel comfortable in the fleeting dating relationship." They move more quickly to "going steady," which is "defined as temporary and lacks the overtone of tentative permanence" it seems to have for the Jewish respondents. Late dating was also a factor in the pattern of the Catholic students. The Catholic male, Bell and Blumberg suggest, "tends to 'play the field' and to seek sexual achievement as early as possible." They add: "It is probably that there is a relatively high degree of religious homogamy among Catholic females and hence, among those subjected to Catholic male sex aggression, which probably accounts for the somewhat higher degree of sexual promiscuity among the Catholic female respondents." The authors liken this sexual behavior to *machismo*, (a Latin definition of masculinity in terms of power and aggression) as reported among Puerto Ricans and, similar to slum sex codes in which status among Italian-American slum adolescents "was defined in part by sex conquest" ("A Slum Sex Code," by William F. Whyte, *American Sociological Review*, October, 1952). This type of behavior, the authors add, "is strongly in *contrast* to the Irish Catholic puritanism."

"fear of growing up, of crossing a threshold when you can't turn back."

Not all virginity is built on fear. It only sounds that way to hear most college girls analyze it. Some girls, however, do prefer to dissect the foundations of chastity in positive terms. They talk about idealism, maturity, responsibility, loyalty to parents, romanticism, Victorian virtue, will power, sensitivity. "I want my first lover to be my only lover," a Kent University junior explained. "I feel I owe my parents something—my virginity—and their influence has been too strong to override," a Wellesley freshman said. "You don't enjoy sex except in love and marriage," she added. "We came to college to leave more earthly things behind," an intense Mt. Holyoke sophomore remarked. "We're here to grasp something more important, aren't we?" "Sex is such a unique and wonderful experience, it should be with one man only," a University of Miami senior said. "I want to be in love first," a University of Alabama sophomore explained, "and I feel if a girl loves him enough to sleep with him, she loves him enough to be married first."

"Virginity is a bargaining position," a Sarah Lawrence sophomore suggested. "After all, there are hundreds of bright, attractive girls around. What do you have? Your virginity. But what about after graduation, when there are hundreds of bright, attractive girls and they're going to bed. Then what have you got? After all, sex is the normal consummation of love," she said.

"So is murder if you're mad," came the response from a recent grad of the Texas Women's University.

The Sarah Lawrence girl, a virgin according to her own confession, sighed. "Girls like you, like my sister, have got to be virgins," she replied. "But I've reached the point where I think virginity for its own sake is stupid."

"But can't you look at yourself in the mirror and tell yourself, some day I'm going to be married and have a family and, knowing that, I will keep my self-respect?" the Texas champion of chastity wanted to know.

"You don't ruin your self-respect by sleeping with the man you love," the Bronxville girl said, a bit impatiently. "And what happens if you look in that mirror at 60 and you never did get married and all you've got is your self-respect?"

Impasse.

Fear of sex itself, the act in its anatomical reality, is the most formidable inhibitor. Coeds themselves rate other factors above fear of sex—fear of pregnancy, fear of public opinion, fear of drifting into promiscuity. Yet the fear of sex, for many virgins the most difficult to put into words, is also the most difficult to dismiss or ignore. Time, environment, persuasive advocates of sexual emancipation, their schoolmates and their dates will tear away other inhibitors one by one. Least affected by this sabotage will be the girl who is conditioned in the reflex of repulsion. There are some girls still being raised to believe sexual intercourse is vile, disgusting, painful, degrading. There are others who reach the same conclusion on their own after being molested by a relative or, as a Northwestern virgin put it, "a dirty old man," in early childhood. For still others though, it is neither reflex or experience, but rather a vague, nagging fear acquired, it might seem, by osmosis. "I went with a boy for six years," a University of Michigan senior said, knitting furiously as if in punctuation. "When he announced he wouldn't marry anyone he hadn't slept with, I stopped seeing him. I have a friend who was fast-talked into it. One month later she and the boy broke up. And she hasn't had a normal relationship with a boy since. With an example like that, you think twice," she said, nodding sternly. And a Bennington coed seemed impressed by the report of a girl who borrowed a white nighty and went off for the weekend with a young man. "She told me after, 'It's not all it's cracked up to be,'" the Bennington virgin reported.

Why such gripping fear?

"There are so many rationalizations around two words—sexual intercourse—and its value as a human experience," an assembly of Harvard and Radcliffe freshmen was told recently by Dr. Preston Munter, a University Health Service psychiatrist. "I don't suppose any combination of human experience could ever hope to meet the expectation that most of you have for the rather commonplace experience we call sexual intercourse," he went on. "It's so highly overvalued that you're frightened of it, you expect too much of it, you can't understand why, once you've had such an experience, it doesn't eradicate all of your relationship problems."

College girls themselves realize that the reasons they advance so glibly for preserving their maidenly state are often rationalization. "Girls seem casual," said a University of Colorado coed, herself a virgin, "but I don't think they feel that way. It's a very tense matter," the tall, rather self-conscious junior explained. "I think a lot of college girls have been raised so that they have no set moral standards when they enter college. From family background, I mean. And if you have no moral or religious reasons for not playing the game, it's difficult to think up other reasons for not playing—other than pregnancy fears."

What keeps this particular girl from going to bed with the young men who seek her company there? "I think I would be emotionally destroyed. When I get depressed, I think I have nothing to offer at all. But that's the one thing I have left—I'd have to know emotionally it would make no difference—and know that I wouldn't completely break down—and I would. There are only two endings to an affair, happy or unhappy. And I think there are very few happy ones."

Most professional behaviorists would agree that pregnancy fears alone keep few girls out of the prenuptial bed. As one Berkeley junior pointed out, "Everyone worries about becoming pregnant—girls who go to bed and girls who don't. Pregnancy is just a handy excuse, easier to say than something hitting closer to home." Moral concerns are a popular rationalization for some to hide behind; for others, morality is reason not excuse. But on many campuses, girls don't like to be caught with their morality showing. To emphasize their emancipation from society's traditional codes and docile fidelity to parental do's and don't's, many coeds shy from any mention of morality. "Your body is so precious, it should be given only to *the* man," they will announce.

Kinsey was also unwilling to accept the ladies at their own analysis. Though the females in his sample listed "moral objections" (89 percent), "sexual unresponsiveness" (45 percent), "fear of pregnancy" (44 percent), "fear of public opinion" (44 percent), "lack of opportunity" (22 percent), and "fear of venereal disease" (14 percent) as reasons for abstaining from premarital coitus or for restricting further coitus, Kinsey had his doubts. Ruling out those factors, which "appeared to be nothing more than rationalization," he listed these primary restrictive or inhibiting factors:

1. The sexual unresponsiveness of many younger females.
2. The moral tradition of our American culture.
3. Lack of experience, and the individual's fear of engaging in an unfamiliar activity.

In today's supposedly penicillin-omnipotent era, nobody seems to be worried about venereal disease. If they are, they're too shy to say so.* Though today's college girls are capable of painful candor about their doubts, lacks, fears, and inferiorities (real and imagined), no one claimed "lack of opportunity." Several girls did say "there just isn't any place to be alone." An engaged senior at Boston University insisted "there's never enough time." But since dozens of girls in the same schools and same situations claimed no lack of "time" or "place," it was plain these girls were actually saying: I really don't want to. Or, an equal possibility; He doesn't want to. There is really no such thing as "too busy with studies" or "too busy making the Crimson" or "becoming editor on the Sun" or

---

* But the fact is reported cases of gonorrhea have increased 20% in the past five years while reported cases of syphilis tripled in the same period.

In "What Parents Must Know about Teenagers and V.D.," *McCalls Magazine,* January, 1963, Dr. Leona Baumgartner, Chairman of the United States Surgeon General's Task Force on Syphilis, writes: ". . . these figures [do not] come near reflecting the true picture, for although v.d. is reportable by law, there is the desire to shun its stigma. Thus, the actual incidence of syphilis, experts agree, is probably three times higher." Among teenagers, syphilis was up 56% between 1960 and 1961. Among adults aged 20 to 24, the increase was 73%. V.D. has "crossed the tracks"— affecting young people "in every social category, including the most sheltered and privileged," according to Dr. Baumgartner. She blames "overconfidence in antibiotics," which "undoubtedly is what led to cutbacks in funds for v.d. control programs. Doctors, health educators, Congress, schools, and churches must also share the guilt, she writes, adding, "Responsibility for its *arrest* now largely lies with another group: *parents.*"

"running for the Student Government," though at least four girls and several young men cited these activities as factors responsible for their virginity.

Rather than say "I'm afraid" or "no one asked me" or "sex isn't nice"—all unfashionable or unattractive positions in many collegiate circles—a girl may say, "I certainly do approve of premarital intercourse, but I must fall in love first." Flying the banner of this popular and loudly approved front, a girl may postpone falling in love indefinitely.

As for "lack of sexual responsiveness," which Kinsey found to be "even more important than the females themselves understood," it would be difficult to judge without a lie detector and mass Rorschach tests. Young women of today do not talk candidly about lack of sexual responsiveness. To admit an underdeveloped libido is taboo. In this orgasm-oriented decade, it would be like denying one's femininity. "I'm afraid I'm much too passionate for my own good," a girl will say, as one Bennington freshman did. "It's hard to resist when you have an affectionate nature as I do," an Ohio State junior said. "I had big plans to be a virgin on my wedding night," a Brooklyn College senior said with a grin, "but no go—I'm just a spineless, lusty broad." The cool coed really warms up when it comes to describing her sexual prowess and the unquenchable fire of her female hormones. "Oh Lord, I've gotta have a man," she moans with mock despair, pretending to climb the wall of the recreation room at a University of Wisconsin sorority house. "I'm not kidding," she insists, "you don't know how long it's been since I got screwed." "Oh, I'm in the mood to discuss sex all right," a Barnard junior announced. "I've just spent half the afternoon at the museum devouring *The Discus Thrower*." A Stanford coed talked about her passion for pornography and a Michigan State senior brushed back a wispy row of uneven bangs with ink-stained fingers and said, "I don't think boys have any idea at all about the female sex drive. There he stands wondering whether he can get away with kissing you and you're already deciding you might like to go to bed with him. Ironic, isn't it?"

Harold Greenwald, the Manhattan psychoanalyst, is not

convinced by such advertisements for sensuality. "I doubt that it is their sexual need that is so great," he commented. "It is their emotional need, the need for affection, tenderness, intimacy." It is tougher, cooler, more in the idiom of the sixties to call it sex. It is also likely that for many girls, sexual intercourse is an act permitted, suffered, endured, or traded unhappily for love, commitment, the security of a date next Saturday night, a marriage proposal. Girls who feel this way are reluctant to admit it, even to themselves.

Nothing about the subject of sex and women is clear or obvious or statable in a simple declarative sentence without qualifiers and dangling "if's" and "but's." Yet even as coeds fired a barrage of their reasons for holding back from the ultimate intimacy—the "dirty deed," the "sexual crime," "*That*," as they put it—it seemed that no fear, no inhibitor was quite so strong that a degree of anonymity could not squelch it.

For pregnancy, the fear of promiscuity, and moral considerations are often forgotten if the occasion is romantic enough, curiosity pressing enough, and the entranced young virgin convinced that "just this once, no one will ever know." Summer vacation or the spring rites at Ft. Lauderdale, Palm Springs, Bermuda, and Daytona Beach offer sufficient anonymity, as one Dean of Women's postvacation campus pregnancy figures attest. Junior year abroad, Europe during the summer, or the postgraduate Grand Tour is for many college girls "the great masquerade," as a recent Smithie suggested. "I suppose you feel as if no one is toting the score," a Bryn Mawr senior explained. "At the end of the year, you will say goodbye to your Italian lover and, if you want to, you can be revirginated on the ship home. No one ever has to know." "Don't get the idea these Geneva Don Juans are using the poor innocent Smithies," a veteran of Junior Year Abroad remarked. "The Smithies are using them, too, and you get victims and shattered morale on both sides."

Several veterans of Junior Year Abroad seemed to feel that European-culture shock has lost some of its force. "If you are wild at home, you'll be wild away," a self-described "straight-arrow" Smith girl observed. "If you're not, just being in school abroad won't change you." And a Sarah Lawrence girl boasted of how she planned to tell her grandchildren some day "that my first great love was a Frenchman, and he truly respected my virginity." And, in fact, certain continental campus followers seem to suffer more from their first exposure to such American courtship customs as petting than do the transplanted college girls from exposure to the blandishments of the European male.

Even so, the fields on the road to Siena and the villas overlooking Amalfi and the small hotels near the Alliance Française in Paris have witnessed the coming of age and the shedding of restraints of numerous "straight-arrows." "It even seems to help if the man doesn't speak English," a peripetatic Sarah Lawrence girl suggested. And a handsome American Rhodes scholar on holiday from Oxford was sure two Vassar maidens had given him icy shoulders because he was "from back home." He was convinced when he later discovered the two girls in Naples "shacked up with a couple of Italian stevedore types—and obviously thriving on it." *

It is not merely anonymity, of course, that makes the European experience a compelling force in the college girl's always changing concepts of love and sex. Exposure to different moralities may make home-grown moralities seem increasingly vulnerable to attack as narrow provincialism. For some girls, discovering the European man is like rediscovering her own femininity, a wondrous joy to the girl who may be deeply troubled over the most pressing and highly publicized problem of the American woman today—role conflict, the feminine mystique. "I adored Italy," a bright Sarah Lawrence

* One hundred thousand high school and college-age Americans traveled to Europe in summer of 1963, "swamping the hard core of 20,000 Americans who live and study there the year around," Geoffrey Bocca reported in "Those Student Tours to Europe," *McCalls Magazine*, July, 1963. "Will Europe corrupt our children morally, physically, politically?" Bocca asks, and his answer: "A well-adjusted youngster probably will not be corrupted. A badly adjusted one *will* be corrupted." He quotes a 21-year-old Chicago girl: "The danger lies for a girl from a very strict home. She might be flattered by all the attention men give women over there, staring at her, compliments. I'd worry about *her*."

girl from Brooklyn said. "Never have I felt so much like a woman. It was very relaxing just to be a girl. Not to be a Sarah Lawrence girl, not to be a 'nice' girl. Just to be a girl, flirted with, looked at, appreciated." "You can always tell an American boy overseas in Europe," a Rochester coed remarked, "They don't even *look* at you. But the Spaniards—I crossed my legs in a cafe and there was a noise like a theater between acts." "Europeans are sensual, Americans are sexual," a recent Stanford graduate commented, making clear her preference for the former. "Italy is just set up for sex," the Sarah Lawrence girl added, noting that she herself did not feel compelled to surrender her chastity.

Some college girls and some standards of sex ethics are easily seduced by the scene, the Man, and the confrontation with the heady notion of being a woman. But the combination is not so overwhelming as it was once regarded. "You hear so much about what's going to happen before you go, you're prepared," the Rochester coed explained. "You don't get swept off your feet." Others tire of being merely women and begin to yearn for, to quote a Northwestern sophomore, "a good hot political argument with an American boy who appreciates that you have a mind." Still others see little or no attraction in either the European male or the permissive atmosphere. A Smith veteran of Junior Year Abroad spoke derisively of "Some girls—Sweetbriar and Stanford, mostly— so hopelessly 'wholesome' they spent six months in Florence without meeting a single Italian and obviously didn't care to." *

Many college girls save the round-trip overseas fare by seeking a taste of sexual adventure with anonymity of a kind at home. Just as a University of Texas fraternity boy may wind up with a prostitute "because you don't do that sort of thing with a nice college girl," the "nice college girl" may discreetly and more-or-less anonymously find similar adven-

* For more on American students abroad, see *From Main Street to The Left Bank* by John A. Garraty and Walter Adams. East Lansing: The Michigan State University Press, 1959, and *Young Americans Abroad*, edited by Roger Klein, N.Y.: Harper & Row, 1963.

tures with a gas station attendant across town or a teenage lifeguard who may or may not know her name. A Temple University junior confided a brief affair during the Christmas holidays with a cabana boy at the hotel where she and her family stayed. "I was curious, I suppose," she said, "but I didn't want to get a name for myself." A Stanford coed mapped out her deflowering, deliberately choosing not the on-campus youth she was "nuts" about, but an Irish tourist who, she knew, would be returning to Ireland two weeks later. "It's difficult to explain," she said, "but I just didn't want someone hanging around—I wanted to do it—and then see. Afterwards he apologized and was all upset because he hadn't known I was a virgin. Then he kept calling the dorm till he left, wanting to know if I was okay. I had no desire to see him."

The sexual conservatism of many college boys and the tacit compliance of many coeds to the double standard prejudices of the boys they will eventually marry contribute to the survival of a cross-culture sexual underground. In her own crowd, a girl may seem to be a staunch and unswerving champion of chastity. Yet in other backyards she may be receptive to sexual adventure, possibly even aggressive with a boy, she regards as an unsuitable mate—a boy of another class or religion or race, a foreign student, a married professor. "If the man is remote enough from your own circle, it's like it never happened," an Ohio State sophomore suggested. Thus a Texas fraternity man will assure you that Northern girls are "easy lays," a Jewish law student at Yale will confide that Jewish girls are "hopelessly middle-class goody-goodies but gentile girls are real swingers," and a Negro architecture student at Columbia will ask, "Who said Jewish girls are square? Not where I hang out."

"I never knew anybody but middle-class Jews," a Barnard coed said. "Older boys, lawyers and doctors who lived with their famiiles, all very proper. Then I got into the theatrical crowd. Bohemians. Classless. I met this beautiful blond Anglo-Saxon. His attitude was if you want it and I want it, it's right. He didn't know I was a virgin. He swears he didn't know. I bled for a week and finally he went to a hospital to find out what we should do. Three weeks later, I was in bed with another man." She shrugged. "It helps to get sex out of the way—to get rid of the problem. But it ought to be a good relationship. Too many girls just go out and get rid of it."

Though all the statistics would indicate that it is love that ultimately leads a girl to revise her sexual ethics to include intercourse, curiosity and the need to "get rid of it" was a recurrent theme in these interviews. Girls speak of Love in capital letters and praise sex in Love's name only. Yet it may be anything but Love:

"I decided it was time," a Boston University junior said. "I felt so left out," a Barnard sophomore recalled. "I didn't want to get emotionally involved," a Bryn Mawr graduate said, "so I chose this most loathsome, unattractive guy." "Everything is so existential and the sophomore year is such a depressed state," a Mt. Holyoke senior explained. "We all look for permanence," a University of Vermont junior observed, "but after a while you become more realistic." "I had to get it out of the way—it was becoming an obsession," a Northwestern sophomore said. "You do it because you like it, that's the only good reason," announced a young lady from Queens College. "Don't think curiosity isn't a big factor—it is," a prematurely pregnant Colorado coed observed, "I was very curious to see what it was like." "It doesn't have to be someone you love necessarily," a San Diego State College sophomore said. "I have some friends I go to bed with I don't even date." "Sometimes it happens just because you both get smashed— which happens too often in fact," a schoolmate suggested. "One day I said 'What the hell am I holding on to it for?'" a Brooklyn college coed recalled. "I'd been saying no all my life. Then I met this boy. For the first time I couldn't think of any reason why not." "He was just so beautiful," a plain-faced, freckled University of Pennsylvania junior reported with a deep sigh. "Lots of girls get talked out of their virginity by boys saying they, the girls, are frustrated and neurotic," a second Colorado coed remarked. "It all boils down to the old view that some people have skin problems because they are frustrated sexually. Girls believe those things." "He was a man and I'd been dating boys," a Smith junior explained. "This thing could be so good, he told me. Nobody had ever said that to me before."

Though these comments seem to have little to do with love, the forces that shove, propel, draw, or otherwise send girls careening along the path to premarital sexual experience is usually tied (even if she herself cannot see the string) to the need to be loved. If a girl cannot love, or has not yet found love, or is in a hurry for love, she can pretend through love's movements. Needing love, needing to be needed, needing to be admired for herself alone (as compared to the male's need to be admired for his abilities and acts), she settles for love-making. Several college girls interviewed were well aware of this pattern in their sexual dossiers. "Sometimes just saying 'I love you' makes it so," a plump, chestnut-haired Cornell history major said rather wistfully. "We are very fond of love in the South," said a Texas champion of chastity with drawled sarcasm. "Some of us manage to fall in love two or three times a week."

Sometimes stated, sometimes merely hinted in the remarks of the sexually experienced is the marriage-panic already discussed, the American cult of popularity (though no girl wants to be popular because boys think she is sexually promiscuous), and pressures that imply a drifting along with the crowd or the bowing to a demanding young man in hopes of keeping him. "Ed wouldn't be pinned to me if I didn't," a University of Mississippi coed said. "You know you're competing with hundreds of girls just like you who are willing," a Goucher junior explained. "The drips keep coming back," a New York University sophomore commented, "but if you only knew how many great guys ask you out three or four times and then just don't call back because they don't believe you can have a really meaningful relationship that doesn't include sex."

Whatever the force that sweeps her into bed, it may be dissolved by her discovery that premarital sex is more than she can handle. "We love each other very much and it just happened," a Swarthmore junior said, explaining that she and her steady decided not to go to bed together again. "We both felt so sad and guilty after, we decided we would wait until we're married." "She was tanked out of her head," a wispy-voiced Middlebury junior said of her roommate, "and she swears she'll never do it again." "It was a nightmare," said a Berkeley freshman. "I should never have gone that far, but I begged him to stop and he wouldn't listen. It was my fault for putting myself in that position."

Some girls do seem to "want to be forced," as a Reed College junior put it, because they prefer to have the decision out of their own hands. But others who enter a sexual relationship more willingly find their own guilt—or the boy's—make it impossible to maintain.*

Other girls set out to embrace sexual adventure and find their determination falters. A determined Michigan State coed made it all the way to a motel before her courage crumbled. "I just couldn't go through with it." But her boyfriend, on leave from the Army, had come 800 miles and she offered to try again the next night. "He said he'd had enough of my tears the night before," she said. Others find it is not their own courage but the young man's interest that has faded. A Wheelock College sophomore told how she decided to sleep with a boy she had dated for two years because she heard he was seriously ill. He refused her. "Imagine," she said, "after trying to talk me into it all those months, he finally told me, 'I just couldn't think of you that way'."

* Kinsey found that among the sexually experienced unmarried females in his sample, 69% "insisted they did not regret their experience. Another 13% recorded some minor regret." Of those who had coitus with fiance only, 81% had no regret, 9% had definite regret; of those who had coitus with fiance and others, 78% reported no regret, 9% definite regret. In the Burgess and Wallin study, *Courtship, Engagement and Marriage,* 84% of the engaged women and 96% of the engaged men did not express any guilt feelings about their intercourse with each other. Bell, in *Marriage and Family Interaction,* reports supporting evidence from another study: "The immediate reaction of 77 percent of the girls to first experience with sexual intercourse was pleasurable." Bell comments: "It may be argued that those girls who say they do not regret premarital coitus are rationalizing their behavior. It is no doubt true that many girls say they have no regrets because they feel they must justify their behavior to themselves and in some cases to others. However, the degree of rationalization is probably much less than many people believe."

What becomes of the coed who experiences premarital intercourse? What about all the imagined terrors, outlined by Mama and most marriage course manuals, later to be analyzed and dissected in those after-hours dormitory seminars. How many of her fears are realized? Fear of pregnancy, for instance—fear of losing control and drifting into promiscuity—fear of being hurt or ostracized?

The mysteries of biology are not nearly so mysterious as many college girls believe.* The Kinsey premarital pregnancy figures—one out of five girls experiencing premarital coitus conceives—seems widely accepted as valid by most professionals in the family field. And the college girl is no more immune than her less-educated sister.

Promiscuity is certainly not inevitable. Marriage may come along before a girl has the time and opportunity to accumulate a scorecard she herself might describe as promiscuous. Or she may be saved from smarting under that epiphet by gradual redefining of the word over the years. Many girls do discriminate between "that very special man" and more casual beaux, saving greater physical intimacy as "very special." Yet many coeds agreed with the Vermont senior who remarked, "It's true that after the first time, the second time is easier. And more fun." And an Antioch sophomore explained, "Once you've been to bed with a man and put sex in its proper perspective, you realize love is The Thing and sex is one small part of it—before that you make such an issue out of going to bed it seems sex is The Thing and love is commonplace." Girls, even those intellectually dedicated to unqualified sexual freedom, do worry about losing control, but the Antioch girl quoted above illustrated determination to hang on to the reins. Bright and deeply concerned, she had left Antioch and was attending a hometown college because, in her words: "I realized that I had let myself drift to a point where I was just going to bed too easily and it wasn't meaning anything anymore."

Hurt? "Of course you get hurt," the slim, curly-haired brunette from Brandeis conceded. "So? What you had for as

* See Chapter 8, Birth Control: The Numbers Game.

long as you had it was far more precious. You get hurt. And you survive." "Reject before rejection," a University of Michigan sorority girl quipped. "And what about the girls who seem to *enjoy* getting hurt," she added. Her companion groaned. "Can't we keep the sickniks out of this for maybe 12 minutes?" "What would worry me," said a third Ann Arbor coed, as we shared a pizza at the Cottage Inn ("home of the intellectual pizza"), "would be the girl who was so casual about sex she *didn't* suffer when a great romance sort of folded." As several girls pointed out, the end of a romance is always painful—whether or not sex has been a part of it—just as divorce or a floundering marriage inevitably hurts.

What these girls had to say about the forces that determine sexual decisions reveals, I feel, the character of sexual behavior in all its elusive contradictions. Their actions cannot be divided neatly into columns headed "moral" and "immoral." If it could, educators now would not be having such a slow and difficult time of finding methods or a value system or even the vocabulary to encourage a dialogue between student and adult. Sex for these girls is carefree and troubled, joyous and traumatic, obsessive, sordid, pure, hysterical, beautiful, deliciously evil, empty, overwhelmingly sinful, intense, meaningful—a hundred adjectives that do not translate well into statistics. What is revealing is how often a girl's sex ethics and opinions diverge from her actual behavior. It is not enough to assume sexual insights are well in order once an investigator has asked young women what they approve or disapprove of. And accepting a coed's comment such as "I don't know any virgins in my milieu" at face value is an insult to the complexity of sexual behavior. With such nuance of meaning and levels of motivation, is it any wonder that pat, all-encompassing solutions and naive preachings parading outdated devils have been just so many wasted words?

Come Live with Me and Be My Love

*Dancing in the snow with no clothes on
and I wasn't cold
snow on my face
and wind making cheeks pink*

snow sitting on evergreen branches
branches like feathers
I am a feather too, feeling beautiful
and I wasn't cold

dancing soft
dancing in sweetness
white powder sprinkles in my hair
dancing
feet singing
arms free
dancing
dancing to the
snow god
and I wasn't cold

Dancing in the snow with no clothes on
and I wasn't cold. I wasn't cold. I wasn't cold
*until I saw them looking at me.**

The poem was taped to the stuccoed wall of the spotless and sparsely furnished apartment high on Telegraph Hill in San Francisco's North Beach, birthland of the Beats. It is the apartment Diana Gaines Brookfield shares with four college boys. To be precisely accurate Diana lives with one young man who lives with three other young men, and they all live together in apparent affection and tolerance and respect.

"No one seems particularly upset or annoyed at having me around all the time. At least they haven't shown it. And I think it would be pretty tough to conceal. After all, this *was* their apartment first. When I came I just had to take it or leave it. They certainly weren't going to leave. There have been relatively few clashes. And maybe they'd never admit it, but I think they're learning a lot about women, having me around. Me? I'm learning what it's like cooking for a family of five. Actually I guess I'm lucky. My obligations don't extend to ironing *everyone's* shirt or scrubbing *everyone's* socks. Only Kenny's—and that's a labor of love."

She smiled, a poster-pretty 19-year-old with a wispy little-boy haircut ("I did it with my own cuticle scissors—at the beauty shop I guess they'd call it an 'Oliver cut' and charge

* "Child Dance," by Carol Mann, *Beatitude*, No. 2, May 16, 1959.

$15."). Diana moved to the heights of Telegraph Hill after one year and three months at the University of California in Berkeley across the Bay. Still officially enrolled there when I was invited for coffee and to meet the boys, Diana had not attended classes in a month and had no intention of returning. She had been living atop Telegraph for six months parttime and "unofficially" (minus such recognition as her name on the mail box), "officially" for three months. Do not be misled by the address. True, Diana and her apartment mates are but a few steps from the Bread and Wine Mission, the Co-Existence Bagel Shop, the tiny hole in the wall where—in the golden days of the early Beats (before the squares muscled in)— citizens of the neighborhood debated "the superiority of the bagel as a contraceptive" and "Where would the world be today if Joan of Arc had had a miscarriage?" They are on the scene, not *with it*. Weekends, college kids from the Bay area's dozens of campuses make the North Beach scene and sometimes the overflow will find its way to this apartment. But a less *beat* female than Diana would be difficult to imagine. Fresh, eager, gentle, well-mannered, radiating joy and contentment, there seems to be nothing forced or exhibitionistic in her nonconformity, her rebellion. It is not the rebellion for the sake of rebellion detected in the sexual adventures of many college girls. Love came first and the nonconformity was incidental to the needs of that love. The rebellion goes deeper: Diana's homelife in a middle-class Bay suburb was underprivileged only in that she never knew where her mother's next husband was coming from. Kenny is more than lover. He is parent, confidante, spiritual advisor, brother, playmate, and beau. He and his roommates attend San Francisco City College, but he was planning to transfer to San Francisco State and Diana hoped to enroll there too if she could convince the Brookfields to restore her allowance.

"Mother realizes now that I'm living here with Kenny but father has to be protected. He's already furious—disgusted, I guess, about my leaving Berkeley, but they've given up pushing me to go back. Mother can accept an awful lot. She may not approve but whatever happens, I'm still her girl. She accepts it, but at times she can be pretty sarcastic, pretty cutting. You see, I've never never tried to hide anything. I never wanted to lie or sneak around behind her back. When you believe what you do is right, you don't want to have to lie. Maybe it would have been kinder—but I don't want to lie about this—lying would cheapen it.

"The first time Kenny and I went to bed it was very simple, very natural, as if we were man and wife. We were both fifteen. My mother was away. I didn't say, 'Well, Mother, we're lovers,' but I didn't try to hide it. She found out for sure when I asked our family doctor to fit me for a diaphragm. Yes, I know I could always have gone to some clinic. But a clinic is not just there to help. I don't want to be a subject for someone's research. It seems to me it should be my privilege to be protected from pregnancy—by my own private doctor. But she refused to do it until I was eighteen unless I had my mother's permission because it would be making it that much easier. 'As if it isn't easy enough now,' I said. 'So why not make it safe too?' When my mother found out she was shocked. She was horrified. It was just awful. She reminded me how, when I was 12, I came home one day and said petting was horrible. That was the way to think, she had told me. 'Are you taking money too?' she wanted to know. Yes, she really said that. *My* mother. They never did approve of Kenny. Not the right background or, you know— I was supposed to date other boys and sometimes when he called, she would say I wasn't home. Anyway, Kenny got disgusted. He lost patience with me for letting her run our lives.

"After he broke us up, I don't know what happened to me. I slept around with too many people. It was too difficult to say 'no.' Oh, there are places, plenty of places to go, even if you live at home. I mean, why do you suppose they have a motel near every bowling alley? The trouble is, I think, too many girls go to bed with boys because they don't have anything to talk about. They go to bed for lack of conversation. I don't think I particularly enjoyed going to bed anymore—not the way I had with Kenny. I liked being cuddled before and after. The middle part was the price you had to pay.

"A few months after I started at Berkeley, Kenny came back into my life. I ran into him at a party here on the Beach and we both sort of just burst into tears and we began to see each other as much as we could. Christmas vacation I told my parents I wanted to spend the holiday with a girl friend in Los Angeles. Then I came here to stay with Kenny. It was like being two kids again. We stood in line to talk to Santa Claus and bought dozens of crazy presents at the dime store and had a tree—a little tree with popcorn on a thread and cranberries. I scrubbed and straightened Kenny's room so many times, the paint started coming off the walls, but it was so great to be doing things for him. It sounds awful, living with four boys, but Kenny and I have our own room, our own home, really. I feel our relationship is much more mature than before. Sometimes I feel a hundred years old. Everything awful I did was like another lifetime.

"I think I even look different. School became so unimportant. All I could think about was Kenny and the weekend and I talked about him—about us—constantly. I was living in this boarding house. Berkeley is so huge. Maybe I would have belonged more if I had rushed a sorority. There were three other girls in the house and we talked a lot about sex. All three of them were virgins—one was even engaged—and they didn't know what to make of me exactly. At first I must have shocked them. But then I guess I became their heroine sort of. Anything they wanted to know about sex, they would ask me. Then one afternoon, one of them said she'd heard a joke and couldn't understand why it was so funny. The joke had to do with the square root of 69. What could I say? I mean, wow. What a place to start the facts of life with. I figured it would be better if I just started at the beginning and worked up to the joke gradually. They thought they knew something from reading pornography, but it was so twisted and they took it all so literally. There really ought to be more sources for kids to learn about love and sex. Those sex manuals are so scientific and cold they make it sound like an operation. But the way I described it, they thought it sounded just great. They wanted me to help them canvas the campus for likely prospects to help them end their virginity—except the engaged girl, of course. Her boyfriend was very prudish and wanted to wait.

"When I left school for the summer I had no intention of going back. I parked my clothes at home and took a job and moved in here. My folks made such a big fuss when I said I wasn't going back I broke down and registered. But I began cutting classes and then not going at all—too bad, we could have used that tuition money. I'm not sure why I left school. Was it just because of Kenny or what? If so I haven't admitted it even to myself. It was so huge. Maybe I was lost there. I know I'm definitely going back to school—the spring semester if we can swing it—financially.

"I still see my mother now and then. We meet at the Mark,* her territory. In a way I feel like she's torn between me and her husband. Not that I can explain it—but he was the one that never gave Kenny a chance. Poor Mother. She just can't let it go. 'You used to hold your head so high,' she says to me. So I told her, 'Mother, I hold it higher than ever now.'

"Sometimes I think how I'd like to get up on a soapbox and tell girls how wonderful love and loving are—they have such twisted ideas about it. I'd like to get up on a soapbox and tell them: What happens in bed with the man you love *is* love."

Most likely the elements of ego deficiency and immaturity in this relationship would be readily discernible to the behavorial scientists. Indeed, there *is* a feeling of two kids playing in a backyard tree house. But love is love whether it thrives on emotional maturity or emotional needs. The physical intimacy between Diana and her Kenny seemed to be neither exploitive, compulsive, commercial, destructive, nor the *raison d'être* of their affair. Rather, it seemed a healthy and desirable expression of their love, respect, and commitment.**

* The Mark Hopkins Hotel
** Ten months after this interview, a letter came from Diana: "Kenny wants me to be sure to tell you we were married last month."

5

A New Style of Chastity

Next to football, there is probably no collegiate sport more popular and less apt to be touted in college catalogues than submarine racing. From Plum Beach in Brooklyn to the shores of the Potomac, along the Charles as it muddles by Cambridge to the shores of Malibu, student enthusiasts gather to watch the big subs race. In Chicago at the University that scorned Big Ten Football, submarine races below the surface of Lake Michigan have never lost favor. "Once someone even saw a submarine," a Chicago coed recalls. Onlookers were reportedly as startled as if the Loch Ness monster had waded into the shallows.

Manufacturers have been inspired to create the submarine racing T-shirt. But uniform is not required—nor are subs. Just a secluded spot by any water larger than a rain puddle, a car and/or a blanket. For an invitation to the sub races (like snark hunting expeditions and dates for the drive-in movie) is just another way to say, "Let's go somewhere and neck."

To examine the rules of such intramural sports as submarine racing is to discover that virgins are not what they used to be. American youth not only invented and patented petting to cope with the unique paradox of contemporary courtship conflicts, they are also the most promiscuous petters anywhere. By the time she marries, the American girl has petted with from 10 to 50 men, and the odds are possibly 50-50, she still remains technically a virgin.* Several sociologists believe that the great increase in premarital sexual behavior is not in actual coitus but rather in the intimacy, sophistication, acceptance, and practice of sexual foreplay. "You wonder how they do it!" marvelled one marriage and family expert. "How do they manage to walk that delicate balance between the sexy seductive appearance and at the same time convey the message, 'I'm untouchable'?"

The answer is: They are touchable.

The complexity of how touchable as a science is staggering. There is no one set of rules. Each girls seems to have her own catalogue of "if's" and "but's" only slightly less complex than the Internal Revenue Code, all of it governing how far to go, how soon, with whom, under what circumstances. "I've discovered there are some boys you can neck with and some you can go almost all the way with and some you can just lead along without even kissing them," an Oregon State University freshman said. "That's how you keep your reputation."

Sometimes a girl's Code and Timetable for Expressing Affection assumes more importance than the moment itself or either of the participants. At least that is how it seemed to a young Yale instructor who, in comparing petting customs East and West, remarked: "I often had the uncomfortable feeling that the California coed dispensed passion by some sort of rule book. It had all been decided beforehand: The first date, so many kisses; the second date, lips part, tongue enters; fifth date, three buttons; next time, one zipper."

* "The Variety and Meaning of Premarital Hetereosexual Experiences for the College Student," *op. cit.*

"It's not a timetable," a Smith junior defended it heatedly, staring into the dregs of a hot buttered rum before the fire of a ski lodge near Vermont's Mt. Bromley. "It's that old cliche 'I'd like to know you first'." "You have to be careful," a by-the-rule-book sophomore at Eastern Michigan defended. "If you're too fast, too eager, a boy may think, 'Wow, here's an easy one.' Then maybe you'll have a hard time convincing him you really are a virgin."

Some call it hypocrisy. Others call it survival instinct. It is a little of both that inspires the staunchly determined virgin to temper her petting pace, though no one described anything like the ultimate of prudence of the Smith girl in the novel *A Step Beyond Innocence*, by ex-Smithie Nora Johnson: One garment per annum was all the girl and her young man allowed themselves.

So it goes. From the shadows of the mausoleum at Stanford to the Airport Road near the University of North Dakota to the University of Chicago's Rockefeller Chapel ("Where," a former coed noted, "more souls are conceived than redeemed"). From the parking lot opposite the Tudor splendor of Sarah Lawrence to the golf course of Cornell, the sand dune haunts of University of Vermonters, the pine forest at Michigan State, in the shadow of the Greek theater at Berkeley, along a lane near Oxford, Mississippi (known locally as "The Hard Road"), at the Educational Testing Center Parking Lot of the University of Miami, the Arb on more than a dozen campuses, and in Swarthmore's celebrated Crum Woods of poetic fame:

> Crum woods is the coed's doom
> Evening shadows fill the gloom
> Suddenly there comes a hush
> The dean is checking underbrush.

At the Radcliffe Fieldhouse, in the Wellesley parking lots ("A policeman comes around and breaks it up if your head disappears below the window—very annoying," a young lady complained). In the mud-rutted roads behind the University of Delaware, in the woods down by the Brandeis infirmary, backstage during rehearsals at the Lydia Mendelssohn Theater in Ann Arbor, on the golf course of Amherst, near the University of Maryland's duck pond, in countless drive-in movies, fraternty recreation rooms, sorority boiler rooms—anatomies meet and hands have a way of losing altitude.

"The thing is to be a great lover," a Sarah Lawrence sophomore practitioner of great love explained. "That's very important. So you have the whole experience up to the ultimate act but not including it. All in neat, progressive installments. Our sex lives are very complicated and defined. Making out —that is allowed. Intercourse is forbidden. Princeton, between 3 o'clock and 4: that is the hour for passion. At Harvard, lust from 4 to 7. Last week a boy told me I was a good lover. I giggled and said, 'Well, thank you' and he said, 'Don't you know that you are? Don't be so ingenuous.' Well, I like to *know* I'm a good lover, but it's embarrassing being *told* it."

While there are still many college girls brooding about the wisdom of kissing a boy on the first date—indeed, some college freshman are only now experiencing their first dates —many are concerned with advanced skills. "How do I learn to be good in bed?" the Sarah Lawrence girl asked. "And you see, someday I want to be very good in bed. We learn by making out—Oh, I hate that expression."

And the American college girl *is* learning. The American college virgin may be a far more skilled and sophisticated lover than her unstudied nonvirginal schoolmate or even the teenage housewife she knew in high school. "It requires skill to satisfy a man and still hold on to your virginity," a sophisticated Ohio State coed observed. Girls acquire these skills in camp, in junior high, spying on the petting parties of older brothers and sisters, from an obliging neighborhood beau, from each other. "I was shocked by what my boyfriend wanted me to do," a Wisconsin sophomore said, "so I asked my girl friend—we discuss all these things together—and she told me. I mean, she practically drew me a diagram." Many college girls are not at all shy about trading technical information. Their enthusiasm for gossipy intimacies of the most clinical nature suggests there may be far less erotic joy in their erotic activity than they like to believe. You wonder, indeed, what a 17-year-old New York City College freshman really means when she says: "I learned about 'everything but—' so fast. I was like a nymphomaniac. I've got the feeling I'm going to be frigid. Everytime I kiss a boy, I get an orgasm."

"Oh, everybody pets," college girls say. Such comments were easily, quickly tossed off, and while not entirely accurate —some girls don't date, much less have the opportunity to pet—they indicate a revision in the traditional double standard of sexual behavior. From "chastity for women, no holds barred for men," it has become "nothing barred but *La Pénétration* * for women," and the college boy is doing his best to cope with the often dubious joys of the evolution.

Everything but—, anything but—, no holds barred but—, and variations suffixed with that great big BUT are current euphemisms for sexual intimacies that range from simple pats and caresses of clothed or unclothed bodies to every erotic act known to man, with one exception: the penis may not enter the vagina. Not completely, that is. It is necessary to add "completely" because some coeds permit partial entry —and still call it "virginity." As long as the hymen remains intact, the dictionary supports their claim.

Rubbing and bumping without clothing ("Have you ever been dry-humped in Atlantic City?" a Hunter junior asked), exchange of genital caresses, mutual oral-genital stimulation— these are a few of the heavy petting practices "fairly common among our virginal groups," according to Ira L. Reiss, professor of sociology at Bard College. The college girls interviewed agreed. A Princeton youth smiled sardonically and nodded, "Oh yes, the American ballet." Heavy petting to orgasm or just short of it seems to be accepted without geographical limitations. But the specific practices covered by the term "everything but—" will depend entirely upon the individual girl's own personal range of experience. "Everything but—" to a Mary Baldwin College freshman might

* As the boarding school girls put it in *Passion Flower Hotel,* by Rosalind Erskine (pseud.). N.Y.: Simon & Schuster, 1962.

seem like "child's play" to the worldly Sarah Lawrence student of technique quoted earlier. "Last week I said I was an 'everything but—' girl," a Boston University girl wrote me. "But Saturday I discovered I had exaggerated out of sheer ignorance. No one ever told me—. Well, I feel it is safe to say the title is probably now accurate. I say 'probably' because who knows what will happen next Saturday?"

An interesting regional propensity was described by a young Mississippi novelist with great experience in the field: "From experience, intuition, firsthand knowledge, trustworthy hearsay and inclination," he writes, "I can assure you that the Southerner loves nothing more than oral activity. I guess this is because there is no oral hymen: I've been to weddings where the bride can really walk down the aisle with her placid smile of virtuous readiness, when meanwhile she has gone down on most of the male guests. There are times when you feel like kissing the bridegroom, too, the feeling being that he is doing more for you by proxy than either you or he might wish."

Sociologists on two campuses volunteered observations that mouth-genital stimulation was probably more common "than most people would guess." In *Sex Histories of American College Men,** Phyllis and Eberhard Kronhausen reported that "a liberal minority" among their Columbia University male sample found "every type of oral eroticism acceptable, including cunnilingus." The "middle-of-the-road majority" found "fellatio considerably more acceptable than cunnilingus." Whatever the incidence of practice, the act is well enough known to prompt one Purdue University senior to comment: "I wonder what it will be like to be a member of the Class of '69.

Petting, certainly in its simpler forms, has become so every-day that the girl who won't is sure to find herself labelled "frigid." On the other hand, if she does, she is just as likely to be called a tease. And, as one cheerful Faulkner fan at Barnard pointed out: "If you don't care enough for a guy to neck with him, it shouldn't upset you when he calls

* N.Y.: Ballantine Books, 1960.

you frigid. I say, 'Frigid, *moi?*' and laugh, very woman-of-the-worldly, as if I were Temple Drake reincarnate and he just wasn't my brand of Popeye."

"If you were ever for a minute worried about maybe being frigid, I bet you wouldn't laugh," a dormmate chided her rather sadly.

Again, what a girl approves of, she may not actually do. And she may not at all approve of what she does. Sex inspires an overwhelming amount of such confusion. There are coeds who flatly disapprove of petting, and pet anyway. "Is petting right?" a DePauw University junior was asked. "Not always. Most guys are out for what they can get. If you want to go along for experience, go ahead, but don't get emotionally involved. It's too traumatic."

"I think personally 'anything but—' is vulgar," a University of Colorado coed began. "The idea of getting as much as you can, yet free without paying is—um—I mean to me, a virgin is in this definition—one who thinks like a virgin. If you do that you're not virginal even if you don't go all the way. It's okay to avoid pregnancy but not that way. Petting has always seemed distasteful to me. I've engaged in it, but it made me feel cheap. I should think the real thing would be glorious and this is just a high schoolish barn hayloft type of fooling around. Yes, I have indulged. It's hard to avoid it because once you start necking, it happens, and the next morning it seems distasteful. It doesn't at the time, especially if you've had anything to drink—occasions after I've had three or four beers, I think I could do anything. Luckily I sobered up quickly. Something just clicks in my mind. This summer I went to the drive-in with a boy and drank four hours and made out for four hours."

Girls who approve only of petting when in love, find themselves petting for countless other reasons. "Ideally, I suppose, the only way to stay out of trouble and avoid ugly scenes would be never to go beyond a few kisses unless you're in love," a Goucher junior suggested. "Then you both take each step together and everything happens naturally—as an expression of your affection and love. But frankly, I've never been in love and I would have been carried to the loony bin in a basket by now if I'd waited."

Drifting with the crowd, "everyone does it," and the acceptance as a fact of life that "boys expect it" are often cited with varying degrees of cynicism and some anger. "Why shouldn't a woman itch as much as a man?" a Vermont junior demanded. Some seem to regard "restricted bodily intimacies" as payment for a pleasant evening or as an advance on anticipated pleasures. "There was this one boy back home who was fabulously wealthy and I thought he would make a fine catch—as a husband, except basically he was pretty stupid," a Rollins junior recalled. "At first I petted with him because, fool that I was, I thought he'd take me out, to the sort of places where I could get in with that crowd. Naturally, once he got me in bed, he never seemed the slightest bit interested in our ever going out. And by that time, I was enjoying it too. The farthest we ever got was both undressed in his bed rubbing against each other till he had an orgasm. But he kept trying to talk me into going all the way. He would put his organ at the mouth of mine and say, 'just the tip, please, that's all, c'mon baby, just the tip.' Finally his whining got to me—the arguments were really spoiling it. Anyway, September came and I went back to school."

When their classmates tended to apologize for petting, several coeds were indignant. "With me it's simply a matter of pleasure," an Endicott College graduate said. "I love to make love. I'm not ashamed or embarrassed by my body. And I want to be a virgin. It's that simple."

For many girls "Everything, but—" seems to be a disturbing and often less than satisfactory solution to a demoralizing dilemma. "All this 'anything, but—' stuff disgusts me," said a DePauw University sophomore pinned to a rabbinical student. "I'm afraid I'll really be repressed by the time I get married—but we always wind up playing the same sex game." "Like everyone says," a sophomore from Detroit said, "petting isn't wrong when two people are in love. It's the only way they can express it. But it does lead to problems and can be terribly frustrating." "Both of us had such high moral characters that after two years of frustration, we finally broke up," a recent Penn State graduate said sadly. "Afterwards, I regretted not going farther." "We finally had to stop petting altogether," an Oberlin couple said. "The tension was threatening our whole relationship. We forced ourselves to avoid being alone." Several girls speculated on the potential for serious frigidity problems after marriage. "My roommate got so used to absolutely wild, uninhibited 'everything but—' with this boy for three years, that when she finally did fall in love and did go all the way, she was unable to enjoy it at all. They're both so upset, she's going to a psychiatrist to get straightened out."

It was a '54 graduate of Smith, novelist Nora Johnson, who noted ironically, "I suppose the ideal girl is still technically a virgin but has done every possible kind of petting while still maintaining her maiden dignity." * But dignity is hardly the word for it, as anxious prima ballerinas of the American ballet testify. Some resent the commercialism of petting. "It begins as kissing anybody as payment for the privilege of going out. And it becomes trading your body," a Sarah Lawrence freshman, garbed mostly in leathers and suedes, observed bitterly as she stood waiting at the edge of a footbridge for a Brattles taxi to the Bronxville train station. Others find it difficult to shed firmly emplanted ideas about the sinfulness of sex. "I just can't shake off my background that easily," a Colby College junior said. My fiance was very patient with me, but after eight months of trying to 'convert' me, he gave up and said we would have to stop seeing each other." Reluctantly, she gave ground, now finds she even enjoys petting, but "He will have to compromise with me about going further as I have already come further than I ever dreamed." What worried a Michigan State sophomore was not her behavior so much as the names for it. "I wish they wouldn't call it mutual masturbation," she said, fingering the cover of a marriage manual in her fiance's off-campus East

* "Sex and the College Girl," by Nora Johnson. *The Atlantic Monthly,* November, 1959.

Lansing apartment. "After all, masturbation is something you do alone. This is a two-people thing and I don't think it is anything we should be ashamed of. We're in love and I feel we show our maturity by limiting ourselves to sexual behavior that can't hurt anyone—as pregnancy would."

The crux of the campus dilemma, as described by Ehrmann, is "that youth themselves are expected both to mix freely males with females in enjoyable social situations, and at the same time to practice sexual restraint." Because the term "promiscuity" is usually confined to acts of coitus, petting becomes an acceptable means of solving the dilemma, he finds. But college girls themselves may come to apply the term promiscuous to petting and from that moment on, you can hear the anxiety in their comments. "You keep trying to pull in the reins," a UCLA Fine Arts sophomore said. "One minute you're in the most advanced state of ecstasy because a boy's hand accidentally brushed your breast and it's the most exciting thing that ever happened to you. Next thing you know your—your, what shall I call it—your private parts, so to speak, are practically a public parking area. It all happens too fast. You're jaded at 19. You decide to slow down. So you say 'no' a few times the next night. Then you say to yourself, 'Oh, sister, who are you trying to kid? You love it and he wants it.' So you say, 'What the hell'."

The technical virgin role becomes increasing uncomfortable when the girl can no longer see any sense or meaning in the distinction between intercourse and "everything but—" As Temple University sociologist Robert R. Bell writes: "The sharpness of the distinction may be dulled by increasing age or stage of emotional commitment, and the girl may be hardpressed to justify the distinction to herself and the boy." * A tall, almost boyishly sturdy University of Houston coed was obviously troubled by the dulling of that distinction. "I can't believe that what I'm doing is the least bit virginal," she said. "I am appalled at myself. I keep saying, 'Joyce, you spineless creature.' A few months ago I practically made a

* *Marriage and Family Interaction*, by Robert R. Bell. N.Y.: Dorsey Press, 1963.

Federal case out of it when a boy tried to unhook my bra, and I practically fainted when the girl down the hall told me how that boy did it to her with his fingers. But look at me now. Doesn't it seem terribly hypocritical?"

During one group discussion a Pembroke girl involved in what she described as a deep, meaningful love relationship with her first and only lover (coital), accused a self-described "promiscuous virgin" of "being totally depraved." "I feel I am much more virginal than you," she insisted. But the object of this attack, a Bennington freshman, held firm in her conviction that a hymen was proper and sufficient virginity for her. Many college girls tended to side with the critical position of the Pembroke coed. And a Barnard senior, sipping coffee in Columbia University's Lion's Den, told how she regretted nothing in her behavior since experiencing inter-course—"only things I did before that." Once she was struck by the hypocrisy of "this mixed-up virginity–petting thing," she was willing to take the next step—intercourse.

For some girls, it is indeed only a question of time to the Fail-Safe point—where the stop-button fails to click and there's no turning back. But it doesn't take a collapse of the hymen value system to bring a girl to Fail-Safe. All it takes is the intensity of her own passion or one Scotch too many or a young man who cannot, or will not, heed her cry to "stop." "She reaches for the brake," as one Bryn Mawr senior put it, "and discovers she has already crossed 'Go' and may not collect $200 or Workmen's Compensation, even, worse luck."

It is the girl's function to say 'no,' according to Margaret Mead. And many girls resent the responsibility. "It's always the girl's responsibility," complained a Temple University coed, eyeing a young man across the aisle in the college-bound subway car. "The boy is willing to go as far as you let him. So you have to fight him *and* your own inclinations." A Penn State coed defined double standard: "The girl has double the responsibility and gets twice the blame." An amply en-dowed sophomore from Chicago, not trusting her own sim-mering passions, adopted a chastity belt of sorts. "I always wear this impossible all-in-one fat lady's girdle," she said, patting a flattened midriff. "It covers me from here to here, which is the entire danger zone, and I couldn't get out of it in the front seat of a car if my life depended on it."

A girl may think she is uttering the final, definitive, undebatable "no" but, to the aroused young man, it sounds more like "maybe." There is no longer a polite (or even hysterical) stopping him. Excessive male aggressiveness— "menacing threats or coercive infliction of physical pain"— is recognized by many college girls as an occupational hazard of campus courtship. Sociologists at Indiana University studied male sex aggression* and reported that 56 percent of 291 coeds were "offended" by some erotic intimacy at least once during the academic year, not only on casual dates, but by steadies and fiances. It may be merely a parallel of that old tale, "The Boy Who Cried 'Wolf' ": The girl who says "no" too many times when she doesn't mean it, is ignored when she says "no" and really does mean it. Or it may be a sheer misinterpretation: "Girls give themselves away in the little things they do," a Stanford youth explained. "When we get into the car and she puts her hand on my thigh or my knee—first date, mind you—she may think it's just a warm gesture. But as far as I'm concerned, it's like a sign that says, 'Here's a live one'."

Promising more than she intends to deliver, or even, as we have seen, *seeming* to promises more, may be disastrous, even if the promiscuous promiser manages to escape, virginity intact. "Once a boy has the idea you're fast and for some reason you brush him off, you're in trouble," a serious and concerned Hofstra freshman noted. "He certainly won't go back to the boys that told him you were fast and admit you weren't. He'll say, 'Boy, was she great.' Then, sister, you've had it."

"Please" and "tease" are the two most popular words in the would-be seducer's vocabulary, according to many coeds. The scenes of anger and fury they describe are hauntingly

* "Male Sex Aggression on a University Campus," by Clifford Kirkpatrick and Eugene Kanin. *American Sociological Review*, February, 1957.

familiar, an echo of the underlying hostility and, often, mutual aggression in the courtship dance. "It is the teaser who is the sexual pirate," a Connecticut Wesleyan teacher said. "It's the one way in which a girl can most quickly destroy herself. She inspires real hatred and justifiably so." Uttered by an aroused and frustrated young man at the half-naked Radcliffe girl pressed against the wall of a Harvard house suite or in a car parked behind a fraternity house on Wisconsin University's Langdon Street, the epithet "tease" is meant to wither. But there cannot be more than a very few coeds who deliberately play *femme fatale* strictly for the pleasure of driving young men wild with frustration. And many girls reject the title. "Sure I've been called a 'tease'," said a Beebe Hall belle at Wellesley. "But I'm not a tease. I'm just a healthy girl who enjoys 'making out.' And I know very well that the boy who calls me a 'tease' would probably be surprised and disappointed if I let us get carried away. It's the only way."

Obviously there is room for great immorality and hypocrisy in American dating. Ideally it offers a framework for making friends, developing social poise, establishing sexual identity, and, as Ehrmann suggests, "is part of a more or less orderly progression from a single to a quasi marriage to a marriage state," with a means of exploring, testing, rejecting, ultimately finding the One. But it can also be a status competition, manipulative, sexually hostile and exploitive—at all levels, regardless of physical intimacy. Margaret Mead, psychiatrist Bruno Bettelheim, psychologist Albert Ellis, and other convincing critics find dating an unfortunate prep school for marriage. Dating is not courtship but a loveless popularity contest, Dr. Mead writes. And to quote Ellis: "Our existing dating mores are almost uniquely designed to sabotage a monogamous marriage. . . . They [American males] develop strong antagonisms toward sex-denying women. . . . As for our females, we make certain, by our courtship rules, that they are sexually tortured and maimed in at least as many (if not in more) ways. . . . They frequently turn out to be orgasmically frigid, both before and after marriage." * Given the complexities of contemporary life and given the greater complexities of being a human being—once Americans were too busy struggling for survival to worry about role conflicts and repression and undernourished ego—it looks as if we're stuck with the complexities of courtship.

But as a single sexual standard of "sex with affection" ** gains greater acceptance, we are moving away from at least some of the evils Ellis describes. Ehrmann is convinced that the greater part of the sexual experience of college youth is with a loved one. In this context, then, the new style of chastity—"everything but—" —has merit. To quote Ehrmann, "It enables the couple to experience in varying degrees the emotional gamut of sex from sensory titillation to a deeply committed love relation without running the risk of an out-of-wedlock pregnancy and the extreme social stigma of promiscuity." ***

There is, as we have seen, yet another risk. Practiced with the frenzy, panic, and compulsion of the "promiscuous virgin," technical virginity becomes increasingly difficult to defend—physically and intellectually. It may not carry the official onus of nonvirginal promiscuity, but it has a similar potential for ugliness and scarring. It becomes an acting out of sex, not an act of love, or even lust. It triggers sordid struggles and shattering hostility in the back seats of automobiles and leafy campus bowers. For the college girl practitioner of compulsive, promiscuous "everything but—," it can set off fierce self-recrimination, disgust, maiming loss of self-esteem.

The new style of chastity does indeed become a perversion of traditional concepts of feminine purity when it rests its claim on nothing more than a slender membrane preserved intact before the aggressions and blandishments of 10, 20, 50 young males.

* *The American Sexual Tragedy*, by Albert Ellis. N.Y.: Twayne, 1954.
** *Premarital Sexual Standards in America*, by Ira L. Reiss. Illinois: The Free Press of Glencoe, 1960.
*** "The Variety and Meaning of Premarital Heterosexual Experiences for the College Student," *op. cit.*

It should come as no surprise then that many girls, a few social scientists, and even some parents, have come to regard the turmoil and troubled existence of the promiscuous virgin with far more alarm than the essentially monogamous and nonvirginal love-making that can be regarded as a responsible and integral part of the courtship process leading to marriage.

Snow Men, You're Melting Me

"Hey wait, who said virgins are afraid to admit it? I'll confess. I'm a virgin. You've heard, of course, about our annual convention—the United Virgins of America—we had to call it off last year because I broke my leg and the other girl couldn't come."

Gracefully seated on the floor in a semi-lotus position, Alexandra Sarah Sweeney seemed both embarrassed and delighted with her own aura of ripe-near-bursting. "Incredible combination, Alexandra Sarah Sweeney, isn't it?," she offered. "But Daddy is a part-time farmer and part-time cabinet maker and full-time self-educated Classicist, and Mama threw in the Sarah just to rile him."

It sounded like the kind of family background that would strike the fancy of the Admissions powers-that-be at Bennington College in Vermont, that fabled temple of self-expression where one-third of the girls are on some sort of scholarship and the curriculum includes periodic tastes of life's realities, i.e., a "nonresident term" of paid employment that might take them as far as Rome and a job making New Wave movies (as it did one resourceful coed).

Alexandra, slender with a tiny waist, incongruously full bosom, and almost Oriental features (made more so by artful cultivation), her straight black hair knotted intricately once about itself, then left to fall unfettered, was a particularly spirited ingenue of a category many supposed experts lead us to believe no longer exists in the elite women's colleges of the East, certainly not in such progressive groves as Bennington. Yet I encountered dozens like her: bright, alive, and sensual, not afraid to confess her chastity, romping in the dangerous country of the promiscuous virgin. Her vision of Bennington's sexual climate as nymphomaniacal would have to be astigmatic. Otherwise there would not be so many girls like her there and at other colleges of legendary sexual abandon.

"Sometimes I think Bennington is too much for me. I have the feeling the girls are deliberately trying to shock me. I mean, if you could just hear the conversation—lurid—geez. One night I made myself so ridiculously nervous, I scratched a run in my brand-new tights. It seems to me they wouldn't talk half so much about sex if they were really doing it. You know what everybody says about Bennington—the Bennington myth—well, *I* think it *is* a myth. You're fighting it all the time. Boys just seem to assume you're some sort of raving nymphomaniac or why else would you ever have wound up in Bennington. Once at the bus station I overheard this boy say to another boy—'See, I told you you'd get laid if we came up to Bennington.' Just because we don't have to sign in at the dorm until 6 A.M., they seem to think we're out every night until 5:59 doing it. I really can't believe, for instance, that I'm the *only* girl that gets put down by this mythical reputation we and a few other schools seem to have. But this man I know, an older man type, New York literary world, that sort, and I trust his judgment because he was around in the old days and he says Bennington is nothing, absolutely nothing at all like it used to be in the late forties. He says the girls used to get tattooed and have affairs and commit suicide, but now we have a school psychiatrist to keep us from doing all those things.

"You feel like an idealistic, emotionally stable girl just doesn't have a chance—I mean, for instance, do you know how our image gets distorted by writers—any kookie sex fiend in leotards in any American novel, without fail, is absolutely guaranteed to be described as 'You know, the Bennington type. ' "

A recent example: *The Magic of Their Singing*, by Bernard Wolfe in which a young Lady Bountiful down from Bennington is welcome in certain Greenwich Village circles, mostly because she buys their marijuana with her allowance. A weekend excursion to Manhattan is climaxed with her rape by a Negro jazz combo. In a more mundane way, the Negro *does* play an important role in the rebellion and idealism of certain college girls. Is there a status date at Bennington? Alexandra was asked.

"Somebody ugly. Especially somebody ugly with a beard. And if he's Negro, that's prestige! If he's ugly, Negro, and has a beard too, like that's the end. Except if he's Prof. X—dating him is the biggest prestige of all. Actually the Negro boy has it made these days. If you say 'no' to anything, he can always throw discrimination at you. No one could bear that.

"I don't know, maybe I'm naive or something, but that first month I got pretty shaken. I was coming out of the library and there was Prof. X., cool as can be, standing against a tree, necking with this girl. He just looked up, cool, you know, and smiled and said, 'Hi there, Alexandra.' I mean, I was hysterical. First my roommate being pregnant and then Prof. X. necking with a student right out in the open in the middle of the afternoon. I wonder if Papa ever dreams what goes on. My pregnant roommate—didn't I mention that? Well, she told me she staged the whole thing with no protection to get this guy to marry her and I guess she succeeded. Actually, she didn't even know for sure she was pregnant until it came out in the physical, you know, the freshman physical. They called me in because they were worried I'd be all psyched up about it—second week of school, first time away from Ohio and all, I suppose. They told me it was all a big mistake—she wasn't even the girl they had interviewed—that's the point I want to make. They really weed you out at Bennington. They are very tough about admissions—it takes two interviews before you can be accepted. I realize that 6 A.M. curfew sounds like they really don't care what you do—why bother having a curfew at all. So you'll get home in time for a good breakfast, I suppose. And so you won't miss class. That's it you see. They are very strict on academics and grades. All the other restrictions come from within. Everything is on the honor system. There aren't any housemothers, just a chairman elected by the girls, and if you find all of a sudden you're going to be away overnight, you just send a telegram collect.

"Naturally, the first two weeks a lot of girls never get in before 6:25—all that freedom goes to your head—but after that you don't have to stay out just to stay out, because you know you can whenever you want to. And you could never keep up the academics if you did it all the time. And anyway, even if there are no housemothers, they must have some sort of spying system because they always seem to know exactly what's going on.

"What bothers me sort of, I guess, is I don't mind immorality, but I wish people could at least be a little bit sneaky about it. I mean they're so open, it's really embarrassing. Like Prof. X. I mean, couldn't he at least keep up some sort of pretense? Like bringing his wife to faculty-student teas instead of coming with his current mistress. I'm not the only one who gets upset about that. Then I have this other professor, and one day out of nowhere, he says to me, 'My don't we look sexy today.' I was embarrassed out of my head. He has this soulful, ethereal expression, you see, and now I find out he isn't thinking of anything the least bit ethereal.

"That's what I mean by the atmosphere. But I think I can swear I'll be a virgin when I get married. The girls keep telling me I'll never make it, but I know I will. Actually, the more they say I won't, the more stubborn I get about it. Once a boy even brought along the pills—birth control pills—that's how sure he was. He's 27 and has two books published, one of them was even eventually translated into Japanese and he probably thinks I'm a fool. But I just know I wouldn't ever have an affair.

"It's not a religious thing. I've never been told it's wrong, I mean Wrong with a capital 'W.' Actually, I think it's fear. Fear of sex. Fear once it's done, you'd lose the boy. Actually, I'm very romantic about love. I think it should be perfect. Not in the back seat of some car. I don't even like to kiss in the back seat of a car. Well, I have, of course—you go along with situations even if you don't approve aesthetically when there's no other way. Cars couldn't be more sordid, as far as I'm concerned. And I wouldn't want it to happen in a hotel either where you'd lied and signed in as man and wife. No. Not even the Plaza. What would be perfect? Marriage. I guess I feel it could only be perfect if you were married.

"That's why I'm so stubborn. Which isn't easy, you know. They call Williams * boys snow men—the way they just snow you into bed. But not me. Oh, boys tell me nobody's a virgin anymore, but I think they're just trying to shock me. Or they give you that line about being the complete, whole woman. So I say, 'Yes, that's what I am, whole and intact, and I intend to stay that way.' Actually a girl shouldn't try to argue with boys because whatever you say, they've got some smart answer.

"There was this one boy, though. He was going overseas with the Peace Corps and like I was biting my nails, I was so close. I really was on the verge. I think the only thing that held me back was he was so huge—6'2" and about 200 lbs. and frankly, I just couldn't see how it could be done, if you know what I mean.

"Actually, I'm very promiscuous. If I like a boy, I pet with him. Which means I pet with just about every boy I go out with because I never go out with a boy unless I like him. If a boy doesn't appeal to me, I won't even kiss him goodnight. I wouldn't even hold hands. But I love to make love and if I like a boy, I do. Everything but—, anything but—, whatever you call it. Yes. Naturally not all boys take it the same way. Some of them get pretty angry. Once a guy hauled off and socked me. Actually socked me. He was so hot, and so furious when he discovered that was as far as I would go. Oh, I see his logic all right. He thought I meant we were going to have relations and he was absolutely livid when I suddenly turned off the passion. Sure, some of them get so angry they don't call back. I find it pretty insulting when I don't see them again. It's like saying, that was all that mattered, being with me as a person meant nothing at all. Who wouldn't be insulted? Of course, I do understand.

* Williams College, nearby source of "conventional" status dates.

"Once I was with this boy who wasn't at all attractive to me, physically, I mean, but we were friends and I refused to kiss him and he was flabbergasted. 'Why did you go out with me then?' he wanted to know. So I said, 'Because I like you —you're sweet.' He was furious. 'Sweet,' I guess being called 'sweet' was a big blow to his masculinity.

"I don't think my position is the least bit hypocritical. Girls keep telling me that what I am isn't really virginity anymore. You know that line—what's a hymen, anyway, when you've done everything else in the book? But 'that' really is the big step. That's it. And boys do have a habit of bragging, you know. Petting is different. You can have all the warmth and affection and your virginity, too. As long as the boy goes along with you and you both don't get carried away.

"Papa says there is nothing as despicable as a c.t. but it's better to be despicable than pregnant—of course, if I should ever change my mind about it for any reason, I think I know exactly who I'd call—Tommy—he's really so sweet!"

Alexandra's reactions are very much those of the college freshman. At times she is a frightened, threatened virgin, describing an atmosphere of carnal anarchy. Moments later, she is a calm, persuasive skeptic assuring you that the legend of carnal anarchy is myth. She debunks the myth because she needs support for her own grip on chastity. Yet she exaggerates the sexuality, possibly to justify her own action should she lose that grip. Fear of sex is a powerful ally of chastity. Yet she flirts boldly with that which she fears.

Everything I have learned about sex and the college girl convinces me that her own intelligence, logic, sensitivity, and promiscuous dalliance with danger will be fatal to Alexandra's faith in the concept of "technical virginity" and to her chastity as well.*

* Two semesters have passed since this interview and Alexandra informs me she has just lost her second roommate to biological reality—pregnancy.

6

Sex as Hobby, Obsession, Part-time Profession

"In the past it has been the perogative of young men—to sow wild oats. Today their monopoly of the privilege is challenged by a relatively small group of girls of their own special world who go wherever desire or the momentum of the hour carries them. . . . These promiscuous girls . . . the Sowers of Wild Oats are only a small minority, and yet they have given popular college girls an undeserved reputation for 'loose living.' " *

* Youth and Sex: A Study of 1300 College Students, by Dorothy Dunbar Bromley and Florence Haxton Britten, N.Y.: Harper & Brothers, 1938. "Actually we found only 25 girls among the 772 undergraduates who admitted they took sex wherever they found it. They made up less than 4 percent of the entire group, but they are the most talked about of all groups."

150 /

These sentences were written in 1938, reminding us that the promiscuous coed is not a child of the sixties nor have attitudes toward her behavior and definitions of promiscuity been significantly modernized. Promiscuity now as then is generally regarded as a sign of deep emotional maladjustment. Casual love-making was and is seen as a desperate search for ego satisfaction rather than obsessive sexual craving. Only a few voices advance the concept of "wholesome erotic exuberance." Their radical departure from certain Freudian theories about sexuality lend support to the coed champion of sex freedom. She chaffs unhappily at being labelled neurotic, asking, "Isn't there something healthy about sex simply for the joy of sensuality?"

Unswerving faith in this kind of carefree sexual exuberance is rare. But discussion of sex for its own sake—sex as just another appetite to satisfy—sex as an act of love one might bestow upon a friendly stranger—is less rare. And I am convinced there is an increase in experimentation. "Sex without love is no good," an Oberlin graduate insisted during one of the interview sessions and was immediately challenged by a Vermont coed who asked, "But how do you know until you try?" "I have tried," the Oberlin girl replied. And that ended the debate.

For the great majority of college girls, sex without love is promiscuity, and promiscuity is undeniably a dirty word. Very few college girls approve of sleeping with just anyone strictly for the fun of it. Even those who do it tend to disapprove. How uncomfortable the role can become was suggested by Harvard's Dr. Graham B. Blaine, Jr., when he revealed that promiscuity among females (and impotence among males) were the problems that most often led students to seek psy-

---

Of the married women in Kinsey's female sample who had premarital intercourse, 53% had only one sex partner before marriage, 34% had two to five; 13% had intercourse with six or more. Kinsey compares these figures to: Davis, 1929 (75%, one partner, 25%, more than one—of 63 females); Hamilton, 1929 (43 to 54%, one; 46 to 47%, two or more partners—of 35 upper-level females with premarital experience); Clark, 1952 (64%, one partner; 15%, two to five; 21%, six or more—of 34 single women).

chiatric advice at the Harvard University Health Service. *

To define the lines that distinguish nymphomania from less compulsive promiscuity, to label one promiscuous coed a female Don Juan or a professional victim (of the male Don Juan) or just an everyday garden-variety coed rebel would be impossible without extensive and professional personality testing. But I would like to distinguish among promiscuity that seems to carry a quality of nymphomania (compulsive promiscuity usually coupled with frigidity), collegiate promiscuity, which seems to be an intellectualized and experimental rebellion that will cease with maturity or marriage; and the girl who drifts from one monogamous love affair to another as she seeks The Right Man. The dictionary labels promiscuity as "indiscriminate mingling." Many behaviorists prefer to avoid use of the word altogether. It isn't precise enough to suit them. Kinsey uses it as a handy tagline when he is counting sex partners, but never defines the word itself. Bromley and Britten referred to "college girls who took sex wherever they found it."

"Promiscuity" as used on the campus can mean almost anything. Many coeds haven't the least idea what nymphomania is, but that doesn't stop them from using it. When an Endicott (Mass.) alumna announces "five girls were really prostitutes," she means five girls went out every night and they didn't talk like virgins, so she assumes they were not. And when a Bennington freshman (struggling to hang on to her virginity, yet constantly putting herself in chastity-threatening situations) says, "Oh, they're all a lot of dirty nymphomaniacs," her remark reveals more about her own state of mind than it does about the pathology of the girls she thinks she is describing. (She seems repelled by the sexual climate. At the same time, by exaggerating the licentiousness, she is hoarding a reservoir of support for her own "fall" when and if.)

A University of Colorado junior pointed out, with an aware-

* At a Queens University conference on student mental health, Kingston, Ontario, reported in *The New York Times*, May 19, 1963. Dr. Blaine also said the male impotence was temporary, caused usually by college customs that pushed boys toward experiences for which they were not prepared. Female promiscuity, he said, was caused by loneliness and need for love and affection, not need for sex.

ness of the irony, promiscuous "means a person who has sexual relations all the time and indiscriminately—and usually the word is used in connection with a woman." "Promiscuous," said a San Diego State College sophomore, "—if you're talking about a man, it becomes virility. About a girl—it means she sleeps around. To my parents, it means she's been to bed once." "With my mother, it would be if you let a boy touch your breast," a schoolmate said. "It means one who is sick and needs sex all the time," several coeds remarked. "To me, it means indecent dress, excessive flirting—she gets around," a Colorado professor's daughter, a junior, said. "I guess it's ambiguous and it means anything offensive connected with sex," a second Colorado coed offered.

"A quick lay"— "a pickup,"—"the campus free and easy" —"like an old beat-up pair of shoes"—"you know, a slut"— "a tramp"—"almost a whore"—"the campus punchboard"— although almost three times as long as a four-letter word, "promiscuity" seems to convey much the same harsh impact. Promiscuous—it's the one thing nobody wants to be. Thus, on a campus where sexual freedom is openly accepted, you won't even hear the word. "We don't use the word at all in our crowd," a University of Chicago sophomore said. "It would token disapproval."

I could use five affairs as the arbitrary boundary line to the no-man's-land of promiscuity. One campus psychologist has suggested that the virgin and the girl with five or more affairs will be more at ease than the girl with two or three. The theory: By her fifth affair, a girl must concede she has cast her lot with sexual freedom. In between, she is wavering and uncertain of what she is in the sexual scheme. It is the sureness of her position that counts. But the arbitrary "five" would surely set off a storm of indignation from such coeds as the University of Miami junior who objected, "What do you mean 'five?' That's not a lot. Every nice girl should be entitled to at least five—in four years? That's practically monogamy."

Since "promiscuous" is such a loaded word, it's meaning evolves gradually during the a four-year college career for some coeds. "I always thought if anything was promiscuous, it's having two affairs simultaneously," a Hunter junior said. "I never dreamed I could handle that sort of madness myself. But I've been doing it the past month and it doesn't seem promiscuous to me, not in the sense of 'indiscriminate.' One is this boy I'm falling in love with—he's not a very experienced lover but I'm teaching him. As for this other one. He's just a big handsome lug and half the time he's stoned out of his head, but in bed—well, I just can't tell you. He's great."

Rather than risk general wrath with an arbitrary numerical definition of promiscuity, it might be better to define it in terms of love. Sex with love is the new morality, at least among most of the college girls we interviewed. Sex without love is re-garded as "a waste"—"nothing more than cold fucking"—"just plain insensitivity"—descriptions offered by girls who should know. They all admitted experiencing it. "If you're not in love, you can't get hurt," at least eight coeds remarked.

For some, sex without love starts as a compromise and soon becomes an inevitable. "Well, there I was," a pretty, painfully candid Barnard junior recalled. "Three weeks before, I'd been a virgin. I'd known this boy a whole year and he had never tried anything. But now he leaped on me. He said, 'If you weren't in my bed, you'd be in someone else's.' He treated me like dirt. I don't know—This set a pattern for me. Once I'd accepted that, I could except anything." Even though this girl could say, "For some reason, I've never been in love with anyone I've gone to bed with," it had not occurred to her that she deliberately—though unconsciously—avoided love. "I want to be in love," she insisted, "and it's not the phonies that worry me, the guys who lead you on to get you into bed. It's deluding myself that I'm in love when I'm not. That's the one thing I want to avoid at all costs. But every time it's the same. Two or three time to bed with a boy and then I'm completely dependent. When I meet The Man, I know I'll have the capabilities of fidelity. I happen to believe in fidelity."

A small group of promiscuous girls are firm believers in capitalism. None of the coeds interviewed admitted merchan-dising sex as a source of income, but college boys spoke of girls who made themselves available for an occasional fraternity "gang-bang." Traditionally, the female involved in this sort of male sexual togetherness is a nymphomaniacal high school girl or a lusty "townie." But a University of Texas graduate told about a coed who had worked her way through college modeling for life-drawing classes, waiting tables in her dorm, and taking on fraternity boys at $5 a "trick." "Bonnie Bang-Bang," a University of Ohio coed, charged $3, according to a recent Ohio graduate. Dina, a brilliant University of Chicago coed, had graduated from high school at 16 and run away to Chicago where she got a job working for an escort service. A client became a lover and, though uneducated himself, he decided a girl with Dina's I.Q. should go to college. He footed the bill.

A New York University freshman said she'd gone to bed with a married man, twice—each time for a pair of expensive earrings. "I probably would have gone to bed with him anyway," she said, "but this way I figured I wouldn't have to get emotionally involved with a married man as long as I kept it on a commercial level."

This kind of promiscuity seems relatively rare. Far more common are the college girls for whom going to bed casually seems to have become the path of least resistance. "I didn't want to make a big, noisy, sordid scene," a Smith junior explained the rationale behind a recent one-night affair. "Sometimes it gets just too banal, too dreary saying 'no,' " a Sarah Lawrence sophomore said. "It had been such a long time and I just felt like it," a Cornell senior said. "I can't see anything so hideous about it as long as you don't feel guilty or ugly the next day," a Wheelock senior offered.

These girls resent the suggestion that any male will do. The sexually active coed of the sixties feels she makes her own bed and has the final say about who joins her in it. "I'm nobody's victim," a tall, lanky, plain-faced UCLA sophomore said. "I don't get seduced. I'm the one who calls the signals."

"I wouldn't even hold hands with a boy I didn't care for," a Bennington veteran of at least a dozen affairs said with obvious indignation. And an Ohio State senior said, "If there's anything I resent, it's boys sniffing around because they've heard you're an easy lay. They just can't believe a girl *wouldn't* with a boy she didn't like—so they ask you out and they're so eager they can hardly sit still through a single feature movie and their pockets are filled with rubbers—oh boy, are they ready. This one boy was so eager he didn't even have on underwear. I was furious. They get absolutely nowhere with me. And if they never ask me out again, well, hell, that's their loss and they just aren't worth worrying about."

For some girls, the pattern of drifting casually from bed to bed begins in high school where, to be more accurate, it should be described as drifting from car to car. But others have never dated until they enter college. A University of Chicago coed described her freshman roommate, a devout Baptist from Kentucky: "She had never even kissed a boy. I went with her through her first date, her first kiss, her first debate of 'Should I let him or not' I went with her through her first affair. By the end of the freshman year she had far surpassed me. Twice now she's tried suicide with an overdose of aspirin."

Even the most conservative college girl is more likely to respond with sympathy or pity rather than moral outrage when confronted with promiscuity. As a Colorado coed remarked, "Sleeping with just anyone is not condoned, but it does happen, and usually the girls feel sorry for the girl it happens to because she feels pretty cheap about it—it is the one thing that can really hurt a girl's feelings of value for herself." Sororities might not pledge the notorious promiscuous girl, but if anyone ostracized her," a San Diego State sophomore remarked, it would be for other qualities—like if she looked cheap or was bitchy. Mostly she would be pitied—you'd feel there was something wrong."

A few of the most promiscuous girls seemed unaware that anything might be wrong. The Michigan State senior who said during a private interview, "As far as I'm concerned, sex has nothing to do with emotional feelings" felt she had explained herself perceptively, brilliantly. But the capacity to separate body from emotion is a feat usually reserved for the schizophrenic, psychoanalyst Harold Greenwald has commented. * "I've slept around some," a Brandeis sophomore said, "but I really haven't spoiled anything because it isn't love."

Other girls seemed a bit horrified by their own behavior. The Ohio State junior who told of keeping a list of all the men she'd slept with, the dates, and how many times remarked, "Actually, it was pretty sick. I finally forced myself to stop keeping track because it was really just too sick. There were 24 when I stopped." "What I was doing, I know it now, was passing myself around like trading stamps," said a shy, soft-spoken, rather plain-looking Antioch junior. "I didn't think much of myself obviously and I felt nobody would stick around long enough to know me and love me for myself—unless I did go to bed. But with my fiance it's different. He's helped me like myself."

The comments of many promiscuous coeds were punctuated with this kind of doubt, recrimination, self-hate, hostility to the man, or all men, rationalization—much of it tossed off in the flip Cool style. "You must think I'm some sort of a sex maniac," a Vanderbilt coed said, wiggling a slender ankle, then adding with a giggle, "well, maybe I am." "I love love," a University of Minnesota senior said. "I love to make love. I love my lover. I love the lover before him. I love romance and mush and I even enjoy a good, clean, hostile fuck. But sometimes I absolutely loathe myself. I tell myself, 'Linda, baby, love is an art not a marathon.' Well, so, sue me." She shrugged.

Though some college girls avoided introspection and remained blind to their own desperation and its genesis, most were eager to analyze. They would talk about themselves and their hungry egos as if they were discussing the case history of someone they had never met (someone they wouldn't like at all if they did meet her). "Talk about Electra," a Southern Cal psychology major began. "The other day it suddenly occurred to me that sometimes, just at the moment of climax,

* The ability to divorce the mind from the actions of her body was a common characteristic of the prostitutes Greenwald reported on in his book, *The Call Girl*, N.Y.: Ballantine Books, 1958.

I get this flash thought like, 'Boy, if only Daddy could see me now.' Think what some evil-minded head shrinker could do with *that*."

To be comfortable with promiscuity was rare. A Smith junior, chic in black crepe and real pearls at a Princeton house party, thought she knew why: "Even if the whole Judeo-Christian culture weren't frowning over your shoulders, you wouldn't relax. You wouldn't let yourself. If I ever found myself hopping from bed to bed without pangs of conscience, then I'd worry about not worrying."

Of course it is much easier to see a pattern in behavior than to break it. "I can see I have been defeating my own purposes," a promiscuous Cornell sophomore said, "but seeing doesn't seem to solve anything." And as a recent Smith graduate said, "If you've been told you're a fantastic high diver, it's hard to stay out of the pool."

But there is the small and articulate core of girls who see no reason at all to keep out of the pool. "It's the unhappy ones who make such a bad name for all of us," a Bard College champion of sexual freedom complained. These girls insist it is fun, fun, fun, every single moment of every libido-free act. Many think it is. Many believe they are free of the nagging awareness of conventional morality. But they tend to contradict themselves in much of what they say. If at the moment a girl is involved in a grand passion of commitment and mutual respect—it may be impossible for her to recall the despair and gloom of the months between this affair and the last. Some girls enjoy a chronic amnesia that erases unpleasant memories, and in some cases this is a fortunate affliction, for the cumulative pain might otherwise be shattering.

If a girl's only ailment is a rash of rebellion, she may graduate from undergraduate promiscuity to a mature and intelligent temperance. If the flaw goes deeper, she may be doomed to a mocking and joyless pursuit of her own destruction.

"Are You a Virgin?" "Not Yet"

" 'One makes love only to confirm one's loneliness.' That's Pursewarden in Lawrence Durrell. But it should be 'One makes love only to confirm one's aloneness,' or [laughing] 'One makes love and manages only to sustain one's aloneness.' I could go on for hours—for days—writing variations on that line, I suppose. It seems to me that I've tried all the variations of living it. I was born not a virgin. Really. I was just never really a virgin ever."

If you were a casting director assessing the possible roles for Karen Marie Hunt, you would type her as the missionary's teenage daughter—the Salvation Army recruit—"Beth" if anyone decides to do a remake of *Little Women*. The most unlikely role you could possibly imagine would be Sadie Thompson. But that is approximately the role Karen Marie has chosen. And she acts it out—the *femme fatale*, the inflamer of men's libidos, the seducer of young male virgins, a fierce, flip combination of clown, soap-opera heroine, amateur existentialist, and the Empress Catherine of Russia.

"What I should do is loan you my diary. That would save time and spare you a certain amount of embroidery. But then again, I might break both our hearts with pathos. Actually, it's probably funny. The tigress in sneakers and cotton underwear. And I can't see across the room without my glasses. No, I'm not tearing myself down. I have to be able to laugh —it's my great strength, that."

Karen Marie, not yet 20, is a senior studying speech correction at Syracuse University (New York). Just below average weight for her just above average height, graceful in worn sneakers, with a plain heart-shaped face, hazel eyes, freckled nose, and a halo of wispy mouse-blonde hair pinned into a slightly messy bun—except for the grace and a dimple, altogether unremarkable. Yet unique—surely the only girl in her sorority who never leaves the house with a date without touching French perfume to the highest reaches of her inner thigh, and surely the only speech correction major in America who now and then rouges the nipples of her breasts because, "I'm so pale—I need a bit of color to cheer us all up."

It was her sorority sisters who suggested I talk to Karen when I asked whether the group would tend to ignore, ostracize, or protect a sexually promiscuous member. "If it were a scandal, she'd definitely be asked to leave," one of them replied. "But take someone like Karen. We all adore her—except, possibly, for a few prudes. And we'd do anything to protect her—we cover up for her all the time. She looks like such a goody-goody—that helps." "Discretion," a second girl said, "that means a lot. There's nothing she won't do and she's always falling in love or spending the night with some boy because she can't say no. But it's never a fraternity boy who might spread it around and give the house a bad name. It's usually someone different, some lone-wolf type or some kook, or if it is a fraternity boy, he's so nuts about her he would die rather than ever blacken Karen's name. None of them lasts too long though." "I wish I had the courage to live the way she does," a third said. "I mean she really rushes into life—she makes you feel like half a person for being so cautious, so intimidated."

"You got me in an off moment. I'm abstaining. It's just that I want to prove a point to myself. That I'm capable of going with a boy and *not* going to bed. Just to show I can do it. That's all. No, guilt and all that hokey jazz have nothing to do with it. What it is, you see, is fidelity to *myself,* not to the man—to myself. I've been running around like this for more than eight years and I want to know: Am I capable of loyalty? You don't believe me? Actually it's almost nine years. Oh, I do believe sex can be evil—definitely evil. Having sex before you realize the implications. This is evil. There is a difference between law and order, and anarchy. For me it was frightening, distasteful. Very-knockdown, drag-out. You see, I was 11. And I used to flirt like wild, you know, the way 11-year-olds can flirt. And [shrugging] I got my due, I guess. He was my piano teacher. From the way he acted, from his guilt, I suppose I must have sensed it was wrong—that my parents would be angry and mustn't know. I didn't feel violated in that sense—what could violated mean to me? But I wished it hadn't hurt so. . . .

"No one had ever told me sex was bad or dirty or a sin, only that it was the way to make babies. The girl down the street —she was about three years older, I think—had conducted a little class in sex education in her garage. Till her mother caught us using her little brother as a demonstration dummy. What a scene that was! Anyway I told her what had happened and she said I was really lucky because now I could do anything I wanted with any boy I pleased because 'the die was cast.' I liked that expression: 'the die was cast.' I doubt that I understood the full implication, but I liked it. 'You'll be so well-liked,' she told me. I suppose I could have become absolutely paralyzed about sex and men but, no—I guess I just always thrived on it. At 12 I had an affair with a college boy —I told him I was 16—then with the husband of a married friend. He gave me what I thought was the absolutely most divine lin-ger-ee in the world and I wore it whenever I saw him—something wild, black gauze, I think.

"Possibly our high school was unusual—maybe not, when I think of all the stuff you read these days about teen-age sex and unwed mothers—but anyway, kids slept around—I mean, if you were going with a boy, it was just taken for granted you were sleeping with him, and girls got kicked out for being pregnant, and there were lots of weddings each spring. Maybe it was only our crowd—at the time it seemed like it was everyone. At 16 I graduated and came up here. By then I was very, very wise. And clever enough to sense that it was different here—most of the kids were pretty sheltered. My roommate was practically committing suicide because some boy tried to put his hand on her bosom. It's the kind of school girls come to willing to waste a few years looking for a husband—if you have money enough for just one year of college, you come up here—if you don't get a husband, it's back to your family, a failure.

"Oh, how I hated this place. The boys are mostly clods. And the girls—what a silly pack of frightened ninnies. You should have heard them the first year—all those long, dreary, soul-searching debates on why a girl owes it to God and Daddy to fight the good fight in defense of her virginity. Sitting around till 3 A.M., arguing over the metaphysical significance of kissing a boy on the third date and stuffing down peanut butter and crackers. I kept my mouth shut. I happen to adore peanut butter myself, you see. Now these girls are seniors and they've stopped debating. They do or they don't. They feel as strongly about the sanctity of discretion as they once did about chastity. I don't know what the girls at the house told you about me. They think of me as some sort of refreshingly amoral nut with this one disarming eccentricity— she can't say 'no.' Actually, they don't know the half of it— I censor my confidences: only the pretty, funny stuff comes through. To me, discretion is getting away with it.

"College revirginated me. A neat trick. I did it once—to see if I could get away with it. The boy felt great. My next three will swear I was a virgin. I've done some foolish things, I guess, but nothing that I'm really ashamed of. Well, once. Once I prostituted my body. I did it to get some information. [Pause] It was pretty essential information. If I had to I think I could give you a good reason for having gone to bed with everyone—well, wait, let me try. Love, now that's unbeatable as a reason. Or the first day of spring. Or the sexiest man in town crooks his finger—or some sad little boy is lonely and needs to be loved. Or once in a while it's just gone too far to pull back—he's all steamed up and I'm near the boiling point myself. Sex isn't just an expression of love, after all, it's a clever imitation of love, too. If you can't have love, you can certainly enjoy the motions of love. Sometimes, the emotion has to follow the motion. You know the so-called sexual liberals who will tell you sex is fine when it's part of love, but without love it's just cold fucking. I say sex is the great thing all by itself, not for love, for itself, the wonderful sensuality of the physical act. Did you ever think that maybe sex *is* love? You can go to bed with an absolute stranger and the two of you are giving love to each other—I mean, wouldn't that be great?"

There was a quality of compulsive confession in her painstaking detail—a willingless to peel away layers of meaning, to expose, defend, possibly to shock. I had heard some of the same sex-freedom slogans from college girls far less qualified to speak than Karen, even from "hip" campus virgins who explained, "I have it all figured out—it just hasn't happened to me yet," or "I'm getting closer everyday." Had Karen discovered any dark corners in the incandescence of sexual freedom? Obviously she thought she had not. Yet there were hints that something—conscience, her sense of propriety, an awareness of flaunting traditional codes (no matter how hypocritical they might be)—made her pedestal of unfettered erotic exuberance somewhat shaky.

"It's funny. I've run around for almost nine years and my mother still thinks I'm a virgin. Oh, I'm sure she does. Once she walked into an apartment I was sharing during summer vacation—with this boy—and all his things were there and she refused to see it. Once she slipped and called me a slut and then she was so upset, she turned and slapped my brother. If I walked in the door dangling a diaphragm on a string, she wouldn't see it.

"You know, sometimes I think it really annoys me that my mother doesn't know. I'd like to scream it at her—she sits there with her ankles crossed, rolling bandages for the Red Cross, bragging about her brilliant daughter. 'My daughter is an angel,' she says. Well, I am an angel. I'm quite a humanitarian. It's my gift—making love. They tell me I'm pretty good at it. And you must admit I'm generous. There was this boy—a brilliant guy—worried about being a homosexual, and he asked my friend to go to bed with him because he just had to try making love to a woman. She wanted to, but she has this Reubenesque body, all bosom, you know, and she thought that was more woman than this boy could take, so she asked if I would be willing—to lead him along—without his knowing she's put me up to it. My friend took the boy's roommate to a concert and I stayed behind with him to study. What a fiasco. The boy was so worried about what his adored roommate might be up to with my friend—he was impervious to seduction. Really. But I *had* tried. I'm growing more like Mother every day. Unselfish, devoted to charitable causes.

"My real problem—my only problem—is I stick with people too long—dragging it out until it's just a habit. I don't eat much. I don't take up much room in bed. I always squeeze the toothpaste tube from the bottom. I'm easy to have around

—I haven't spent a spring or Christmas or summer vacation at home since my freshman year, and it's easy really to get out of the sorority house. You just don't sign out at all. Or you sign in at curfew and then sneak out the back stairs—the fire escape. Weekends you sign out for home. I don't think the school cares that much about what you do as long as you pay lip service to their silly regulations to get them off the hook if anything should happen.

"I date a lot off-campus—college boys are so square, hopelessly square. And professors. There's something about a man on a podium and he's teaching you. It's very masculine. You want to drain them of all they know. Oh, I don't deny there's something in being able to bring the world's expert on medieval linguistics or whatever down to a human level. A lumpy mattress or the floor of his living room and maybe he has a rip in his underwear. Celebrities? No. But there was a certain playwright the year I went to Barnard. [She named him.] I really went after him—gave him some work to criticize and went back and—I must say I was persistent. I saw him a few times in New York after that. You don't believe. The girls didn't believe me either, but one night when we were talking about it, he called. The girl that answered almost fainted when she heard the name.

"One thing I never do. I don't go around proselytizing. If a girl asks me should she go to bed with someone, I always say no. I say 'If you have to ask, then the answer is definitely no.' I don't want the responsibility of someone's virginity. I don't have to run around justifying my own life by converting people. What's right for me might not be right for her. But I get nauseated by the professional virgin. As the man told the girl in *The Moon Is Blue:* 'You don't advertise unless you've got something to sell.'

"Marriage. Oh, yes. Of course, I want to get married and have children someday, and fidelity is very important to me. I don't for a minute doubt that I'll be a faithful wife. I mean, I won't have reason to fool around. It's only the virgin bride who gets to wondering what she might have missed. I don't believe I've missed out on anything." *

* A few months after this interview, Karen was married.

7

The Men—and Boys— in Her Life

> By Gis and by Saint Charity,
> Alack, and fie for shame!
> Young men will do't, if they come to't;
> By cock, they are to blame.
> Quoth she, before you tumbled me,
> You promised me to wed.
> He answers:
> So would I ha' done, by yonder sun,
> An thou hadst not come to my bed.
>
> Ophelia in *Hamlet,* IV: 5

"They're either animals or worshippers," the University of Pennsylvania coed said. "You have to fight them off, or else they put you on a pedestal and then are afraid to approach." "Boys are really quite prudish," a Radcliffe girl observed, eyeing a trio of Harvard youths dashing across the Yard in the bleak chill of the January cram-time. "They're a lot more strait-laced than they'd like you to think." "They're all out to make you," a dimpled University of Indiana virgin insisted, "but the average guy, if anyone took him up on it, wouldn't know what to do." "Boys have a habit of bragging," a Bennington freshman warned, with an expression of distaste clouding her peach complexion. "Boys 18 and 19 know what they want," a sophisticated Cornell alumna pointed out, "but not what to do with it." "Strangely enough, the boys here are more narrow-minded about sex than the girls," an avowedly conservative University of Mississippi coed said slowly, as though the idea had never occurred to her before. "There are many unscrupulous fast-talkers," a University of Colorado junior said. "I know one man who cracked a virgin a week," a Barnard sophomore reported. "At Harvard that would be considered the absolute cardinal sin," a vivacious blonde from Radcliffe responded. "Boys do want to marry virgins," a Michigan State junior said, rather sadly, "but if they wait too long, I don't know where they'll find them." And at Valade's, a coffee shop at the Burlington bus terminal, a slender, athletic University of Vermont junior announced: "A good man could make any girl on this campus. I said m-a-n, not boy."

Man, men, a particular man (as mate, lover, companion, buddy, or escort) is the object of much of the trauma, joy, confusion, and determination already documented. And this is Joe College as the college girl sees him: a most unlikely candidate, a drag, a drone, a dullard, an incurable Don Juan. By her testimony he is an insufferable prude, sexually backward, incurably narrow-minded, staunchly conformist, mama's boy, lady's man, con artist, sex maniac, moral hypocrite, satyr, and insensitive lover. Examining this dissection, it would seem that 90 percent of America's male undergraduates must be social dead beats and presumably the other 10 percent are married, engaged, pinned, or very busy.

It would seem so. But appearances are misleading. College girls are not above exaggeration to prove a point. A girl's perception will, of course, be distorted by her own fears and prejudices. Further, the female on campus and off makes do with the material at hand, sometimes grudgingly, sometimes gratefully. "The Man" girls bemoan the rarity of would be too much man for many of them. The Don Juan wants to know if there isn't a girl somewhere who can't be easily tumbled into bed.

Everyone knows what familiarity breeds. Bryn Mawr girls regard nearby Haverford men as weekday material only and "good enough to practice on." Smithies express similar sentiments for their neighbors at Amherst. Swarthmore men write off the Swarthmore coed as "sheltered, naive, and dull." Harvard men may tell you, "Cliffies are dogs." And the University of Michigan male may have much the same to say of the Ann Arbor coed. But Smith marries Amherst, Harvard weds Radcliffe, Michigan male pairs off with Michigan female. The snide remark, the sneer, the misunderstanding are the unfortunate—and seemingly inevitable—symptoms of young American courtship. The venom is half pose, half genuine hostility. But the misunderstandings are quite real.

One of the most striking characteristics of sex on the campus in the sixties is the widening gap between the conservatism of the college boy and the increasing sophistication of the coed. It plagues the girls. It threatens and paralyzes the boys. It inspires trauma, guilt, compromise, and makes seasoned actresses out of young women with no theatrical ambition.

The implications of growing up male create many of the problems of growing up female. To quote psychoanalyst Bruno Bettelheim: ". . . Many of the special difficulties of women—particularly their emotional difficulties—are timeless and practically inevitable, springing as they do from the distorted images of females which preoccupy so many men. Freud was probably right in thinking that the male infant's overattachment to his mother projects him into a continuing emotional predicament which is peculiarly difficult for most men to solve and often warps the demands they make of women." Man is, Bettelheim observes, "bound emotionally to the infantile image of his mother as unassailably pure."

The female who wants a man is often "placed in a sadly absurd position: she must shape herself to please a complex male image of what she should be like—but alas it is often an image having little to do with her own real desires or potentialities; and these may well be stunted or concealed as she grows into womanhood." *

Enter, the offstage coed actress. She will be what he wants her to be. Her resentment echoes throughout this book. And when she dares to break out of the complex male image of what she should be—when she becomes the cool coed with her Peter Pan collar, her Lorelei hairdo, and her sex manual-wise caresses—she is a threat to the lusty but less liberated college boy. "Modern women are making sexual demands on men never dreamed of by the previous generation, and larger numbers of women are displaying a degree of sexuality which was unheard of and unthinkable only ten years ago," write Drs. Phyllis and Eberhard Kronhausen in *Sex Histories of American College Men*.** "It seems," the Eberhards continue, "as if the male sex has not had sufficient time to assimilate these changes in the sexual behavioral pattern of women. There has therefore developed a curious cultural lag between the sexes that is not infrequently the cause of wonder and embarrassment on the part of the male, and a source of trouble in many heterosexual relationships." There was, indeed, a quality of this wonder in the voice of the lanky blond undergraduate, sprawled in the unyielding angles of a contemporary modern arm chair in a tutor's suite at Harvard's Leverett House. "I wouldn't worry too much about guys leading the Cliffies astray," he said. "What worries me are the three girls so far this semester that tried to seduce *me* —and one of them was a virgin."

Even though Kinsey exposed Joe College fifteen years ago as sexually retarded compared to males of lower education levels, the myth of collegiate carnality persists. In a spoofing back-to-school mood recently, *Esquire* *** magazine posed a

* "Growing Up Females," *op. cit.*
** N.Y.: Ballantine Books, 1960.
*** September, 1962.

flapperish Julie Newmar knock-kneed and bosomy, beside a
poem, and the instructions "to the tune of *The Sweetheart of
Sigma Chi*":

> The girl of my dreams is the hippest chick.
>> She really reads a lot.
> She's made Phi Bete and she'll only date
>> Pacifist boys who smoke pot.
> She's made no fuss on the Freedom bus;
>> She's nonviolent and so dear.
> Oral pills she's bought, so she'll never get caught;
>> She's the Sweetheart of the New Frontier.

Here, I suspect, is the college girl college boys want to think
they want. Possibly she is the girl most likely to amuse and
delight the ex-college boys who edit *Esquire*. But the average,
ordinary, everyday college boy, especially the frosh and sophomore, would be treading water to keep from going under in
the company of *Esquire's* Miss New Frontier. Still the myth,
nurtured in tabloid headlines and *Playboy*,* is so widely pro-
mulgated that many coeds do not realize how virginal, strait-
laced, and sexually conservative many of these male undergraduates are. Girls often mistake male aggression for sexual
experience, persistence for sophistication. It was a recent graduate of the University of Ohio who wanted to set the record
straight. "You'd be surprised how many guys are virgins," he

---

* Playbody's editor and publisher, Hugh M. Hefner, has been attempt-
ing in a series of monthly statements under the heading "The Playboy
Philosophy," to "explicate the Sexual Revolution" and his magazine's "part
in this search for a 'new morality.' " Tracing sex morality through the ages,
Hefner finds: "Modern American morality is an amalgamation of the
superstitious paganism and masochistic asceticism of early Christianity;
the sexual anxieties, feelings of guilt and shame, witch-hunting sadism
and sex repression of the medieval Church; the desexualized love of the
troubadours; England's Romantic Age, wherein love was presumed to con-
quer all; and the prohibitively strict, severe, joyless, authoritarian, un-
responsive, book-banning, pleasure-baiting dogma of Calvinist Protestantism, Puritanism and Victorianism" and "virtually assures us our high incidence of unhappy marriages, frequent divorces, impotence, masochism,
frigidity, frustration and perversion." (From Hefner's editorial in the
Playboy of September, 1963.) How the double-standard male responds to
the "new morality" remains to be seen.

said. "And 90 percent of those that start out virgins graduate that way. The older a guy is, the tougher it is to take the step —maybe he's worried about his masculinity, how he'll stack up with the guys she's had before. Unless he gets involved in some kind of gang-bang with his frat brothers and is forced into it, he may figure it's easier to just marry a virgin and fumble along together."

There were usually snickers, giggles, and free-flowing braggadiccio whenever I talked to boys in a group. Their comments on the motivations and behavior of the college girl were quite valuable, but I could pick up only hints of an individual youth's actual experience. Alone with just one boy, I was touched, and embarrassed too, by the intensity and intimacy of his confidences. As with many girls, it wasn't merely a telling, it was also an asking: the slight, baby-faced, and I was told, brilliant Stanford junior, who seemed to be saying, "Am I really much different from other guys because I haven't gotten around to it yet?" One of the most disturbing conversations was with a tweedy and attractive Harvard senior. I had come to him as a campus leader, asking for his observations of sexual attitudes among his peers. But he would not, or could not, talk about anyone but himself, and it was as if I had opened the floodgates. Boys at Harvard do not trade lockerroom tales of sexual prowess, he was saying. There is too much respect for privacy and the intellect. I had the uncomfortable feeling he had never told anyone what he was telling me. ". . . I must admit I was tempted to see how far she would go," he was saying, "but when we reached the point where she was willing, ready, and I knew she would go all the way, I said to myself, 'you rat.' " He leaned against the wall and stared out the window. " 'You rat, you can't do this to a nice girl like this, a Foxcroft girl, a virgin." So I told her I'd changed my mind. "But you say she wanted you," I said. "Yes, but you mustn't take advantage of girls," he replied. "When you've got them like that, spread eagled, it's so easy to take advantage. They say they don't care if it isn't love, but afterwards they can't help falling in love with you." Some twenty minutes later, he finally cleared up some inconsistencies in his comments by confessing that he was a virgin. "You might say I'm cheating nature by the vice—you know Rousseau's *Émile,* 'cheating nature by the vice.' " He paused to make certain his reference to masturbation was not beyond my erudition. I apologized for taking so much of his time and offered to leave. He said, no, he wanted to help me. The conversation not only pleased his interest in scientific inquiry; it was, I felt, becoming a sexual experience for him. "Why do you think you've never had an affair?" I asked. "Too busy," he said. "Getting into graduate school and running ————." He named the campus activity that had consumed his passion. "I just wouldn't want to hurt anyone," he repeated, "and it's inevitable that the girl will become emotionally involved. They tell you it's just for the moment, but girls will give anything to marry a Harvard man, you know." "I hadn't realized," I said. "It's a great responsibility, being a Harvard man," he said. "I hadn't realized," I said. "They're waiting out there for us to take up the world's burdens," he said. I shook my head. "They are," he said. "We're already running Washington, you know."

Forgive me if I have devoted inordinate space to this young man. I have done so because I suspect he speaks for a significant number of the intellectual elite and ambitious college men who may devote their high school years to "getting into Harvard" or "getting that scholarship" while other boys are thinking about "getting the best of the neighborhood easy make." He might very well be one of the boys, described with impatience and sarcasm by a Radcliffe girl as, "those Harvard men who are always telling you how important it is to hold on to your virginity and not make a mistake you'll be sorry for." His comments on lack of communication between Harvard men was reasonably accurate, according to a graduate student I talked to later that day. "I know more about a girl I've dated six times than about guys I see every day," this student said. "Women tell men how women feel. It just pours out. But men have to go out and get drunk before they open up. Otherwise it isn't manly."

As manliness is a deep concern, and sexuality inexorably

linked to manliness, chastity in the male goes unappreciated. Studies * find "little support" for the male virgin, not only among his peers of both genders but also among adults, including parents. "I never yet heard a girl say she wants to marry a virgin," a Rollins sophomore said, and at least two dozen girls made similar remarks. "I don't want some idiot slobbering all over me and not knowing what to do," a Brooklyn College freshman announced. Unencouraged and unsung, it should be no surprise then that many college boys yearn to shed what is virtually a stigma. And some approach their sexual adventures as an unpleasant duty—like ROTC, only a bit more unattractive. "I have to learn about sex for my own good," an Ivy League freshman from the Middle West said solemnly. "I will have to take advantage of every opportunity I get with girls who are the type you go out with for sex. It may be selfish and it may be dangerous, because it gives you a hollow feeling to make love where there's no love. But lust will carry me through until I'm married." "It was awful. I hated it—I don't exactly appreciate screwing that kind of pig, but I do it," a Princeton sophomore said.

Sexual intercourse seems to stir up more repulsion than erotic joy in many of these boys. "A man must have release from sexual tension," a University of Texas senior explained, adding, "You have to forgive us our animal appetites." He knows what a man is supposed to feel but somewhere along the way he has been convinced it's all a dirty business. He may be unaware of his own disgust for the act, but he expresses it in his contempt for the girl who services him or falls for his line. He, of course, is the flag bearer of the traditional double standard—sexual freedom for the male, chastity until marriage (or engagement) for the female—or, as a Harvard graduate student put it, "It's okay for me to sleep with your sister but it's not okay for you to sleep with mine." "I believe completely in freedom in sexual relations," said a Long Island University psychology major. "There should be no restraints at all," he added. But the girl he marries must be a virgin.

* "Male Virgins: Conflicts and Group Support in American Culture," by Irving B. Tebor. *Family Life Coordinator,* March-June, 1961.

An LIU freshman agreed, saying, "Sex freedom is appropriate for a fellow, but not for a girl. The girl I marry—I want her to be pure. But if something comes my way, I'll take it." "I wouldn't even *try* with the girl I was going to marry," a New York City College sophomore said. In sociologist Winston Ehrmann's comparison of "Premarital Sexual Behavior and Sex Codes of Conduct with Acquaintances, Friends and Lovers," all coital experience of the double-standard males was with nonlovers. Of the seven experienced coeds (out of 50), four had coitus with lover only, three with both lover and nonlover.* In a society that professes to exalt love—and with the unshakable romanticism of many college coeds for whom sex and love are inseparable—it is no wonder that the double-standard male is regarded as an unattractive relic of Victorian days.

"Why do boys think a girl is either a virgin or a tramp?" an Elmira College freshman asked. "They don't see how you could be somewhere in between." Her observation seemed at least partly justified. As many boys put it, there are "nice" girls, and then there are the "sluts." With a "nice" girl, some boys won't even try. Other young men take nothing for granted: no girl is innocent until she proves it—by resisting his advances. "It's the boy's privilege to try and the girl's privilege to stop," said a City College of New York youth with a shrug. "I would have been very disappointed in her if she had let me," an Ohio State lad remarked. "I really flipped for that boy," a Temple University coed confided, sipping her Coke in a booth at the crowded Campus Sandwich Shop on Philadelphia's Broad Street. "And I was really ready to go all the way but something—I don't know exactly—somehow I got the feeling he was testing me. If I let him, I'd flunk." From the remarks of college men, such testing is common, and when girls he identifies with "mom" and "sis" melt in the warmth of his attention, he is appalled, sometimes shattered.

From the ranks of these double-standard stalwarts and the sexually intimidated come the panty raiders and the piano tuners. Piano tuning was popular in college curricula in win-

* *Social Forces,* December, 1959.

ter, '62. Tuning, a team effort, calls for chopping any available piano into pieces small enough to pass through a specified hole in a sheet of cardboard. "What could be more fraught with sexual implication?" asked a Vassar junior, sighing behind her cloud of cigarette smoke. The glorious symbolism of the panty raid has been well documented— "ritual rape," *Mademoiselle* reporter Nancy Lynch calls it.* As an Antioch junior remarked, "You pull a panty raid only if you can't get panties any other way." "If we were getting laid, we wouldn't have the steam left to tear the town apart," a tall, bespectacled Princetonian remarked in an epilogue to the spring, '63, campus riot. ". . . red lights blinked on and screens and panties came down," runs a panty raid account in the University of Michigan Daily. "Fights broke out over them. One student walked around with a pair on his head." Often it is a girls' dorm that provokes the skirmish for lingerie. A trumpet, a catcall, any provocation will do on the first balmy day of spring. Girls wave bras and cry, "Chicken." "The boys broke in," a recent University of Delaware graduate recalls, "but they didn't know what to do once they got there." "Barnard girls have never respected Columbia men," a Barnard girl reported. "Not since the guys stormed toward Barnard on a panty raid and then stopped at the corner when the traffic light turned red." So essential are panties to prestige for some lads, a market in underwear flourishes. Or so a Wheelock sophomore reported, telling about a young man from Dartmouth who stopped by to say hello, bringing with him a suitcase load of ladies panties to sell to Harvard men—guaranteed "used," he informed her.

The frustration of Joe College reaches an awesome height in the more isolated men's schools. Dartmouth is one. Girls say the men stand in the railroad station panting like so many beasts when the weekend contingent of dates pulls in. At Bowdoin, bus loads of "pigs" are imported from nearby colleges for occasional sexual release, a recent graduate said. But by the big weekends, when girls converge on the isolated

* "Lady Chatterley Goes to College," by Nancy Lynch. *Mademoiselle Magazine,* August, 1963.

Maine campus from miles away, frustration reaches such a height that, according to one instructor, there is communal masturbation and a core of homosexuals is kept busy after the dates are bedded down for the night. "It's the nice girls who get asked for the big weekend," the faculty man explained, "and guys may make a token pass but most of them never expect to get anywhere."

Even so, boys are trying.* It often *does* seem, as one battle-torn Purdue sophomore complained, "All boys want to do is screw." And as dozens of coeds remarked: "They're always trying to talk you into bed." To the sexual provocateuse— the promiscuous virgin, the tease, the siren, the reputed "nympho"—it will seem especially so. "If she seems to be asking for it, who am I to worry about her emotional state?" a Michigan State youth asked. It is not merely the exploitive double-standard would-be seducer the coed must contend with. She is under a spirited attack from male disciples of the new sexual freedom, and the attack is especially persuasive because it responds to her emotional needs, hits her on an intellectual level, and, as a clincher, is devastatingly sincere. The most persuasive force of all, love, attacks on a third front, and, when both boy and girl are dedicated to a single standard of chastity, they may find themselves taking turns, as a Penn State coed described it, at applying the brakes.

The Kronhausens, Reiss, Kirkendall, Ehrmann, and other behavioral scientists find a sharp trend among college males away from the traditional double standard toward a single standard of sexual behavior, which may be chastity for both, sex with affection for both, or sexual freedom for both—with the majority favoring the middle stand. A University of Colorado coed advanced one theory behind the change: "It's that petting has become so acceptable. It takes a lot of mental gymnastics to 'respect' a girl with whom you've had contact almost to the point of intercourse, then lose respect for her

---

* In "God on the Secular Campus," Father Richard Butler, chaplain of the Newman Club at the University of New Mexico, reports that one of the fraternities on his campus "used to distinguish the member who 'made out' most often every seven days with the coveted title 'Bastard of the Week.'"

as soon as she goes all the way." No less an expert than author Glendon Swarthout (having taught honor students at Michigan, Maryland, and Michigan State), offers, in *Where the Boys Are,* as blasé an advocate of sexual freedom as any cool coed could hope to meet: one O. O. Ryder, fictional Brown University seducer. "My God," declares O. O. "Virtue can't be a physical thing . . . It has to be spiritual. It isn't whether you have sex or not, it's your attitude . . . If you do it unselfishly, to please someone else, it's got to be virtuous . . . It's like contributing to charity, darling," he assures his be-dazzled date from the Middle West. "Or working on a civic committee . . . Sex isn't a matter of morals anymore. It's a part of personal relations. It's the pleasant, friendly thing to do . . . like shaking hands or making sure you catch the other person's name when you're introduced . . . Saying 'no' is anti-social."

In my rather limited sample of college men, however, I spoke to few college boys claiming to believe in the single standard who didn't expose themselves as false claimants a sentence or two later. A University of Michigan youth, who described himself as "much more liberal than my friends," explained he didn't bother using a contraceptive when having sexual relations with a certain coed because "she was just a vegetable and I couldn't care less." And when he described meeting a good-looking Brooklyn College coed in a Green-wich Village bar during Christmas vacation, he wound up the account saying he was "disgusted" when she proved "so hot to get me to bed with her."

Boys who think they are "emancipated" may discover, and even concede, they are far less emancipated than they thought. "I used to say it didn't matter if my wife were a virgin," a Harvard youth said. "But now I'm engaged and I realize it matters *very* much." It is difficult, of course, for girls to dis-tinguish what is temporary emancipation from what is sheer seduction in the guise of sexual freedom. A Baltimore sorority girl expressed the coed's dilemma when she asked, rather plaintively, "Is it true boys just say they wouldn't dream of marrying a virgin to get you to go to bed with them? My father says so, but—well, he's my father. I'd like to know what you think," she asked me.

It would be grossly unfair and inaccurate for me to write off the college boy as all fears, confusion, naivety, hypocrisy, and sexual chicanery. As a recent Wellesley graduate pointed out, "There is a world of difference between the Dartmouth sophomore and a man in Harvard Law [School]." Even among Dartmouth sophomores, there will be many levels of sexual honesty and sophistication. Possibly there are even undergraduates who would say, with conviction equal to that of the European photographer who *did* say it: "If you love a woman, you must love everything she's experienced. Nothing is less interesting than virginity." And I was impressed by the sincerity of the Michigan law student who chided a prudish youth with the comment: "I feel there must be a special space in hell reserved for the man who would refuse a woman."

But to view the college man through the eyes of the coeds interviewed leaves us with the picture of a majority more conservative and passive than otherwise. So passive, indeed, that even though all the traditional cliches of campus courtship still flourish—the male aggressor, the Don Juan, the make-out artist—the female as seductress and the coed on the prowl stand out most vividly. The Kronhausens "were struck" by the number of their Columbia University youths "who had been seduced, not only by older women, but also as children and adolescents by their female age-mates." And again, "The underlying theme in most of the case histories was . . . that the girl had been the initiators, teachers and leaders in their various 'games of sex'—from kindergarten right through the grades, high school and into college . . . The kind of female sex aggressiveness of which the students told is also an indication of the cultural changes which are forcefully influencing the sexual behavior of our generation."

Because the role of passive female is traditional does not make it preferable. But the abandoning of traditional male-female roles is easier accomplished than adjusted to. It is an accepted pattern of the American courtship dance for the boy to advance three steps and retreat two in the face of female rejection. For a young man to fight off the sexual advances of the female is a step that has not yet been properly choreographed. An Oberlin boy told of sharing an apartment with two nurses who took turns adding to his sexual sophistication. And a Yale sophomore confided, "I couldn't believe she was really asking me to do what she was asking me to do." "I know it sounds impossible," a Rochester sophomore reportedly told his roommate, "but she practically tore my pants off."

An author and his wife visiting Dartmouth were taken on a tour of a fraternity house, including a quick stop at the darkened "Sex Room," where they were astonished to see "dozens of girls crawling all over guys—practically attacking them." What kind of homes, what sort of mothers produced these lustless young men? they wanted to know. I posed the question to a Princeton instructor. "It's the contemporary image of love-sex," he said. "They read it and they see it in the movies, *Nouvelle Vague,* the hot female, the passive male. You can dig deeper to more significant layers, but that's the surface of the phenomenon."

"I seduced mine," a Michigan State girl trilled, describing her first lover. "I seduced mine, too," a recent Vermont graduate said. "It was a lemon." "I guess you could say *I* made it happen," a Radcliffe sophomore chimed in. "Nothing gives a guy a bigger kick than holding you off," remarked a Brooklyn College junior with a pretty heart-shaped face and a young man waiting outside for her. "They like to make you feel like some sort of sex fiend."

It is neither particularly new nor exclusively contemporary, but still important to remember that even when they meet in bed, boy and girl often do not speak the same language. Kinetically they touch, emotionally they may be riding on two different planets. To the boy it is sex; to the girl it is the beginning of a relationship that might even lead ultimately to marriage. Even the coolest of the cool coeds often finds herself in bed with a stranger trying his name with a "Mrs." in front of it, just to see how it sounds. "I hate it when they make you say 'I love you,' " a University of Ohio lad complained. Kirkendall's case histories of what he calls "Level III Liaisons" (defined as "casual acquaintance who was perceived merely as a potential sexual associate with no affectional attachment on the part of the male") are studded with such comments as "I told her I loved her and all that baloney"—"She was pushing me all the time to get me to say I was interested in marriage. I never agreed or disagreed. I just listened and went along for the sex"—"I just let her talk. She was making lots of plans about us. She wanted to date steady, and to really make something out of the relationship—I just didn't go back."

"Man's love is of man's life a thing apart; 'Tis woman's whole existence," Byron said. "Men are freed by the fulfillment of sexual desire, women are committed by it," Theodore Reik suggests. No wonder, then, that they speak in different languages. So strong are these pressures for a girl she begins to see the possibility of permanence in almost any pleasant relationship. "you're divine! said he (you are Mine said she.)*

The boy may react with resentment and hostility at being pressed too quickly. Or feeling guilty may tell himself he has lost respect for the girl—this permits him to withdraw gracefully. Some boys confessed to letting relationships drift into a semi-engagement strictly for sex. A New York bachelor had little difficulty seducing a Barnard junior who was obviously "mad about me." To her it was a sign their might be promise for the future. To him it was a new aesthetic kick because, "We were in her folks' Park Avenue apartment and, to tell you the truth, I'd never laid a girl under a Picasso or a Renoir." A University of Ohio lad described his impassioned courtship of a persuadable coed in a wooded area near Athens. He had bet some fraternity brothers he could bring home the girl's panties. "I was worrying so about how to get the panties, I didn't enjoy it too much," he confessed. "But when I had them off, I yelled, 'Someone's coming,' and stuffed them in my pocket." He won the bet. "Girls can be cruel too," he defended himself. "Once a girl I'd had no success with at all

* e.e. cummings.

called and said, 'Sorry you didn't convince me earlier, Billy. It's great!' Talk about hostility." He grinned.

The who-can-break-whom-down-first exploitive quality lamented so fervently by Dr. Albert Ellis * moves on many paths other than the traditional one Ellis describes as sex teasing followed by "a dearth of sex pleasing" with the female as sex pirate. Both sexes promise more than they deliver and demand more than the orginal contract specified. "He only wants sex," the coed may say. "She doesn't give a damn about me," the boy replies, "only wants to know where I'm planning to take her." The problem is that antagonism becomes habit-forming and hostility, a way of life. The brutal competition, as it is played out in bed by the young man and the cool coed, is etched with acid in "The Time of Her Time," a fragment from Norman Mailer's novel-in-progress. He is Sergius O'Shaugnessy, "messiah of the one-night stand . . . one of the Village equivalents of an Eagle Scout badge for the girls." She, Denise, a junior at New York University, "one of those harsh alloys of a self-made Bohemian from a middle-class home . . . far from formed . . . she made love as if she were running up an inclined wall so steep that to stop for an instant would slide her back to disaster." He must prove himself a man by clawing, pummeling, tricking her to a first confrontation with her own femaleness, and she must punish him for his gift by emasculation. Mailer's document of the duel between these two killers is so vivid, it tastes hate, and so accurate, you suspect he does it not with typewriter but with tape recorder.

Sergius is an important man in a college girl's life. For the Denises and for the less driven coeds awakening to sexual freedom on slumbering fields, the typical college undergraduate is fine material for coffee dates, pledge formals, and marriage. But for less fettered sexual attachment, she may be attracted by a Sergius, an older man, an emancipated graduate student, a faculty member, a uniform from the nearby Air Force base, a ball player, a visiting novelist or playwright

* *The American Sexual Tragedy, op. cit.*

or folk singer. The appeal of a heterosexual and willing literary lion was demonstrated recently at Pembroke. A student there reported that a visiting novelist had gone to bed with 12 Pembroke ladies in a four-day period, adding: "But one of the girls told me he wasn't all that good."

Some coeds seem drawn by the compelling appeal of the faculty lover. "Radcliffe has Harvard, Barnard has Columbia, at Sarah Lawrence we marry our professors," a Sarah Lawrence junior said, paying tribute to popular legend, which is not totally alienated from the truth. "There is something about a man on a podium," a Barnard coed explained. But the Sarah Lawrence girl rarely gets to see her professors on a podium because of the school's unique set-up that requires not homework but "contracts" and regular conferences with her "don." "You're supposed to tell him everything," one Sarah Lawrence girl said. "And when you're discussing why you didn't hand in that last contract because you had a nervous breakdown, things get pretty intimate." Girls go to Europe in summer with their professors—not necessarily in a capacity less academic than advertised. But there have been enough faculty-student marriages to perpetuate the legend and more than enough affairs or, at least, gossip. "You get two tickets for something you know he wants to see and that's how it starts," one knowledgeable junior reported. At Scripps, one of the Associated Colleges at Claremount, Cal., girls, David Boroff writes, "like their Sarah Lawrence cousins, have the opportunity for a sustained I-thou dialogue with their professors." Boroff tells of a girl who asked her humanities instructor: "Aren't you going to discuss Dante and the modern world?" A talk session was organized at his home where, "sprawled on the floor, they did a remorseless job of assigning each other to appropriate circles of hell."

The more innocent chums of the girl so involved often see the professor as Svengali. "I don't know what he did to her," a Mt. Holyoke girl remarked of a dormmate's affair with her music professor. "She became thin as a rail, withdrawn, almost mystical. Poor girl. She said it was so wonderful, they could talk of death together." At Stanford there was one nice professor with four kids who chose one girl a year for an affair and then converted her to Catholicism, a faculty man reported. A Barnard girl described her affair with a Columbia department head "on the floor of his living room with the kids asleep and his wife having a baby in the hospital." He kept leaving her notes, she said, attached to corrected exam papers and stuck in the pockets of her coat. In her tone was a hint of the triumph in bringing a great man to his knees—not to mention on his own living room floor.

Even a faculty man who resists may be marked for attack by the aggressive coed. A Southern professor described walking into his apartment one evening with the eerie sensation that someone was in the room. Someone was—naked, in his bed, a fact he did not pin down until he himself slid under the covers. He leaped back. "Don't go, Dr. L.," the girl cooed with a soft drawl. "Ah been listening to your talk. Now I want to feel your body." "I tried to talk her out of it," the professor said. "But sexually deprived as I was, I finally gave in. Teaching," he added, "is extremely masculine. Those passive little minds and you're impregnating them. Juicy pink—you just want to put it into them. I think many of them feel it too."

The potential for scandal in faculty-student affairs is great, of course. At small, conservative colleges, it would be more difficult to maintain the essential secrecy. But in more sophisticated circles, neither students nor faculty seem either shocked or alarmed, only somewhat disenchanted if a likable faculty wife is unnecessarily hurt. On the sprawling campus of a state university where a breath of scandal could have economic repercussion during legislative budget hearings, it is possible to become lost in the enormity of the machine. But even then it may be difficult. One jealous or offended witness may expose the relationship, as one jealous or offended coed did recently at a California school where boys and girls room in segregated areas of a coed dorm. A former student, now transferred to San Diego State College, told how one girl's parents came to call on their daughter and her roommate came downstairs to explain, "I'll have to run and get her— it's her turn to sleep with the dorm daddy tonight." The dorm daddy, a resident counselor, was fired and replaced by a dorm mother. "I won't name the school," she said, "because I don't want to hurt its reputation."

These are some of the men—and boys—in the coed's life, the objects she struggles to fashion into her "whole existence." They are mostly seen as she sees them, and while her vision is distorted, it is supported, at least in part, by reality. Perhaps it is impossible for men and women ever to explain fully men and women to each other, to ultimately clear up conflicts of gender and misunderstanding. But the academic atmosphere *should* provide ideal conditions to get a genuine dialogue going. Sex, as we have seen, is a constant topic of discussion for the college student. Young people are able to speak freely with each other about sex, far more candidly than adults speak, as Oregon State's Prof. Lester Kirkendall suggests.* One boy and one girl involved in a meaningful and sincere love relationship should be able to shed superficial pose and explore meanings and motivations that might otherwise build a gulf between them. But some of the courtship situations that call themselves "love" might not survive if all pose were abandoned. Thus, a basic dishonesty is encouraged: In the female, any dishonesty may seem justified as long as it leads to marriage. Here is where sex education must branch off from mere biology and examine the psychology of gender.

Certainly the arguments advanced by the double-standard male to justify a position essentially insulting to the female would be exposed under such examination as mere folklore. In his interviews with double-standard men, Bard College sociologist Ira L. Reiss found two main arguments: 1) "The female sex drive and sex desire is not as great as the male's, and thus the woman has less compulsion to such behavior. 2) The female takes a greater risk because she can become pregnant and she is more easily condemned. Thus she has reason to abstain." **

The difference in risk does exist, Reiss points out, but "with

* *Premarital Intercourse and Interpersonal Relationships.* N.Y.: Julian Press, 1961.
** *Premarital Sexual Standards in America. op. cit.*

the development of rational means of contraception" its significance is lessened, and he adds: "From a strictly logical approach, woman's chance of becoming pregnant may merely mean that she should be cautious or that man should not tempt her."

As for faith in the less compelling sex drive of the female— it is indeed widespread, but I was taken aback when a psychology instructor at Yale said his students wondered if it were biological and what did I think. I had the uneasy feeling he himself was not sure. Hadn't the anthropologists long done away with the myth of a lesser female sexual desire as biological? "There is much scientific evidence which indicates the female sex drive (that which is inborn) is not by nature significantly less than the male's . . ." Reiss writes. In *Sex and Temperament in Three Primitive Societies,* Margaret Mead advances a concept similar to that of Clellan S. Ford and Frank A. Beach in *Patterns of Sexual Behavior:* that differences are due to learned, not inborn, factors. Reiss suggests that boys raised as we raise girls would be as sexually inhibited as are girls. He refers to Kinsey for evidence of the speed of arousal and the capacity for orgasm in the female and to the incidence of heavy petting as an indication that many young women have strong sexual desires but strive to keep them within bounds.

Kinsey's findings that the male reaches a peak in sexual outlet in the late teens while the female's outlet peaks in the late twenties and early thirties, is not, as Reiss notes, conclusive evidence of sex-drive differences. "Sex outlet is not necessarily a reflection of sex drive," he writes. As inhibition is an important factor in sexual outlet, it seems quite likely that a sexual age gap will be narrowed with a greater acceptance of the new sex morality. Possibly it has already narrowed.

And Then He Blushed

"I was so sure I would never be a virgin when I got married. I thought—when I fall in love, then I'll— yet here we are. It's harder than ever to find the time or a place. You just wouldn't believe it. I mean, Freddy and I have been so busy running back and forth meeting each other's families since we announced the engagement. You might say, at first it was fear. Now it's Freddy."

Sharon Pearlman glanced at the modest diamond solitaire placed less than 138 hours earlier on her engagement-ring finger. Then, caught in the act of admiration by her roommates, she grinned and clowned with sweeping, mock-elegant hand poses.

"Maybe I'll even stop biting my nails," she mused.

Obviously many forces have gone into the preservation of Sharon Pearlman's chastity through four years at Boston University and six months in Manhattan—where she has lived a kind of extension of sorority house camaraderie with seven coeds and working-girl roommates, six of them at varying stages of sexual emancipation and erotic exuberance. The strongest force at the time of this interview was probably Freddy, her fiance, soon to graduate from the Massachusetts College of Optometry. Cultural traditions, family loyalty, a vague but tenuous religious code, pragmatism, and no particular passion to deny these forces preserved her chastity before Freddy came along. And Freddy had now assumed the burden of that defense. Freddy's is not at all an unusual role for the American male.

"We've discussed it—Oh, have we talked and talked and thought about it—and Freddy feels as long as we've managed to last this long, we can stick it out a few months longer. It's a funny thing about virginity. Sometimes after a while you can get almost stubborn about it. It becomes a cause. Freddy is an essentially conservative guy. If he thought we should, we would. But he likes the idea of my being a virgin. And I always thought it would be nice to be a virgin on my wedding night. I don't mind that he isn't. I want the first time to be not fumbling-bumbling but smooth. And I would like my first man to be my last—my only. Hell, it's only a few months more."

Doesn't she feel pressured by the surrounding atmosphere of sexual emancipation?

"What's right for one person isn't necessarily right for another. I've learned a lot—but Freddy has convinced me I'm really the last woman in the world who could carry off an affair. It's funny. I dated him for a while when I was a sophomore and he was trying to persuade me to go to bed practically from the beginning. You know how guys are—they always feel they have to try. Always on the make. Then when I ran into him again my senior year and we started dating, it was different. When that kind of boy starts thinking about marriage, he treats the girl with—I don't know—respect."

For some girls college is Vassar or Bryn Mawr, a particular college. For other girls, college is education essential to the well-rounded housewife—college is a marital shopping mart, a playpen without responsibility, four walls to protect in the move from the four walls of home to the four walls of her own home. For some, it is a degree, or the first step toward career or profession. To some, knowledge. To some, it is most important of all, close to Harvard. And that, Sharon feels, for most of its coeds, is the most obvious attraction of Boston University. After Radcliffe's, 1,800 or so women and Wellesley's 1,700, claim their share of Harvard's forces, there are still, numerically at least, surplus enough to inspire hope in the hearts of BU coeds.

"Harvard, Tufts, MIT, but never the boys of BU. It's a question of values. BU boys are so middle-class. They have no drive, no particular ambition. They're doomed to go into their father' business. The typical BU girl is husband hunting. Frankly, I never thought going to bed with a boy was the way to get him interested in you. Necking? The Charles River is very romantic. Parties? When I was a sophomore some MIT boys had a black mass. It was wild. There was this guy nude and some Radcliffe girls and all sorts of things supposedly going on behind the door. I was a sophomore and I didn't know what was going on actually.

"One day, though, I decided it was time. You know, I just decided I was going to do it. So I looked around for someone, preferably foreign. And I picked out this Turkish boy. He didn't speak English, but hell, I didn't plan to *talk* about it.

We went out and I knew I was going to sleep with him—
I mean, I'd made up my mind. It was really going to be wild.
He picked me up and we started walking in toward town.
'No,' I said. But I couldn't explain what I meant in English
so I just turned him around and aimed him toward the
Charles. Well, we were necking and I finally managed to get
him down on the grass—"

"Sharon," a roommate squealed. "You never told us."

"He spread his coat and there we were—and I panicked.
I just froze. I thought, How am I gonna get out of this? Maybe
he'll rape me. So I whispered 'No, no,' but he thought I was
just kissing his ear. And I said, 'Not tonight. We'll have other
nights together.' So he took me home. I never saw him again."

Petting, everything but—?

"Well yes, and I've always been humane enough to think
if a guy goes home in agony, I'd feel terrible. No one told me
exactly, but I just assumed it could be done—without going
all the way. Freddy and I spent the night together and we're
very close. We went on a ski trip to Vermont. We were so
casual about it—so matter of fact, my parents didn't think
twice. I don't think they think I would ever do anything they
wouldn't approve of. We sort of created an innocent rapport.
I was packing for the trip and my mother said, 'Be sure to
take your red flannels.' My red flannels. They're like Dr.
Denton's and I wouldn't have worn them even if I'd been
going to share a room with the girls. But I took them.

"When we told my parents we were going to get married,
my father said to Freddy, 'You sure you know what you're
doing—she snores in her sleep.' Without even thinking, Freddy
started to say, 'I know—' And then he blushed. What a girl
does depend a lot, I think, on the kind of boy she falls in
love with."

8

Birth Control: The Numbers Game

She may be a whiz at logarithms, but the college girl is apt to be totally misinformed about the rhythm of her ovaries. Contraceptives are, she may suggest, "a perfectly divine solution to the economic woes of the underdeveloped nations and the population explosion of the Orient." Obviously it would never occur to the college girl who wrote this answer on a mimeographed questionnaire that population expansion might become a personal problem.

By her own description, the average college girl is "pitifully naive" about conception and "even less informed about contraception." "It's not just the virgins," as a Brandeis senior noted. "The rest of us often act like we still think the stork brings babies and screwing has nothing to do with it." "It frightens me to think how little we know about birth control," a Wellesley junior confessed, "And I'm a biology major." "Just a few days ago I read an article about the menstrual cycle, in one of the ladies magazines," a Brooklyn College sophomore reported. "According to the newest theory, I should have been pregnant a dozen times at least by now." "I don't blink an eyelash when the girls talk about diaphragms," a Northwestern University "Beauty Queen" confided. "But frankly I wouldn't know a diaphragm if I tripped over one." "I get so upset when people talk about that subject," an Eastern Michigan University sophomore said, "I don't want to even think about it." This last girl said she felt relaxed, "sort of," and confident because her fiance had said they would marry at once if she accidentally became pregnant. I felt she would be almost grateful if the "crisis" came soon.

Even the coolest sexual sophisticates of the campus are "apt to be as ignorant of the facts as the poorest Indian peasant," Cornell Pediatrician Milton I. Levine writes. Despite exposure to high school lectures on the romance between sperm and egg and to sociology courses on marriage and the family— despite the availability of *Peyton Place* and *Lady Chatterley's Lover,* students, Dr. Levine suggests, "are not much better off than in the quaint old days when hygiene courses simply taught girls to say something like 'I am a Wellesley girl, and, I hope, a lady.' They are worse off, in fact, since times and the definitions of a lady have changed. . . ." *

Science continues to come up with increasingly effective and easy-to-use oral and mechanical contraceptives. It is almost impossible to pick up a mass circulation magazine these days without coming across a chapter in the annals of birth control. How does the college student respond to the contraceptive revolution?

"Some of the kids have been using Saran Wrap," a Wheelock college sophomore reported. A Cornell youth confirmed her finding. "It's neat, it's inexpensive—and most girls get clutched if you even mention diaphragms."

Say "birth control" to a college girl and the reactions range from "abstinence is the only way" to "I have the diaphragm Mommy bought me when I was 14" to "I used a ginger-ale douche once in an emergency out in the woods." On the more conservative campuses, no "nice" girl would want to seem too well-informed. In hip circles an equally "nice" girl might accumulate dribs and drabs of information (misinformation)

* "Sex: The Problem Colleges Evade," by Milton I. Levine, M.D., and Maya Pines. *Harper's Magazine,* October, 1961.

rather than come right out and admit her ignorance. First day of her freshman year at Sarah Lawrence, a blue-eyed 17-year-old from Brooklyn was greeted from across the hall by an upperclassman busily hanging African masks on her bedroom walls. She recalls the upperclassman's asking: "Do you have the name of our official school doctor for diaphragms?"

"What do you mean official?" the freshman stammered. "Does everyone *have* to get one?"

The Africanophile sighed. "No, but everyone eventually does."

It is easy to be misled by the weary, matter-of-fact sophistication of such remarks. The Brooklyn freshman was. Young men who date the sexually emancipated coed are misled too. A man-about-Manhattan (Yale grad) noted that girls can no longer get away with pleading fear of pregnancy as a reason for not going to bed—"They know very well and they know you know they know all about contraception. One girl told me she wears a diaphragm at all times; another one, age 17, said she takes a contraceptive along whenever she goes out 'just in case.' " *

There are, indeed, plenty of cool kitties for whom the diaphragm is a status symbol, others who regard its use as the duty of the sexually mature female. But those who have a contraceptive device do not always choose to use it; those who talk about maturity may revert to adolescence; those who seem knowledgeable about contraception may be merely faking it.

"We don't know half what we pretend we know—and we won't admit it even to each other," a Sarah Lawrence junior said. "I just know this girl hasn't the least idea how the seed gets planted in Mother's tummy," a University of Indiana senior said, "but she sat there while some girls were discussing contraception and nodded her head like she knew everything and never said a word." "It was coming home from her second abortion trip to Tijuana that my best friend decided no more lying 'it's safe' when it isn't," a UCLA design major said. "It seems she wasn't even sure what 'safe' meant."

Conception and contraception as a topic of after-curfew

* "The Moral Disarmament of Betty Coed," *op. cit.*

gossip sessions know no geographical boundaries. They are subjects some girls would feel free to discuss only with roommates or closest friends. But obviously many girls are so eager for reliable information that a *tête-à-tête* may soon grow into a seminar. One well-informed or textbook-coached coed may educate an entire corridor of interested females. But often the facts get twisted and girls wind up debating old wives' tales and folklore. "There's nothing to worry about," a Radcliffe sophomore was assured by her roommate, "I mean you can't get pregnant unless you make love during your period." "You should hear the kind of questions these supposedly knowledgeable girls ask," a Sarah Lawrence girl said. "Like 'Can you get pregnant from a toilet seat?' and 'If you're making out and the boy has an orgasm near you, can you get pregnant?' " "A girl told me you can't get pregnant unless you have a climax," a chaste San Francisco State sophomore said. "I told her, 'Don't count on it, dear.' "

It might seem incredible that college girls should be so ill-informed. Educators had hoped marriage and family courses, introduced in the thirties, might provide students with the sex education so often disastrously lacking. But it is in this area that educators have "fallen down most seriously," according to many authorities.* Studies show there is "continuing but not too great improvement" in the level of reproductive knowledge in the past 25 years.** The dearth of information even among medical students is regarded by educators as particularly appalling.***

Many of the girls I spoke to were distressed at their own ignorance. For some it was a matter of principle, not need. "True, I don't *need* to know about birth control methods at the moment," a Purdue senior said, "but I can't think of one

* "Are Educators Afraid of Sex?," by R. A. Harper and F. A. Harper. *Marriage and Family Living,* August, 1957. "Family Life Education in This Scientific Age," by Thomas Poffenberger. *Marriage and Family Living,* May, 1959.

** "A Survey of the Public's Knowledge of Certain Aspects of Human Reproduction," by H. F. Kilander. *Journal of School Health,* June, 1959. "Sex Ignorance of College Students," by W. L. Stone. *Family Life,* October, 1960.

*** "Sex Education in Medical School," by H. I. Lief. Unpublished address before American Psychiatric Association, Toronto, May 10, 1962.

earthly reason why it shouldn't be taught." For other girls, the need is more pressing. They beg for frank and thorough sex education—including birth control information—from the schools. Some get it. Others get tea, not much sympathy, and morality sermons. As Cornell's Dr. Milton Levine * notes, "Some colleges create a very tense and punitive atmosphere in their 'sex education' lectures. 'Go ahead and do what you want,' " he quotes a physician addressing male students at a Midwest college. " 'But we'll be treating your psychiatric disorders, your pregnant girl friends, and your venereal diseases!' " This is the kind of approach almost guaranteed to rub college youth the wrong way. The appearance of Drs. Sylvanus and Evelyn Duvall, two well-known family counselors, at Oberlin in spring, 1961, aroused the campus newspaper to editorialize: "Although we were amused by the Drs. Duvall's statements, we also see serious overtones in them. Here, as in the freshman seminar program, the College seems to be trying to inculcate students with a specific moral view under the guise of sex education." Oberlin has not abandoned this approach to sex education, according to the testimony of two recent Oberlin graduates. "But to answer the criticism, they also brought in Dr. [Alan] Guttmacher who set the tone with his opening remark." She quoted: " 'With one ejaculation I could impregnate every girl in this room.' " A Sarah Lawrence girl described recent campus lectures conducted by the local Planned Parenthood group as "a big joke." "The girls wanted to know: 'Why won't you fit us?' 'Where can we get a diaphragm?' 'How long does it take for a woman to learn to enjoy it?' 'Why aren't we as good as men—in sexual response?' But they always came back to the same theme: 'Where can we go for a diaphragm?' 'Do you want us to get pregnant?' 'Why won't you help us?' "

But if pregnancy or, as Margaret Mead writes, the potential for illegitimate children is "the real issue" of sex on the campus, sex education is not enough. Not even handing out birth control information during freshman orientation week would eliminate the potential for unwanted pregnancy.

As worried about pregnancy as she seems to be, and as

* "Sex: The Problem Colleges Evade," *op. cit.*

much as she talks about it, and as often as she grows hysterical the day *before* her menstrual period is due, the college girl often has the utterly unrealistic "feeling" of: It can't happen to me. "It's like a superstition," several girls said. The phenomenon is difficult to explain. Fear of pregnancy is vivid, real, one of the factors most often cited when girls analyze what keeps a college girl out of the premarital bed. Virgins worry about pregnancy and the most sexually sophisticated worry too. "If I took birth control pills and wore a diaphragm and he wore a condrom, I'd *still* be afraid of getting pregnant," one coed told Manhattan analyst Harold Greenwald.

For this girl, as for those who rely on what they called "Vatican Roulette," those who prefer "to leave the whole ghastly subject to the fates," and even those with diaphragms unfailingly used, periodic pregnancy panics occur as inevitably as final exams. As a tall, freckled Antioch junior put it, "I go through the wringer practically every single month even when I know—I mean I just *know*—I couldn't possibly be pregnant. Sometimes I even get to feeling dizzy and I imagine I can see my waistline thickening. Once I was a week late and I almost singed my bottom sitting in red hot baths and lifting heavy furniture and throwing myself around. When it finally does come—my period—I close my eyes and say 'thank you' and swear never to take chances again." "Chances" she had no intention of eliminating included sleeping with her young man of the moment, she confessed with a wry grin.

At a school where open acknowledgment of premarital sex is publicly frowned upon, this girl would probably suffer in silence, tugging at the furniture in a self-imposed exile of sorts. But where affairs are regarded as "inevitable" and "enviable," monthly panics may inspire great camaraderie. "I was pretty disgusted my first year at Brandeis," a senior recalled, "when I walked into one of the rooms and found four girls sitting in a circle clutching their calendars and moaning how they were sure they must be pregnant. It wasn't so much the pregnancy that annoyed me; it was the element of group therapy, the *en masse* seance. I found that distasteful."

Thus pregnancy as a monstrous specter of doom hovers menacingly, and yet individual girls almost seem to be saying,

"Not me—it can't happen to me." Pregnancy is something that happens to the girl down the hall. "It's like nuclear war," an American University (Washington, D.C.) coed tried to explain. "You're scared stiff and sometimes it seems inevitable, and yet you have this faith, somehow you will survive." "Everyone knows he's going to die," a Barnard senior put it, "but who really accepts his own mortality?" "Girls talk and act as if each one were somehow magically immune," a University of Chicago junior observed. "It's as though they were unable to connect this passionate and meaningful act with anything so clinical or anatomical as ovaries and semen. Girls don't even seem to learn from their closest friends' mistakes," she added. "My friend's roommate got pregnant and then one week after the roommate's abortion, my friend discovered *she* was pregnant. She kept saying, 'I just don't believe it.' "

Then there are the mystics, the romantics. They may know a little about contraception—maybe even enough. But they couldn't care less. Or what they know offends their aesthetic sense. "Girls want to justify this terribly natural act by doing it in a terribly natural way," a bright-eyed Berkeley brunette observed with cynicism. "There's this big thing about there shouldn't be anything mechanical between you and romance," a Brandeis senior said. "It's too clinical and unaesthetic," a Queens College freshman insisted, "and so we just trust to rhythm." (There was a suggestion that ignorance and not aesthetics was the real explanation in her case.) "Birth control. It's just too embarrassing," an Ohio State junior said. "A lot of us trust to the guy and the gods," a University of Maryland coed remarked. "You hate to spoil a great moment by even mentioning it," a Wisconsin University junior said. And a Maryland sorority girl told of a girl she knew who was having intercourse on the living room floor when the young man suddenly produced a canister and sprayed foam into the young lady's vagina. Afterwards, the girl murmured huskily, "What was that stuff you had?" and the boy told her it was a new contraceptive. "Imagine," the Maryland girl who told the story said, "Why, it could have been anything and she was too carried away to even ask."

"It's pretty stupid to risk pregnancy," said a petite blonde

University of Colorado coed in a maternity dress. "But most girls risk it because they don't want to ask a boy to use contraceptives or the idea doesn't appeal to them." "I don't like being a victim or a target in a battle plan that would make D-Day seem like a kindergarten exercise," a Smith junior said. "It infuriates me when a boy comes all prepared with something *before* he has any reason to think I am willing. Contraceptives make it seem so calculated."

From remarks like these (and I heard them again and again) it becomes obvious that many college girls—and a shocking number of college boys—are far more intimidated, frightened, apathetic, or foolhardy about contraceptives than the alleged sophistication of their sexual behavior would indicate. And everything that is written—and whispered—about shotgun marriage, illegitimacy, and abortion suggests that these college girls were truthful in describing the ambivalence toward birth control on the campus.

Where there is love, affection, mutual commitment, respect (for the act itself or for biology, if not for each other), real or imagined aesthetic qualms and emotional blocks are overruled. And students make an effort to avoid conception, though such efforts may be makeshift at times and, with the best intentions, often ineffective.

Abstinence, rhythm, withdrawal before ejaculation, the condom, foams, and spermicidal jellies, with or without a diaphragm—each has its champions and its detractors. Abstinence: "The drawback should be obvious," was how a Sweetbriar senior put it. Rhythm: "Haphazard, and anyway, does anyone ever take the time to figure out exactly when you ovulate?" a Stanford University sophomore said. Withdrawl: "Inexpensive," a Brandeis senior suggested. "It doesn't always work as planned," an Ohio State sophomore offered. "A middle-class perversion," was a Yale law student's pronouncement. "Pretty unaesthetic," a Brooklyn College freshman said. The condom: "Depressing," said a bronzed, silver-haired UCLA would-be starlet, a junior, criticizing the interruptive nature of the male sheath. "Just at that wonderful abandoned moment, he starts fumbling in his pants pocket and then you hear sounds like a doctor pulling on his rubber glove. Ugh."

"You just can't do it with a rubber," said a Cornell sophomore who described herself as "maybe promiscuous by some standards." She explained: "The man's pleasure is like—half as much—I mean if you enjoy love making at all—you just wouldn't want to use one."

Statistics indicate that use of birth control increases as education and income increase.* With greater education and income, contraceptive control shifts to the wife. The same shift might be expected with the unmarried female, especially at the college level. The more sexually sophisticated the girl and the more permissive the climate of her campus, the more likely there will be a flat plastic diaphragm box tucked away in her bureau. But the average sheltered and conservative coed who finds herself suddenly involved—eagerly, willingly, or half-heartedly—in intimacies she never dreamed she would experience before marriage, is likely to be uninformed or grossly misinformed. It took forty years and a major campaign by such pioneers as Margaret Sanger to overcome the ignorance or indifference of the American female to the vaginal diaphragm. Women of the upper classes were first to accept it, the idea took even longer to filter down to the middle class. The college girl is expected to pick up the necessary information at the traditional moment—just before the organ breaks into the wedding march or shortly after the honeymoon. To ask questions "prematurely" is embarrassing to some girls. "Four of my friends, at least, kept telling me to get a diaphragm," a Hunter College senior said. "But none of them bothered to explain exactly what it was. I had this picture of something metal about eight by ten inches—it sounded horrible. Then this gynecologist got hold of me and said I was out of my mind to take chances—she showed me one. It wasn't anything like I'd imagined, of course."

But there is an even greater block to the popular acceptance of the diaphragm by the single and sexually active college girl. Girls can be as emotional about a diaphragm as they are about their virginity. Maybe more so. Treasuring virginity is

* "Growth of American Families" study, quoted by Dr. Alan F. Guttmacher in *The Complete Book of Birth Control*. N.Y.: Ballantine Books, 1961.

not too fashionable. But carnal anarchy is rarely approved. And for many girls, the diaphragm is official recognition of innocence irrevocably lost and a commitment to uninhibited sexuality. "Yes, I have had an affair," said the Rollins University senior with the auburn bouffant mane. "But the diaphragm says I am a girl who has affairs. I haven't accepted that about myself yet." And a Barnard sophomore echoed her reasoning. "It's one thing to be in love, to be swept away by love," she said, "but once you start planning ahead to the extent of a diaphragm, it's like wearing a sign: 'I'm a girl who screws.' " "I would feel guilty having a diaphragm," a George Washington University freshman said, "It doesn't seem right to be that safe." A Northwestern University English major, who begged off from an interview because of finals, offered one comment: "Put me on record as saying all college girls should be issued diaphragms freshman year along with class schedules. I'm not just kidding either. I'm sitting here right now," she said, "trying to study Chaucer and keep my roommate from jumping out the window because she's three days late and sure she's pregnant." (Later I learned the English major had passed her Chaucer exam and her roommate, the pregnancy test. Neither had any plans for obtaining a diaphragm.)

Many girls will assure you they would like diaphragms, but doctors refuse to prescribe them. Or they will explain as did one Goucher junior, "If I knew I wouldn't have to answer all sorts of embarrassing questions, I would go to a doctor." But there is in most campus residences an underground that passes along names and addresses of cooperative doctors in the campus area for a girl who wants a diaphragm. Most girls who say they cannot obtain contraceptive devices are probably saying they do not want to. "I don't want to lie about being engaged," a Hofstra freshman said.

It is true that Massachusetts and Connecticut prohibit the sale of contraceptive devices and many doctors will prescribe diaphragms only for engaged girls or the single girl over 21. Many girls are willing to lie if necessary. "When the nurse asked if I was planning to be married, I said yes," a Vassar junior reported. "It wasn't a lie. I *am* going to be married.

Some day, that is. I just haven't met the man yet." One doctor remarked that he would love to assure nervous young ladies who come to him there's no need to lie. "But I don't want to embarrass them. They like to think of us as kindly old idiots." A Boston doctor says he prescribes diaphragms for anyone who asks. "I don't know a doctor who demands a marriage license before giving contraceptive advice or prescriptions. The law says 'health reasons' and leaves the interpretation up to our discretion. We proceed on the basis that unmarried women need medical contraceptive methods for their own and society's health." The Planned Parenthood Clinic of Ann Arbor even advertises its services and hours in the classified columns of the University of Michigan student paper, *The Michigan Daily,* among the notices for pizza and photography staff tryouts.

For some college girls, buying a diaphragm is only the beginning of the trauma. "First time I go to bed with a new man, I wouldn't want him to know that I have a diaphragm," a University of Ohio senior said. "I would play very naive. Later on, when I know it's right and we're right, I would say, 'I bought it for us.' Boys like that." "I played the rhythm game for four years," a recent Barnard graduate said. "Then I finally broke down and got a diaphragm. On Friday I looked at that ugly little flying saucer and I hated it. By Sunday afternoon, I looked at it again and I had grown to love it."

A minority group, but one that would seem from this research to be growing, tends to regard use of the diaphragm as the only sane and responsible choice in premarital relationships. On the campus where a diaphragm is a status symbol, the highest status rating goes to the girl who got her mother to foot the gynecologist's bill. At least a dozen coeds said they knew girls whose parents had initiated the acquisition of their daughter's diaphragm. And a University of Texas coed gave a beer bust for her closest girl friends to celebrate the mail delivery of her new "heat shield."

Even these girls are wary of seeming too wise. "You know how square most college boys are," a chubby Berkeley sophomore remarked. "If you appear too knowing, they get the wrong idea—they figure you must be some sort of campus punchboard." Most of the boys I spoke to seemed rather cavalier about contraception. The staunchly double-standard Joe College who recognizes no middle ground between virgin and tramp was quite unconcerned about the possibility of pregnancy. "I figure if she's that kind of girl," a University of Houston junior said, "she will have her own protection, and if not, that's her problem."

"If she becomes pregnant, it could be your problem, too," I suggested.

"Not when my five friends here get finished testifying how they laid her too," he said.

Other college men, partly from compassion, mostly from a passion for self-preservation, take the opposite tack. "I just don't go to bed without a condom," a Middlebury (Vt.) youth said. "I just know if some girl calls and says, 'Mike, I think I'm pregnant,' I could never be a bastard and say, 'Oh, really, whose do you think it is?' I know I'd take the responsibility and wind up paying the doctor bills."

This sort of caution was interpreted by a Temple University junior as more of an insult than a compliment. "My boyfriend won't listen when I say it's safe," she complained. "He uses one of those things every time. If he loved me better he wouldn't worry so about my getting pregnant." Her analysis is sharply contradicted by the findings of the University of Oregon's Lester A. Kirkendall, the sociologist who attempts to set up a value system for judging boy-girl relationships.* At the highest degrees of attachment, boys were most likely to willingly assume responsibility and to protect the girl from any unfavorable consequences of their relationship—gossip, possible pregnancy, and guilt. With pickups and girls dated "strictly with sex in mind," boys were apt to be rather lackadaisical about contraception. "She said 'It's up to you,'" one boy reported of the girl's response on the subject of a condom. He used none. "If she had got pregnant, I wouldn't have married her and she wouldn't have expected it." "If she wasn't going to make a point of it," another youth remarked, "I certainly wasn't. It was for her, not me." A recent Vanderbilt graduate, a Nashville deb, was highly cynical about this

* *Premarital Intercourse and Interpersonal Relationships, op. cit.*

kind of attitude. Girls who intend to leave the birth control question up to their bed partners "should date only Boy Scouts," she said. "Because Boy Scouts are supposed to 'Be Prepared.' But I've heard my brothers talking and it frightens me how callous boys can be."

The new birth control pills seem to have had little impact on campus sexuality. The pill that would prevent ovulation and make pregnancy impossible has been described as the ultimate weapon in "the moral disarmament of Betty Coed." Writer Gloria Steinem, an alumna of Smith, suggests * that girls "can afford to view affairs as a natural part of their development because science has removed the physical consequences of sex." But as Ellen Willis,** then a college student herself, reported in *Mademoiselle Magazine,* and as my own interviews corroborated, fear of pregnancy has never been a major factor in keeping girls from premarital affairs. Tabulating the results of questionnaires sent to college girls across the country, Miss Willis concluded: Oral contraceptives would have no effect on the idealism ("as distinct from morality and fear") that influences many college students. Many girls told Miss Willis they thought ethics would change but not their own behavior. "Premarital relations are immoral because of the possible consequences of having a child without being able to give it a normal home and maybe being a financial burden to relatives or the state," a Wellesley girl commented. "But with 100 percent birth control, you are not running the risk of hurting anyone by your behavior; therefore it is not immoral. Still, such a pill would not alter my conduct, because my upbringing is too much a part of me." "My attitude would not change," a Mississippi student wrote. "But many people don't have moral principles strong enough to overcome the temptation that safety will offer." Just looking at words typed on a mimeographed questionnaire, however, fails to provide total insight into the mind of a girl who says, "Not me. But everyone else, maybe."

"The Pill" is very much a topic of discussion, debate, and

* "The Moral Disarmament of Betty Coed," *op. cit.*
** "The Birth Control Pill," by Ellen Willis. *Mademoiselle Magazine,* January, 1961.

curiosity among college girls. No single contraceptive agent has ever received the kind of attention in the mass magazines, and certainly Dr. John Rock's *The Time Has Come* (a Catholic doctor's personal comment and challenge to the traditional birth control teachings of the Roman Catholic Church) will have considerable impact on college-age Catholics. The collegiate passion for scientific inquiry, collegiate distaste for calm and unquestioning acceptance of absolutes tend to transform many once-docile followers of all faiths into campus agnostics. It may be only a temporary transformation. No one age group has a priority on far-fetched rationalization to justify behavior. But a Harvard professor seemed to be particularly struck with the remarks of a Catholic Cliffie. "I have to use birth control now because after I'm married, my religion does not permit me to," she told him. A Sarah Lawrence junior said many girls, "even Roman Catholics," were interested in the contraceptive pills, but no one she knew had used them. Several girls mentioned fear of "playing around with hormones" or said, "My doctor isn't convinced about the safety." Only one girl, a recent graduate of Oberlin, said she had taken Enovid. She quit because of uncomfortable side effects. A New York University coed said a pharmacy student dating one of her friends had given the girl pills "for a whole month before they went to bed." And a San Diego State University sophomore responded, "Pills, oh yes. Guys will get you pills. 'Here, dear, a Valentine present. Take one a day,'" she giggled.

But the sweeping sex revolution the contraceptive pill was supposed to trigger has yet to make itself felt. Educators and scientists who suggested the campus was the spot most logical for this radical shift in sexual mores neglected to take into account the illogic, the myth, the superstition, and the emotional blind alleys that influence sexual behavior. Attitudes toward contraception, as expressed by the college girls in this study, provide striking evidence of this illogic. Denial of honest and complex sex education does not seem to be the answer. Obviously lack of information has not kept many college students from premarital affairs. Sex education at its best, and it is rarely available "at its best," would provide not only the technical information to prevent the disaster of premarital pregnancy. Ideally it would inspire youth to consider sexual behavior in terms of self-interest and to recognize patterns of self-destruction. The college girl who bemoans the possibility of becoming pregnant often seems to be fighting two adversaries at once: biology and herself. Again and again she offers herself as the amiable target of that which she professes to fear most. Her worst fears are realized more often than available statistics can possibly reveal.

I Myself Get Kind of Sad

"Doctors here won't give pills or diaphragms, you know, until they've seen the marriage license, and some hesitate even then. One doctor told me not until I was married would she give me anything because doctors don't encourage promiscuity. The majority of girls think, 'Oh, it can't happen to me.' I did. But you see, there was a doctor who told me I *couldn't* get pregnant and well—as you can see. . . ."

She is small, brunette, vivacious, matter-of-fact, and pregnant. She is a junior at a Western state university, daughter of a professor, wife of a pre-med student two years her junior. Living at home until her recent marriage cut her off from most campus activities. Or rather, it seems she always cut herself off. Her friends, she says, are older women, more town than gown. In their company she may have cast off certain layers of naivete but not the all too common conception mystique of it-can't-happen-to-me.

"You can't afford to be too narrow with this new trend of thinking about sex and morals. So many things used to be taboo and now everyone is so casual about it. No one is shocked over abortion or living in a man's place unmarried or having a baby without a husband or having a baby two months after marriage.

"I myself get kind of sad when I realize how blasé I've become and how nothing can shock me anymore—I met a little girl over at the Catholic instruction class who had been raped and was here to have her baby. She was so naive and innocent and it was such a tragic thing for her to go through. But I wasn't too shocked. After my affair nothing shocked me anymore. And I could only feel sorry for girls because I remembered how innocent I was and now . . .

"When I was a freshman I dated my English professor. You know it's funny. The girls who get involved with professors are usually freshman and usually virgins, and the professors are older, established men, not just young instructors. We both liked opera and that's how it got started. I never had a thought of an affair because keeping my virginity was very important to me.

"I had even quit dating my freshman year because I had so much of that in high school and I wanted to make good in college, and I didn't want to risk getting too involved with anyone because I'm pretty passionate and I was afraid I might give in—

"But this backfired on me because I got so lonely, and my professor and I began to see each other constantly and he told me he loved me. I know I didn't love him then, but when he said it I felt I ought to reciprocate but I didn't expect anymore to come of it. He had the most beautiful wife, but she was cold sexually. At the time I thought his and my love was so perfect, and I never realized the reality of what I was doing.

"After five months we made love, and then we did it all the time. Now I realize he was starved for affection and sex— Don't get me wrong. The odd part was I really became fond of his wife and began to see her side of the picture and how they had lost their chance to communicate and how difficult he was—he wouldn't even give her a chance. He went to Europe, and I fell in love with someone else and never saw him again, but I had a breakdown over my loss of virginity, and it was a long time before I could feel physically toward a man.

"Oh, I forgot to say. This professor introduced me to a boy he wanted me to date so things would look right, and this boy and I became the closest of friends. Later he went to Europe with the Professor and his wife, and when he came back I told him the whole story. The professor tried to start the relationship up again, but this boy said if I ever did, he'd blow the whole thing wide open, and he told me some of the pro-

SEX AND THE COLLEGE GIRL

fessor's activities in Europe, which made me know that he
was somewhat perverted. This really destroyed me because
my eyes were opened to how sordid the affair was. This boy
stood by me the whole time and helped me reorientate myself and have a normal outlook on life.

"Two years ago I became engaged to a boy who was away
at school. We set a definite wedding date and were all ready
to get married, but then we got scared and we didn't. He
came home last Thanksgiving and we made up. That was
when I got pregnant.

"By the time I found out, for sure I mean, the boy was
back at school again. But there was another boy, Perry, I'd
become very attached to. He knew my whole story and he knew
I was afraid I was pregnant. So he took me to a doctor, and
when we learned I was, he asked me to marry him.

"But I felt I should try to marry the father of my baby even
though I no longer wanted to. Being pregnant had changed
my whole outlook. Looking at the situation coldly, I didn't
think that this boy could care for me and a child. I didn't
think we could make a good marriage.

"I want this baby and I want desperately to be and do all
the right things for it, and I knew he just wasn't the boy who
could do it. My folks were insisting I marry even if it meant
leaving him immediately after the wedding. They never had
approved of him. And this really set them against him, but
they said for the child's sake I must give it a name.

"The day I was to leave—we were supposed to elope—
Perry insisted that I marry him and I couldn't bear to leave
him. It was a weepy, hysterical, just awful time. Everybody
was pushing me in another direction. But Perry's folks knew
he loved me and knew my situation and were very sympathetic.
So he asked my folks permission and my folks were delighted
to have him marry me instead of the other boy.

"So then we went down and broke the news to his folks—it
was a terrible time—they were kind, truly, but you see their
son is two years younger than me and an only child, and he
being only 19 they weren't sure what it would do to him. But
when they saw he was determined, they came to see my folks.
They all got together and talked everything over and then
talked to us quite seriously to make sure we were aware of

what we were doing. Then they gave us their consent and have backed us all the way. They even sent us both back to school and plan to get care for us until we're through.

"We had some trouble with the other boy. He wrote everyone I knew trying to get them to convince me to marry him, and he wrote one woman the whole story and she viciously gossiped to some friends of mine, but they shut her up. I told them the story and they said nothing to anyone and are on our side—It's funny. Men forget it takes two to tango and the woman always gets blamed. Women should remember this when they get involved—they must be ready for any kind of blame put on them whether there is a true basis for it or whether it is unfair. It still happens.

"Nothing is fair in the relationship of sex between men and women. In the first place, men can enjoy sex more because they can get pleasure from orgasm easily—many women never experience orgasm and many don't even know it exists! It's only when you get a good man who is aware and full of love and who wants you to have happiness too, he will go out of his way for you and he will want you to enjoy the sexual relationship too.

"My husband was a virgin when we were married. But he is a good lover—I used to tease him that he couldn't really be a virgin because he could make love to me several times a night and he could make me have an orgasm, too.

"My husband is a wonderful person and I shall try my hardest for him. He is very ready to accept the baby. It was a long, hectic, and sad thing but my husband and I went through a lot to get married and I think we will stay that way. With real love, the past is of no concern. Only the future."

Does she seem too calm, too matter-of-fact, too resigned to a bizarre and painful situation? Or would numb be a more accurate description? Obviously many of the comments are accurate only as they reveal what she *wants* to believe. If the world is not as she must see it, she might lose her fragile shell of composure, her faith in happy endings.

9

Babies and Abortions

"In March, 1955, Smith College invited Saul Bellow, Alfred Kazin, William Maxwell, and other *literati* to hold a symposium called "The American Novel at Mid-Century" for the benefit of its two thousand lady students. As soon as speeches were over and questions were allowed from the floor, Smith girls got down to the real, burning literary issue of the day, and it dominated the rest of the symposium. The question: 'Was Franny pregnant?'

"It was clear from the debate that followed that author J. D. Salinger, whose short story *Franny* had first appeared in print a month or so before, was a little ahead of the time. Quite a few girls had not caught his hints that Franny was having an affair and were shocked at the idea. The majority was sophisticated enough to recognize the affair but was misled by Franny's faint on the way to the ladies' room. (Who, brought up on Hollywood, could fail to take a faint, any faint, as clear evidence of pregnancy?) Only a handful of Smithies understood that the affair was incidental to the point of the story, that Franny was not pregnant but had fainted from the strain of having, or trying to have, a religious experience." *

What writer Gloria Steinem is getting at in this excerpt from her *Esquire* article, "The Moral Disarmament of Betty Coed," is that all this innocence was "in another time, a different era, which college administrators and other romantics already look back on with nostalgia," an era in which Miss Steinem was herself a Smithie. The Smith girl has caught up with Franny, she believes, and now regards sex as "just another area" in which to "pursue truth and not be a phony." The conclusion is not that American girls faint less because they are pregnant less, but that American girls are merely swooning less. If Franny were of real and not literary flesh, class of '63 for example, she might very well be pregnant. I suspect that those girls who would faint, if they were the fainting type, at Smith today or on any other campus, are more likely to be pregnant than to be straining for religious truth.

There are no recent authoritative figures on college pregnancies. Most college pregnancies end in illegal abortion, making accurate statistics impossible.** Some girls quietly drop out of school without explanation and disappear under a new name to have their babies and surrender them for adoption. No one can pinpoint how many: Unlike the expectant high school girl, relatively few enter maternity homes. If a bride can zip up her wedding gown, no one judges too harshly when the heir arrives six or seven months later. One out of six brides is pregnant before a single grain of rice is thrown, the younger the bride, the higher the odds she may be pregnant.*** But even these statistics include some guesswork in the light of "indisputable evidence," as reported by Purdue's Harold T. Christensen, "that physicians sometimes 'doctor up' birth records to support parents' claim to a 'premature' infant."

Citing what he describes as "rough student estimates," Dr.

* *Esquire Magazine,* September, 1962.
** "Sex: The Problem Colleges Evade," *op. cit.*
*** "Pregnant Brides," by Harold T. Christensen. *Sex Ways—In Fact and Faith: Bases for Christian Family Policy.* N.Y.: Association Press, 1961.

SEX AND THE COLLEGE GIRL

Milton I. Levine, the Cornell pediatrics professor who has expressed great concern over failure of schools to provide frank and thorough contraceptive information,* concludes there are "well over a thousand" unwanted pregnancies among college women each year. But the obvious familiarity with which the girls I interviewed talked about the pregnancies of their schoolmates indicates many may have even more intimate knowledge than they admit. Dr. Levine's estimate thus seems highly conservative. Equally unrealistic (one hopes) was the figure of 400 pregnancies annually among 6,000 Syracuse University coeds, advanced in a student-written expose that appeared last spring in *Sword of Damocles,* an off-campus publication that notes it has "on occasion been charged with muckraking and sensationalism." The authors arrived at their pregnancy estimates on the strength of a quote from a social worker at the Syracuse Memorial Hospital who said her office was receiving from three to four cases of unwed, pregnant Syracuse University coeds each year and, according to the article, added: "However, this is probably only about one percent of all of the University pregnancies." Anyone can multiply by 100 without benefit of a college degree, and that apparently is what the authors did. If their method were reliable, we could multiply by the national census of females on campus and come up with 90,000 unwanted pregnancies annually. Whatever the accurate figure, many educators and sociologists are convinced the number is increasing. It need not be 90,000 or 9,000 or even 90 to legitimately concern us.**

* "Sex: The Problem Colleges Evade," *op. cit.*
** "Premarital Pregnancies and Their Outcome," by Cornelia V. Christenson. *Journal of the National Association of Women Deans and Counselors,* January, 1963.

In this article, the author summarizes findings on the 5,293 white, non-prison females of the over 7,000 whose pregnancy records were described in *Pregnancy, Birth and Abortion,* by P. H. Gebhard, W. B. Pomeroy, C. E. Martin, and C. V. Christenson, Harper-Hoeber, 1958. Since the 5,000 women are mostly "drawn from the socio-economic upper 20 percent of the urban white population of our country with emphasis on youth, Protestantism (62% Protestant, 28% Jewish, 10% Catholic) and college education, the data seems especially pertinent to this research on the college girl. "Since the midpoint for the interviews was 1945, the data cannot be considered a current picture, but unfortunately, there is no comparable later survey . . ."

Our public moral posture implies that only "bad" girls become pregnant. But pregnancy pays little attention to public postures. If "bad" implies promiscuity, the posture is equally misleading. Certainly there will be promiscuous females among this year's crop of college girls who will become pregnant as a result of their own ignorance, carelessness, or drive for self-destruction. But consider this varied sampling of last year's unwed expectant mothers, as described or encountered during this research: a small-town doctor's brilliant (I.Q. 142) daughter, for the second time—a member of the Women's Honor Court at a large Eastern State University—a vivacious, pretty freshman, daughter of a prominent churchman—a pre-med student by a fellow pre-med student celebrating the end of exams over grain-alcohol punch—a plain-faced Kansas girl on her first date after her first kiss—a returnee from Junior Year Abroad by "she wasn't sure who"—several contemporary Marjorie Morningstars too concerned with shedding the shackles of middle-class morality to consider the calendar—any number of pinned, lavaliered, engaged to be engaged, and ringed young ladies of all ages, faiths, classes, and ethical traditions, a number of whose pregnancies could be traced to spring or Christmas vacation—a self-styled contraception expert who "remembers reading somewhere that the second ejaculation just doesn't have the fertility potential of the first"—and a sorority house officer on a California campus who didn't think the semen could "get there if you did it standing up."

It might seem that the college infirmary or the university health service would be the last place an anxious girl would go if she suspected she were pregnant. But apparently enough wind up there, complaining of vague and vaguely traditional symptoms, for it to become a joke in some circles—a joke that fails to amuse many college girls. "Mono or pregnancy?"

Twenty-two percent of the girls with from 9 to 12 years of education who were 20 years old and who had had premarital coitus reported premarital conception. The figure for the similar college-educated group was 13 percent by the age of 20. "Slightly over a fifth" of these pregnancies were resolved in marriage, 69% in induced abortion, 6% in the bearing of an illegitimate child, 3% in spontaneous abortion.

is the standard greeting at Health Service, an editor of the (University of) *Michigan Daily* reported (Mononucleosis being a common campus ailment). "Frankly, I wonder if they're equipped to deal with anything else," she added. A rather cynical virgin, she was not amused either by the humor or the phenomenon that had inspired it. A recent University of California at Santa Barbara graduate recalled how furious she was when a doctor responded to her complaints of dizziness and nausea with one word: "Pregnant?" "He didn't even look at me first, and what really made me angry was I hadn't had a date in six months."

A staff doctor at one university health service reportedly took care to reassure a tearful coed after delivering the dreaded verdict. "You're not alone," he told her. "This happens to 15 or 20 girls a day. (It wasn't clear whether he meant on that campus or throughout the nation.) I don't know what you plan to do," he went on, "but I just want you to be aware that once an abortion has been performed, if anything should go wrong, no doctor may refuse to treat you."

From the moment the confirmation of pregnancy is made, a tense drama begins. What to do? Who to tell? Is marriage the answer? Abortion? Do I want to have this baby? Could I raise it on my own? Am I willing to give up college? Should I—must I—dare I go to my parents for help? To him? She may sleep through morning classes and let term papers go neglected, or she may throw herself into school work with unaccustomed vigor. She may lock herself in her room, lifting and dropping heavy furniture, leaping off the upper bunk, creeping down the hall after hours to the pay phone to make long, painful, weeping phone calls in the smoke-thick booth—sometimes to The Man.

What about the unexpectant expectant father? A graduate student involved in the hysteria of half a dozen pregnancies in her role as a dormitory house mother at Brandeis observed: "Often it seems to me the boys were far more concerned than the girls." But many girls are shocked and converted to premature cynicism by the chilling response of a boy who turns away from what the girl thought was their common predicament, "revealing," said a Rochester (N.Y.) junior, "as he

heads for the door, that white stripe down his cowardly back."
"Well, what do you want from me?" the Northwestern coed
was asked by the indignant, indifferent young man she had
simply assumed would be eager to marry. "How do I know
it's even mine?" a Louisiana State athlete said to the tearful
coed at the other end of the long-distance line. A Boston University graduate told how her Harvard beau had said, "We'll
get married, if you want to." "His face looked like he'd just
agreed to be a pallbearer at his own funeral," she said. "I
wasn't what his family had in mind or him either—I guess. I
let myself fool myself. So I wrote him a note saying something
like 'I'm not marrying martyrs this year—just put a blank
check in an envelope or whatever heels like you do.' I couldn't
resist that 'heel.' He paid for everything. He even gave me a
little ruby pin that was supposedly his grandmother's and said
he was sorry. Maybe it was his grandmother's. Who knows?"
She shrugged.

What about parents? Is it wise to tell them? Is it right to
tell them? Most of the girls asked felt they would try to avoid
"bringing my family heartbreak"—"getting them involved in
something they could never understand"—"flaunting my behavior in their faces." "It would only be cruel"—"My mother
would die if she thought . . ."—"I would try to avoid going
to my dad." "Only as a last desperate resort if the boy walked
out"—"only if there was no other way to raise the money."

"That's what's immoral about pregnancy," a recent Oberlin
graduate pointed out. "So many people have to get hurt."
"My mother would disown me," a Brooklyn College coed said.
A 22-year-old veteran of "sleeping around," a Barnard graduate, was certain her mother "would never believe it. If I
walked into the house with a baby in my arms looking just
like me, she'd say, 'You picked it up on the street.' "

Several girls announced with evident pride that their parents would want to know, would want to help. "My mother
told me, of course, she would be upset," a Pembroke junior
said. "But she would want me to come to her first if anything
should happen because she would know where to go and how
to handle it." A doctor's daughter said her dad had instructed
her, "You can bring one bundle home but no more." "He said

it flip but he meant you can be forgiven for a mistake once, not twice." A pharmacist's daughter said her father had mentioned he would be able to help her "with some sort of pill or shot, I guess"—if anything happened.

Some coeds spoke of the hurt-potential in bringing home the problem of a pregnancy, and a University of Miami sophomore said: "I would want to be a big girl about it and handle it on my own, but I have a feeling that I would forget all about being brave and noble and run right home bawling for help."

That is what most pregnant college girls apparently do. That is what most of the girls who admitted pregnancies or described those of friends did. "Her parents arranged for an abortion in Puerto Rico," a Sarah Lawrence girl said. "Mother was devastated," a Vanderbilt coed recalled, "but she was glad I came to her, and if I dared ever let my dad know, she'd never forgive me." "Mothers can stand it better," several girls said. "Fathers have to be protected." In many cases, mothers whose daughters predicted "She'll have a heart attack" (interestingly, they told her anyway) often showed far more sympathy and strength than expected. But some who sought comfort and support encountered shattering anger. The mother of a Long Island college girl reported her daughter's condition to the police. "After an hour's intensive grilling on possible abortion contacts, the police tried to bully the pregnant girl into signing a rape complaint against the prospective father, a man with whom she was deeply in love."* An Illinois coed came home from college to be married at a big garden party wedding, but when she confessed her pregnancy, her mother promptly cancelled the formal ceremony and was so vehement about not attending even the small informal wedding "if you have the audacity to wear white," the bride became hysterical. Glassy-eyed and tranquillized, she was wed in a beige wool suit.

Such unyielding devotion to the tradition of bridal chastity among mothers of today is exceedingly rare. "The college," writes anthropologist Margaret Mead, "has turned from a

* "Mothers Without Joy," by Jonathan Rinehart. *Saturday Evening Post*, March 23, 1963.

place where girls were protected from pregnancy to a place where pregnancy—if it ends in marriage—is not penalized, but rather, rewarded. The college, in effect, helps the girl to get her man."* The dean of women may even officiate as a sort of matchmaker, too aggressively, some coeds report.

Pregnancy has become a legitimate "social shotgun." To quote Miss Mead again: "We have slipped into a position of accepting the idea that the most important thing in the world is to get young people, boys and girls, married. Premarital sex and premarital conception, as a means to an end, have become acceptable. . . . What we are dealing with today is not a pregnant girl, but a pregnant couple, effectively blackmailing a society . . ."

It seems to me that as recently as seven years ago there was still something of a stigma attached to the hasty wedding, but college girls today are mostly matter-of-fact about "instant motherhood." "Who doesn't know at least one girl who quit school to marry and had a 10-lb. premature baby like maybe six months later?" said a plump Kent University junior.

The gossips still gossip. And the bride's mother may be a bit embarrassed to find herself a grandmother-to-be and a mother-in-law all in one harrowing week. A few seams may be let out of the wedding gown and Lohengrin echoes through sacred halls. No one would dream of halting the ceremony to cry "hypocrisy." It is pure Twentieth Century Americana.

There is a school of thought, popular in some college circles, that no premarital pregnancy is strictly an accident. Unless a girl is "outrageously naive and sheltered," as a Sarah Lawrence sophomore put it, "you figure that consciously or unconsciously she *wanted* to get pregnant." In some cases there may well be a deep psychological craving for motherhood. And in many campus pregnancy stories, one detects a feeling of guilt relieved by punishment—the punishment of pregnancy. But often the wish is not at all unconscious. Some coeds are quite frank in confessing that they have used their biological potential as just another weapon in the arsenal of the husband hunt. A recent Endicott (Boston) graduate told

* "Sex on the Campus: The Real Issue," by Margaret Mead. *Redbook Magazine*, October, 1962.

of a friend, frustrated by her parents' veto of her chosen mate, who managed to get pregnant, and walked majesically down the aisle three months later. "What could her parents say?" the Endicott informant asked. "I planned it," a pregnant freshman confessed to her wide-eyed, now a little wider-eyed roommate, as she prepared to leave Bennington, only a week or so after the beginning of the fall semester, for home and the wedding. "I don't think my parents will have any more nasty remarks to make about Freddy," a Wisconsin sophomore confided to her dormmates, "now that he *has* to marry me."

A Vanderbilt University professor tells of being greeted by a coed who bounced into his office and announced happily, "Well, Dr. L., I think I'm pregnant." Hoping that a touch of wry humor would suit the occasion, he replied, "Well, should I congratulate you?" "Of course," she cried. "Dr. L., I think I've got him now." A few days later when the girl slipped into his office, this time downcast and red-eyed, she said: "Oh, doctor, it's just no good." "What's the matter?" the professor asked. "Won't Henry marry you?" "Hell no," she said. "It's that I'm not pregnant after all. Damn."

Possibly only a few campus pregnancies are this calculated. But others are open to suspicion. Certainly many college girls regard marriage as a pretty, moonlight, orange-blossom, and happy-ending solution to premarital conception. "He didn't want to marry her," said a Swarthmore sophomore describing a classmate's pregnancy, "but he finally came around and it's just great. They have the sweetest little girl."

Of course, many hasty, forced marriages *do* survive and thrive. Though even where there is love and a sincere prior commitment for the future, there are problems created by the biological pressure. Too many responsibilities too soon. Education threatened, possibly ended. Too many adjustments in too short a time. A Hollins College girl, describing her older sister's hasty marriage, said: "They really are extremely happy now—the only complication is celebrating two birthdays for the baby—the actual birthday and then a later one to keep the great-grandmothers from being upset."

Several college girls sternly rejected shotgun marriages as "strictly frying pan to fire, an out for babies and fools who let their parents push them around." "Even if I loved him and we were planning to marry later, I would never agree to a hasty marriage," a Stanford sophomore said, and several others made similar comments. (They were divided on whether to have the baby and place it for adoption, or undergo abortion.) "You wind up making so many sacrifices and compromises for the baby you weren't ready for, you wind up hating each other," a Penn State junior said. "You need time to be just two before you start being three," a recent Reed College graduate suggested. A Hunter coed told about her sister, married eight years, in a sanitarium with her third nervous breakdown since the wedding. "They've got three kids now," the girl said, "and he's mad about her, but she's got this idea he married her only because she was pregnant."

The divorce rate for early marriage—and even higher breakup figures for marriages hastened by conception—have alarmed the clergy and triggered a new concept in religious counseling. "Pastors are increasingly unwilling to perform marriages just to 'regularize' an illicit pregnancy," says the Reverend John C. Knott, director of the Family Life Bureau of the National Catholic Welfare Conference. "Rather than push immature youngsters into a marriage that has little chance of success, I would much prefer to let the baby be born illegitimately and placed for adoption." In a 1961 Church of Christ workshop discussion, delegates were urged to be forgiving with couples forced into marriage, while avoiding marriage as the only solution for premarital pregnancy. "What has occurred," Presbyterians warned in a discussion of pregnant brides at their 1962 general assembly, "should be the occasion for a grave self-examination and for serious repentance. A tea party and a bridal shower are not enough." Where the immaturity of one or both partners makes marriage "unwise," the Church "must be prepared to help" the young couple in following the alternative—illegitimate birth and adoption.

Only rarely does the pregnant college girl chose this alternative. The older the unwed mother-to-be, the less likely she is to seek marriage as a solution, the higher the reliance on illegal abortion.* "I'm afraid I'd never have the courage to carry a

* "Premarital Pregnancies and Their Outcome," *op. cit.*

child for nine months and then calmly give it away to someone else," a Sarah Lawrence girl said. "I would want to keep it and that would be a mistake, for the child and for me." "Maternity homes for unwed mothers are for 12-year-olds, kids who can't find any other way," a UCLA coed said. "I think abortion would be far less of a trauma than knowing you have a child growing up—somewhere," said a slender, somber Radcliffe freshman.

One out of 20 babies is born out of wedlock today,* triple the 1940 rate although the total birthrate is up only 25 percent. Few of these will be born to college students. Of all the hundreds of pregnancy accounts offered by our coeds, there was only scattered reference to illegitimate births. One girl interviewed had left a Midwest college to bear an illegitimate child and was raising it herself. Another's life was "ruined," according to her schoolmates, because her father, a state supreme court judge, had refused to let his daughter undergo illegal surgery. Forced to bear the child, she refused to give it up. But it was possible she might not have agreed with the analysis of her friends that her life was thus ruined. A University of Colorado coed quit school and went to Los Angeles to live with an aunt, bear the child, and give it up for adoption. She met and married a Los Angeles man two weeks before entering a maternity ward to deliver. A girl who knew she was pregnant but didn't say so during an interview session, decided against "a quick trip to Tijuana" (the likely spot for an unwed mother, her classmates had agreed at the session) and was planning to move to a nearby small town, pose as a naval wife, and bear the child. A spontaneous abortion changed her plans, she told the coed who gave us the account.

What a girl thinks she might do is not always what she does do. Once marriage has been ruled out, all the alternatives of the predicament she may once have courted so casually seem grim and ugly. Many college girls—including some who have undergone abortion—have no idea what the surgery involves. They only know it means traffic in the medical underworld, back alleys, and risk of death, disability, sterility, and

* Population Reference Bureau

psychic scarring. When the decision is no longer theoretical, she finds herself pushed in the direction of abortion. Her family doctor may himself dictate an address to her. Her parents may urge it as easier to conceal than a full-term pregnancy. The boy may press her to have an abortion as the alternative in which he can least likely become entangled in the future—no blood tests, no paternity suits. After listening to a friend tell about a friend who had an abortion and "it was really nothing," she herself may wish to seize upon the solution that will end the matter swiftly rather than prolong the punishment for several more months.

In certain circles she won't even think twice about seeking an abortion. She has the addresses of two local abortionists in her address book, under "B" for babies (as did one University of Chicago sophomore), or she knows a boy who took his girl to Puerto Rico just last October and he will have his girl write her a long letter with all the details. Addresses and names are passed around. If she hasn't the money, kids will pass a homemade collection box in the student dining room, as they have done at Brandeis, or solicit funds along the dormitory corridors, as was reported by a freshman at the University of Michigan. If she is really cool, she may even have a piggy bank on her dresser, as did a Berkley coed who confided she was "saving for my next abortion."

A patrician rebel from the sheltered exclusivity of Grosse Pointe, Michigan, described the fervor of a fund-raising campaign at the University of Michigan. "We thought it would be a great idea to collect all our old clothes and sell them—so we got together a mountain of stuff and a couple of us drove into Detroit to see what we could get in the pawn shops on Third Avenue. What a blow—they wouldn't give us anything—50 cents for a cashmere cardigan, $2 for a custom tweed jacket. So we decided to sell the stuff to each other. We were having such a fabulous time with the whole glorious adventure, I'm afraid we really lost track of how deathly serious the whole thing was. I mean, here's the girl sitting around weeping and we're having a ball."

Such "team spirit" is rare. Most pregnancies are solitary and desperate. Girls who insist morality has nothing to do with sex may turn away from the pregnant girl, in anger, fear, or disgust, declaring: "Getting caught *is* immoral."

If she goes to her parents, the pregnant coed may discover that legal abortion is available in certain cases—to families with money and influential connections.* But on her own, with only gossip to guide her, she gambles with her life. Abortion, as she may or may not know, is minor surgery—a routine and common procedure performed daily in almost any hospital without complications. As Dr. Alan F. Guttmacher notes, "a therapeutic abortion is a safe procedure—illegal abortions are desperately unsafe," and may (because of the furtive nature in which they must be performed and the questionable qualifications of the beauty operators, manicurists, amateur midwives, phony and actual doctors involved) "cause illness leading to permanent, incurable sterility or even death."**

Riskiest is self-induced abortion, Dr. Guttmacher points out. "Hat pins, knitting needles, splinters of slippery elm, a sharpened goose quill—the methods are legion," he writes "and vary geographically." One coed interviewed told about a dormmate "pinned to a boy she was madly in love with," who tried to abort herself with a hanger. "It didn't work for some reason," the girl said, "and she left school to get married— but to a different boy." A Boston University junior recalled bitterly the case of a friend whose young man told her to use a knitting needle. "She miscarried and almost died. One girl who was there was so furious with that boy, she sent him a bloodstained pillow case with a note that said something like, 'Sleep well, you Bastard!' "

Several girls spoke of a drug supposed to trigger abortion and that they would seek an injection of the drug from a family doctor, but no one knew anyone who had ever done so, successfully or otherwise.

Many girls seemed to have become intimately, emotionally,

* "Abortion—Medical and Social Review," by Alan F. Guttmacher, M.D., from *Sex Ways—In Fact and Faith: Bases for Christian Family Policy* (eds.: Evelyn M. and Sylvanus M. Duvall), Association Press, 1961.

** Vivid in the minds of several coeds were the 1962 headlines reporting the death of a New York coed on the abortionist's table and the doctor's attempt to dispose of her dismembered body before fleeing the country.

involved in the pregnancy experiences of their friends. A recent graduate of Cornell, a campus leader and honor student, told of helping a numbed friend locate "the most competent" abortionist possible. She collected names from sources at half a dozen colleges and her own hometown—"Everyone knows someone," she explained. "Then I set out to New York to interview them. Oh, I had nerve all right. It's easy when you're not the person directly involved." She had five names. "Two didn't even pretend to be doctors—one was a manicurist, one sounded very suspicious. Another address was a terrible neighborhood and I decided to save it for last. The one I chose had an office in a magnificent old town house in Manhattan—furnished in antiques. All very posh. I figured anyone who's been around long enough to collect all those antiques must know what he's doing. His price was $500. That's where she went." A Brandeis house mother said she was threatened with the loss of her job when she refused to reveal the name of a student who had gone to New York that day for illegal surgery after she, the house mother, had tried in vain to set up a legal abortion. "I should never have called the dean of women's office in the first place," the dorm counselor said, "but with all their psychological counselors I thought they could help."

In describing the abortion experiences of friends, several girls told harrowing tales. "I had a friend who died after an abortion," a Barnard graduate offered when someone remarked that abortion was rarely dangerous. "She left the doctor's office, tried to lead a normal life, then infection set in. She didn't want to go to her parents or the school. I was with her when she bled to death. And another girl I know really flipped her lid after an abortion. She came in with a smile on her face and locked herself in her room for days, crying. After that she just wasn't the same. When she saw a baby on the street, she would imagine it was hers. She kept saying how she could hear it crying at night."

Yet the girls who described their *own* experiences with illegal abortion rarely spoke in terms of horror or strong repulsion. They seemed matter-of-fact, at least superficially unaffected, and emphasized the ease, the disparity between the imagined nightmare and the reality, distasteful yet rarely as ugly as anticipated. "I thought the money was the absolutely last thing I'd ever regret," a recent University of Florida graduate said with a smile. "But honestly, it's the only regret I have. It was my summer-in-Europe money. It just wasn't sordid the way everyone wants you to think it will be." "When I look back," a Wisconsin junior said, "I can only remember some worry, but great warmth. I never realized how many friends I had or how much they would do for me." A University of Michigan coed had only one comment: "You'll never guess who paid for mine," she said. "The boy borrowed the money from the University's Office of Student *Affairs*." One girl described a trip to Puerto Rico for surgery as though it had been a glorious adventure. The prospective father, a New York bachelor, took a week off from his ad agency job. She, a Smith College senior, was free for the spring vacation. "It was a clean, modern clinic and the doctor charged only $165," she said. We stayed the rest of the week sunning on the beach and I had to keep reminding myself we were here because I was pregnant. I really should have had the vacation first and saved the abortion for the weekend before we went home. If you've been stupid enough to get yourself into this kind of jam, I can't think of a better way to get out of it," she said.

There are at least one million illegal abortions in the country each year—some set the figures even higher. Psychoanalyst Theodor Reik has written: "A woman going to have an abortion may feel she is going to her own funeral. They feel a part of themselves is about to die." It is difficult to explain the seeming nonchalance of the girls who actually experienced abortion in the light of Reik's analysis. Aren't they even scared? Yes. If you ask that specific question, the girls admit they were frightened, "scared stiff," "petrified" before the operation. But in their relief at escaping physically whole and exposed to a minimum of horror, they forget the fear.*

* "No unfavorable results" were reported in two-thirds of the 220 cases of induced abortions in the Kinsey Institute Study. Physical ill effects were reported by 18 percent (severe physical damage 6.4%; moderate, 7.7%; mild, 4.1%). "With some overlap, since some individuals reported multiple types of consequences, 4% reported unfavorable social consequences . . .

Is it possible to be that unscarred by the experience of an illegal abortion? "A lot depends upon the circumstances of the surgery," according to Harold Greenwald, Manhattan psychoanalayst, "whether or not it is performed by a doctor, the atmosphere of the setting, the support a girl has been given, her knowledge of the actual procedure." Either these girls who seem detached and blase are *so* deeply disturbed by the experience, they cannot concede the horror, or they are truly unscathed, as they claim. It would be impossible without digging deeply into the individual psyches to choose one possibility over another, Dr. Greenwald said. What of the girls for whom abortion was a nightmare, traumatic and lingeringly painful? I cannot say. If there were some among the coeds interviewed, they did not, or could not, speak out.

A Visit to a Shy Abortionist

"Surely, you don't believe college girls get accidently pregnant by accident?"

Four girls, (two Barnard seniors, a recent graduate of Penn State and a wide-eyed freshman home on vacation from Goucher) stopped talking and turned to stare at Annette Marie Thompkins caught by the bitterness in her voice. She paled, leaving two red circles like wind rash on high, fragile cheekbones, the skin stretched taut by the weight of lemon-colored hair in a heavy twist of braid. Twenty-two, skinny, with the lingering nobbiness of an adolescent boy and the beginning veneer of Manhattan-acquired chic, Annette was seven months out of the University of Wisconsin.

"I'll always be sorry I didn't have the courage to go to Radcliffe," she had said earlier. "I was too bright for Wisconsin. I really wasted it. Silly, really—but my friends from home (Kenosha) were going to Wisconsin and I guess I was

---

gossip, family rejection, a loss of friends, having to leave school, and subsequent difficulty in marriage over the abortion. Unfortunate psychological after effects were described by 14% in all . . . the subject was emotionally upset, depressed, nervous or had guilt feelings. Some worried about subsequent sterility in marriage." This fear was not substantiated by the data. No difference in fertility in marriage was shown in comparing two matched groups of women, between 26 and 30, one without abortion, the other with. Cornelia V. Christenson, *op. cit.*

afraid to go away from home and start all over again with strangers."

We had been talking about campus pregnancies.

"I just don't think it's ever an accident," Annette said. "If a rubber breaks—well, granted, that's an accident. But when you're making out like mad and some boy thinks your 'no' means 'maybe' and the next thing you know, you've been had. I don't call that rape—I don't call that an 'accident.' When I think of the girls I know who got pregnant, and all that led up to it—it's as though, consciously or unconsciously, they let it happen."

A heated debate broke out. The young lady from Goucher singed her thumb lighting a cigarette (with one still burning in the ashtray beside her). A few days later I phoned Annette, told her I needed an intelligent account of a college pregnancy, and asked if she would be willing to discuss the experiences of the friends she had referred to.

"What the heck," she said. "I'll tell you about mine."

We spent an evening together and I learned a thousand details of the accident which was not an accident and the mechanics of terminating a pregnancy, but very little about Annette herself. Recalling what must have been a time of panic and strain did not noticeably upset her, although it did inspire a certian amount of contradiction in her remembrance of reactions. She might have been describing a nuisance of no more account than fixing a few traffic tickets. She seemed untouched by the horror or remorse we are assured inevitably accompany abortion. Frank as she was about her pregnancy ("I'd like girls to know it just isn't that shattering."), she had little to say about her promiscuous pursuit of—of what?—of intimacy, tenderness, affection, love? Yet it would appear that this promiscuity was another aspect of the same pattern, hinting at a maze of motivation she was unwilling or unable to reveal.

"When I got pregnant, it was no accident. Oh, at the time it didn't seem like anything else but an accident. The meanest, dirtiest, lowest trick Fate had ever played on me in a lifetime of some pretty low tricks. If you had asked me then why—why does a girl practically get down on her knees and beg for disaster, I wouldn't have known what you were talking about. But since then, I've thought about it a lot—going through my best friends's second abortion just last summer—imagine, twice. That's no accident. It brought things into focus. Behavior patterns.—how we seem to punish ourselves."

"Punishment for what?"

"For going to bed, of course. We like to feel how wholesome and modern sex is—how going to bed with The Man is—ah—right, proper—healthy. Unfortunately, you can take the girl out of Kenosha but you can't take Kenosha you know . . . Something deep down in the back of your head just won't let loose—it's back there bugging you—your insipid little conscience. So then one night when you get mad enough at the world and really down on your folks and you can't stand yourself, you anesthetize yourself with too much gin and fall into bed with some guy, any guy, some animal you don't even know his name and—"

"You didn't know his name?"

"Oh, we were introduced, if that's what you mean. I just can't remember the name offhand at the moment."

"You were introduced and you went to bed?"

She laughed. "Almost. But not exactly. From the beginning? Well, I had broken up with this great huge Teddy Bear of a bastard just before the end of the school year. By broken up I mean it had seemed sweet and beginning to be serious—at least on my part—at which point he sort of disappeared.

"I was so blue about the break-up, I couldn't face Kenosha the whole summer so I decided to stay in Madison and take some courses. Madison is great in the summer. Everyone's so much more relaxed and school doesn't seem particularly real. The second week of the semester I was picked up—so to speak—at a garden party one of the History men threw by the most unlikely man a girl could possibly meet in Madison, Wisconsin. I mean he was strictly Manhattan Ivy League Social Register. One look at him in those custom tailored madras walking shorts, it was plain that he was a tourist in the provinces and I decided to do my best to sort of orient him to the local peasant customs.

"You make him sound impossible."

"Oh no. He was really a warm, charming, bright, likable guy. He'd come to Madison to work with this history prof on some book he was writing and the only problem was he nearly drove me out of my mind. He just wouldn't do the Thing. At first I was flattered. We spent almost every evening together and I kept telling myself, 'Isn't it nice to have a man love you for yourself alone and not your yellow hair.' You know. Then we started going away weekends—to Chicago twice, to little theaters, once to one of those super posh resort places. We would sleep together wherever we went. Once in a while he even slept over at my apartment. (I won't go into how I managed to get away with an apartment—but it's easier in summer.) We would pet like mad and one night when we were swimming—*au naturel,* me, him in his underwear, he got very amorous and for a minute I thought he was going to give in, but he sort of pulled himself back together and swam away—left me hanging there, so to speak, at the end of the pier. Oh, it was insane. Then I thought of all the boys in my life I'd teased and led on and on till they practically jumped out of their skin from agony and I had to laugh. Poetic justice."

"Did you ever ask him about it?"

"Well, at first I figured he just wasn't interested in women. It turned out he was in love and practically engaged to a girl at home and he was being faithful. Very simple. We were supposed to be just good friends. I was so frustrated I was practically climbing the walls. Then one weekend when he was working on the book, there was a wild beach party, and afterwards a bunch of the kids came back to my apartment. There was gin and a slight, sort of quiet, ordinary looking boy, and next thing I knew we were lying on the bed and he was struggling with my bra hooks, and I'm not sure how potted I was because I remember thinking how I ought to say 'excuse me a minute' and go do the diaphragm scene because—and

I was trying to remember what day of the month it was—and I also remember saying, 'oh, what the hell!' "

"Do you mean that you convinced yourself it wasn't a time of the month when you could conceive so you wouldn't have to bother going for the diaphragm, but you really knew?"

"No. Well, in a way, yes. I think I knew it was a very ripe time. Somewhere in my head I knew very well I better drag myself out of there but I just let myself say, 'oh, what the hell!' I'd been late before. There's a sort of panic almost every month, even when there's no reason at all for panic. But this time when my period was late, I knew it wasn't nerves. I was calm at first. Then it hit me—pregnant. It had just been a word. Now I finally was forced to consider all the implications. Time. What to do? Money? Where to go?"

"There wasn't any thought at all of marriage?"

"Marriage? To whom? My writing friend had gone home to marry his fiancee. My strong, silent Teddy Bear stopped by now and then to say hello and drink a beer, but that was definitely over. As for the boy—no name—I never saw him again. I never for a moment considered telling him. I felt it was really none of his business. What happened was my fault. I had the diaphragm. I hadn't bought it just to decorate the medicine chest. I had simply been too lazy, too stupid to use it. As far as I could see, abortion was the only possible solution."

"You never considered having the child and placing it up for adoption?"

"That's for brave girls. Or martyrs. I'm not either, I'm afraid. In fact, I was such a coward, such a rat, I went home to Mama. There was really no reason to. Kids I know had addresses of abortionists. But I guess I wanted to be comforted and babied. Now, of course, I realize, I was actually trying to hurt her. I was saying, 'See! See what you made me do? If you'd been nicer to me I wouldn't have gone out and done this.' "

"And your father?"

"Heaven forbid. Father must be protected. We both agreed on that. My mother cried a lot. So did I. My brother kept sniffing around wanting to know what the hell was the matter.

I looked at myself in the mirror and the loathing was practically three-dimensional. Though I must confess I was sort
of pleased to see what was happening to my bosom—maybe
I only imagined it—I remember even feeling sorry no one was
getting to see them besides me.

"Mother gave me the address of a doctor in Chicago—She
said my Aunt Marie had gone to him the year before because
she thought it was ridiculous to start having more babies at the
age of 44. Then she gave me an envelope with money in it—
saved from her house allowance, she said—and talked my dad
into loaning me the car to drive down to Chicago.

"It was an office in the basement of a big old Victorian
house. Grimy, seedy neighborhood and the receptionist-nurse,
whatever she was, was exactly the sort of person you'd hire if
you were casting the movie. A square, burly redhead with
orange lipstick pointed in a sloppy bow and iridescent finger-
nails. I didn't see the doctor. Just some ordinary looking people
sitting in the reception room—two women alone and a couple.
The nurse called me into her office and asked some questions:
'How many months? How did I know I was really pregnant?
Why didn't I want the baby?' "

"What did you say?"

"I don't know what got into me. But I just couldn't walk in
there without a wedding ring. I realize it was silly. They didn't
care if I had four husbands as long as I had the money. But
I made up this complicated story about how I was married—
I said my name was Margaret Richardson and my husband
was Andrew—and we had still two years of college and
couldn't afford a baby yet. I'm sure she didn't believe a word
I said but the minute I mentioned a husband, she pulled out a
mimeographed form and said he would have to come in and
sign a release for the surgery. I practically had the baby right
there. But I stammered and blushed, and then I said I hadn't
told my husband yet because he'd be furious. And she said,
'It takes two, dearie. So you better tell him and it's $450 in
cash and come back in the morning.' It was really fraught with
Freudian implications, my using that name. It just so happens
Andrew Richardson is the persuasive young man who talked

me out of my virginity my freshman year. I really just gave the name without thinking but on the way back to the hotel it occurred to me that in a way I was obviously blaming Andy for the whole mess I'd gotten myself into. After all, he'd started it, hadn't he? I ought to call him and make him come sign that paper. Instead I called Teddy Bear. He wasn't too keen on the idea of coming along—but he knew Andy and he seemed to get a kick out of the idea of signing Andy's name to the consent papers. I wanted him to rush down and spend the night with me because I was scared. But he said no, he'd take his time and come for me in the morning."

"Were you worried? About the operation?"

"Well, I was sure the police would pick tomorrow morning to raid the place and I lay awake for hours wondering what would happen if they walked in when it was only half-done. I was sure the redhead would want a driver's license or something to prove it was really Andy. But they didn't. Teddy Bear signed the paper, Andrew Richardson. I gave the woman the money. She told him to come back for me at 4—that I'd be sleeping off the anesthetic. He sort of snickered and drove off.

"I never did see the doctor at all. The nurse put me on the table and propped my legs in the stirrups and gave me a shot and—darkness descended. It was incredible. So fast. When I came to I was in bed in a little room, and a maid in a white uniform was asking if I would like some tea."

"How did you feel?"

"Groggy. Angry. Actually, I'd been feeling anger for weeks —anger at my own stupidity, at biology, at fate. They told me to get up. I dressed. There was a sort of dull pain—like menstrual cramps, that's all. And a stain on my slip. They gave me pills for pain and a penicillin shot—that is, the red-head did. I never did see the doctor. She told me not to let my husband near me for six weeks or I'd be back there again before I knew it. 'If you don't get your period within six weeks come back and we'll give you an injection,' she said. That did it. The minute she said that I got the awful thought that nothing had happened—that they had knocked me out and then not done anything. I asked her was she positive it was really all right. She laughed and said, 'I could show you, if you like—' A sensitive creature she was.

"Teddy Bear was late coming back with the car and not particularly appreciative of my emotions when he arrived. The whole thing had been very anticlimactic. I didn't *feel* like anything had happened—but I thought I should. So I sat there brooding. He kept acting like it was nothing. I was furious. I muttered something shatteringly brilliant like, 'It doesn't hurt to be nice.' And he said very cooly it wasn't his fault and he wasn't going to get involved. I said nobody said it was his fault and couldn't he please just pretend for a few miles that he was distantly involved. After that he was more himself—gruff, teasing, gentle."

"What about the summer session? Your classes?"

"I'd only missed one exam and I went back to Madison and made that up. I stayed in a friend's apartment and I was really down. Postpartum depression, they call it. Bad joke."

"There was no physical complications?"

"No." (A long silence)

"I'm sorry. I've kept you too late."

"No. No. I was just thinking. People aren't going to like what I've said. They don't like to think it isn't unbearably sordid and it doesn't haunt you long after. I used to wonder myself—was I some sort of monster because I wasn't more upset about it? I suppose I ought to have felt something. I was sad that Teddy Bear wouldn't start up again. He said I ought to see a psychiatrist. Last fall when it was exactly a year, I thought about it again. I said to myself, 'Shouldn't you sort of be thinking, if I hadn't murdered my baby, it would be one year old today.' That was not only bad mathematics— now that I think of it—it would have been six months, I think—but it just didn't come. The image, I mean. It was never a person to me. I'd asked myself at the time, Is it murder? and I couldn't see that it was, not in any way. But I had to force myself to think about it after a year had passed, to see if it was too much with me. And it didn't make me sad at all. Not sad for it. Just a little sad for me."

10

Now, What Were You Saying, Miss Sarah Blanding?

"Ladies of Vassar and your guests from Harvard and Yale. I would like to say that premarital sex is indecent, immoral, and wrong—and the least you could do is stop while I'm talking to you."

President Sarah Blanding's ultimatum to the young ladies of Vassar had become a part of the repertoire of off-Broadway's irreverent revue, *The Premise*. The point was well taken. Stern moral pronouncements have become little more than background orchestration to the sexual drama of the campus.

For Miss Blanding's off-the-cuff lecture was merely a blunt airing of policy stated in most college rule books. Although such statements are usually couched in the lofty ambiguity of language that fails to stir student ire until policy is spelled out by invoking it—as Cornell did recently in suspending a graduate student who admitted sharing his off-campus apartment with a coed from a nearby nursing school.

Glancing through back issues of *The Daily Californian* (Berkeley), *The Cornell Sun*, *The* (University of) *Michigan Daily*, *The Wisconsin Cardinal*, *The Harvard Crimson*, and a dozen other college newspapers, not overlooking *The Vassar Miscellany News*, reveals that the debate over *in loco parentis* and sex are hardy perennials. Overardent kisses have been forbidden at Long Beach (California) State College and lolling on the greens, or more specifically "uncontrolled public displays of affection," outlawed at the University of Connecticut. Girls at Wisconsin were debating whether lockout (curfew) was a "social crutch" or "a vestige of high school." A *Michigan Daily* editorial writer was calling for "the inalienable right to privacy" and scolding the Administration because, "they, by their narrow suspicions and militant vigilance, are offending the laws of decency far more than any of the moral culprits they seek to restrain." At Berkeley, students were going to ask the Dean of Men to define "illicit cohabitation" but withdrew the request, deciding it might be better to let sleeping dogs lie. And a Vassar journalist pleaded for extension of the hours girls may entertain male visitors in their rooms—in verse:

O grand and glorious Warden, you've no idea how fine
T'would be to have our menfolk within our rooms 'til nine.
Though we'd like to be alone, it will not be immoral,
We simply want to talk, we'll keep it strictly oral.

In the role of policeman, baby sitter, and guardian of female chastity, the colleges have come up with often woolly and wildly varying rules and regulations. Increasingly, as Margaret Mead points out and coeds themselves observe, the college rules seem designed to protect the school from blame rather than the students from any social disaster. *

Many colleges have abandoned once sweeping restrictive codes and seem content with jurisdiction over on-campus be-

* "Sex on the Campus: The Real Issue," *op. cit.*

havior or blatant mischief reflecting directly on the school's reputation. The dean of one coed school in the Midwest tells parents he is sorry but sexual matters that do not directly affect the campus community are not his problem. "When they're off the hill, the hell with them," was how one Wisconsin faculty man expressed his own position. "We're not in the business of building character. I doubt if some of us are qualified. Instead we should be building minds." * In several of the elite women's colleges, where there is a tradition for scholastic fervor or high enthusiasm for the school's philosophical goals—as at Bryn Mawr, Radcliffe, Barnard, Sarah Lawrence, Bennington—social restrictions may be relaxed. From the beginning of their freshman year, Bryn Mawr girls may, if they like, stay out every night until 2 A.M. and go away every weekend. At Bennington, girls need not come home until 6:30 A.M. Strict and demanding academic requirements become an indirect social discipline, limiting potential for the abuse of freedom. "You'd flunk out of here in no time if you tried the 6:30 A.M. bit too many nights in a row," a Bennington sophomore explained. At the same time, student griping about college apron strings is eliminated, and with it any need to break rules just for the principle of anti-maternalism.

For the simple, unavoidable truth is most rules are ignored, overlooked or simply broken, sometimes with righteous indignation. "We feel such rules are an insult to the academic tradition," a Purdue sophomore said. Few girls indicated they felt even the slightest attack of conscience at breaking rules and many get a kick out of flaunting their defiance. Only at schools with what coeds describe as a "true" honor system, was there any respect for the administration regulations. "If

---

* *Campus U.S.A., op. cit.* Wisconsin's "Committee on Living Conditions and Hygiene" continues to tackle rules governing students living in apartment houses—rules, Boroff commented, "that smacked unpleasantly of a police state." A student living in a building into which an unmarried woman moved was required to move out. The rule has been liberalized. Now, if he is a graduate student and over 21, he may stay. Chaperones are no longer required for entertaining guests of the opposite sex in apartments —a rule that was "contemptuously ignored" at Wisconsin as it is everywhere, most recently curfews have been sweepingly liberalized.

the honor system means you turn in your friends, it's not really an honor system," a Pembroke coed said.

Nor is it particularly difficult to break rules against drinking, unchaperoned weekending, automobiles, and the presence of females in the Law Club or above the first floor of the fraternity house. One Michigan graduate student told of having intercourse standing up in the boiler room of a sorority house. And a Bennington girl noted there are no housemothers or chaperones in Williams College fraternities. "When it's curfew, time for girls to leave, some just don't. You hear the giggling for hours." Coeds leaving the DePauw University campus overnight must have a note from their hostess. "One fraternity cleaning lady writes twenty house notes at a clip," a DePauw coed reported. "There's nothing to it," a Smith girl insisted, "if you can't get home by sign-in time, you just sign out for overnight." Harvard allows women in the Houses 44 hours a week. When Columbia University instituted its slightly open-door policy (girls allowed in the rooms between 2 and 5 P.M. alternate Sundays, doors to be opened the "width of a book"), one student promptly adopted a matchbook standard of measure. The rule is lights on, door open at least six inches at Brown, but Pembroke coeds report: "You get by that with lights on in the bathroom and the *closet* door open six inches." A necktie hanging over a doorknob—from Harvard to Antioch and wherever closed-door privacy is permitted —is a universal language, warning: Keep out. Male visitors are supposed to sign in at Sarah Lawrence and leave the dorms by midnight, but girls are not surprised to hear masculine voices or run into a man coming out of the shower in the early hours of the morning.

Abolishing privacy is a hopeless task as long as there are cities, motels, and woodland retreats nearby. But it can and does have an effect on campus courtship. "You change your concept of what may properly be done without privacy," an Oberlin girl said. Dormitory and house councils strive to maintain decorum in student lounges, requiring, for example, "four feet on the floor at all times" or, a University of Rochester dorm's homey variation, "at least three feet on the

floor." That they are often less than successful—aesthetically
—is suggested by students dubbing the lounges "passion pits,"
"the snake pit," "the zoo," and "the make-out room."

The "Lockout" scene—the *en masse* final embracing before
curfew in the women's dormitories—is regarded by most coeds
as a grim and unaesthetic, but essential, feature of campus
romance. A Wisconsin student editorial decried "the immorality of mass passion." And a recent University of Michigan
graduate swears he witnessed a couple engaged in "the ultimate
intimacy" under a blanket in the shadows just beyond the
brilliance of Alice Lloyd Hall near midnight—certainly the
ultimate adaptation to lack of privacy.

Students suggest that the mass "make-out" scene is the last
desperate resort of couples who do not have—or do not seek
—real privacy elsewhere. "When a guy sort of gives a girl a
quick peck on the cheek and nothing else, you figure he's just
a good buddy or they've just come from a nice warm bed in a
nice warm apartment," a Northwestern senior explained.

Opposition in the battle over the University's proper role
in a student's private life is by no means clear-cut. Many
girls welcome curfews and chaperonage—"to protect you from
yourself, I guess," as a Hollins freshman put it. "Goucher
protects us here but nobody cares what happens to us on a
Princeton weekend," a Goucher girl complained to her mother,
"For a sheltered girl, the first exposure to an Ivy League weekend can be quite a shock," a Vanderbilt junior recalled. "I
walked into this Princeton house party. There in one corner of
the floor were a boy and girl making love—and in another
corner, a boy and a boy. Talk about coming of age in Samoa!"
Radcliffe's liberalization of social restrictions stirred loud
protest, much of it coming from the reputedly Brahmin-deb
confines of Briggs Hall. "Of course, we are supposed to be
adults and should be able to take care of ourselves," a Briggs
junior conceded, "but not all of us can." Support for this
position came from Harvard's Social Relations department in
the concern of Prof. George W. Goethals: "Some of our girls
have led pretty sheltered lives," he pointed out, "and they
are still trying to answer questions other girls may have an-

swered at 14. Sexual arousal in girls follows a much more quixotic pattern than with boys. Boys have been coping with sexual drive for some time but most girls don't run into the problem until much later, when it occurs in circumstances where they don't have control. There can be some pretty devastating consequences. I wouldn't like to see anyone panicked into bed."

No one would disagree with Dr. Goethals' thesis: "A girl must have the right to say 'no' as well as 'yes.' " But not even the toughest restrictive codes guarantee the right. There seems to be a sharp dichotomy between the college that is a playpen for adolescents, or to quote Boroff, "the idea that the college years should be a kind of moratorium . . . before the encroachment of adult responsibility," * and the college education that represents a transition to adulthood. I wonder which concept emerged first: The student's idea of college as a four-year vacation from responsibility or society's faith that irresponsible youth must be shielded from realities of adult life? We grow up thinking of college as a time for football, panty raids, pushing beds down a highway, serenades at midnight, and plush pandas on bunk beds, and we offer ourselves to society as models of the image they seem to have molded for us. Where schools demand more of students, students give more. In his calm and reasoned questioning of a Cornell policy in suspending a graduate student for an off-campus affair, Max Lerner makes an essential point: "The faculty does have a moral role to play in the life of the student far more important than any disciplinary role it may have. I mean the image of a man which the teacher projects, not only in his teaching but in his thinking and living . . . In an open society, where the professors have a tolerable degree of maturity, their aim should be to help the student achieve some maturity, too."

Lerner specifically excepted "Vassar turtledoves" from his commentary. But it seems to me it follows from his thesis that undergraduates and "turtledoves" need not be "squeezed dry of all intellectual color" either. There must be some attempt

* "The Case for 'The Asphalt Campus,' " by David Boroff. *The New York Times Magazine*, April 21, 1963.

to distinguish between the need for supervision of a panic-prone freshman of 17 and the need for autonomy of the responsible and maturing sophomore and junior. How can we defend the kind of half-hearted hit-and-miss discipline that leads to Pembroke girls being suspended and Brown boys being merely scolded, when all of them are found together partying in a motel?

Lerner asks, "If a young man who has been through college and is in the last stages of preparing himself for life cannot be trusted to make his own personal decisions, then how will he ever learn to form his own intellectual judgments? If he isn't allowed to organize his own life off-campus, what chance has he of doing his own thinking, away from textbooks and lectures?" * But does it make sense to wait till "the last stages of preparing for life?" The transition from playpen mentality to adult responsibility dare not be postponed until commencement day.

Dropping the restrictive reins altogether or pulling them tighter is not going to solve all the problems of sex on the campus. Sex is not a problem. But the abuse and misuse of sex creates genuine tragedy that college deans and counselors have finally warned us we can no longer ignore. Pregnancy, illegitimacy, early marriage and forced marriage, abortion, and venereal disease—the reality middle-class girls don't seem ever to worry about—are only the most readily identifiable symptoms of the ignorance, pretense, anxiety, hostility, and self-destruction revealed in the confidences of the American college girl. A boy and girl go to bed because they have nothing much to talk about. A young man and his fiancee decide they must determine their sexual compatability before marriage but are unable to meet sexually unless, in her words, "We're both absolutely blotto." A Barnard girl says, "I never wanted to be promiscuous but now I find it almost impossible *not* to sleep with any boy I like more than casually—and it means very little to me—I don't feel guilty, but I can't say I'm happy either." These are not "believers in the unbelievable sweetness

* "Cornell Story," by Max Lerner. *The New York Post,* October 15, 1962.

of sex love." Nor are they the healthy, mature, and idealistic young lovers they claim to be.

The pressing need for sex education is obvious. Educators agree most sex education efforts fail miserably. Often lectures are conducted in a tense and punitive atmosphere. Many marriage and family texts occupy themselves with facts that tend to uphold conventional morality to the neglect of evidence that might lend the spirit of scientific inquiry to their lessons. Even some of the most thorough courses in the biology of reproduction scrupulously avoid any reference to contraception; Cornell pediatrician Milton Levine reports, "because of pressure from outside groups" and the fear that "merely mentioning the words, 'birth control,' would tarnish the good name of their college." * Yet much of the leadership in sex education is coming from religious groups. The National Council of Churches has "done much to foster sex education classes and counseling in both churches and colleges."

But as anthropologist Ashley Montagu warns, " . . . sex education—and also the cultivation of judgment on sex—is not something that can be taken up all of a sudden and disposed of neatly at college, like a course in calculus or Greek literature." ** Dr. Mary S. Calderone, Vassar '25, and director of the Planned Parenthood Association recently urged that sex education start in elementary school when "emotional connotation and reaction is at its lowest." Addressing public health doctors and nurses at a workshop on sex education, Dr. Calderone said, "It seems incredible . . . that we are unwilling to ground our children in the basic facts that man at all ages has a sexual drive that must be accepted, understood and welcomed in order to be controlled." For parents who worry that sex education for grade school children might force knowledge on youngsters before they need or want it, there is an important message in a report by Prof. Thomas Poffenberger of questions eighth grade girls submitted in writing to their teacher before a scheduled sex lecture. "What happens when you're seduced?" "What do you do on your wedding night?"

* "Sex: The Problem Colleges Evade," *op. cit.*
** "Has Chastity a Chance at College?" *op. cit.*

"How do you have intercourse?" "Is it safe for a young girl to have an abortion?" "Does it hurt to have intercourse?" "How do you stop from having a baby after you are pregnant?" "How does a boy rape or fuck you?" "What does fuck mean?" The teacher was shocked, Poffenberger writes, because these girls were from "very nice homes." Why shouldn't they ask these questions, and why shouldn't they be given frank answers? Poffenberger wanted to know.*

Yet some educators protest that school sex-education courses are a too-little-too-late effort to assume responsibility shrugged off by parents. And middle-class parents, who have come a long way in giving their youngsters honest answers to questions about sex, wonder where they have failed. Oregon State's Professor Lester Kirkendall is convinced that youth is totally "alienated from adult contact and influences." **

Most of the girls interviewed seemed to feel they are indeed "on my own" in matters of sexual ethics, although many acknowledge an awareness, and some a lingering loyalty to parental teachings of traditional sex morality. "My parents have contributed their puritanical standards to my values, which were discarded my sophomore year," said a Wellesley virgin, "but they still run around in the back of my mind despite whatever I do." She believed in "everything but" petting. "I appreciate my mother's views," a recent Middlebury College graduate remarked, "and she doesn't know mine." I wouldn't dream of going to Mommy for information on birth control, "or even the basic facts of life for that matter," a University of Maryland coed said. "I probably know more than she does by now." "I can talk about sex to my friends but not to my mother," said a Long Island University girl of 17. "It would embarrass her," she added, "so why should I discuss it—but if I'm in a nasty mood, I'll ask her questions and see her squirm." "I think parents don't want to know what you believe and what you do," said a Sarah Lawrence junior. "We tell our parents wild, shocking stories about other girls. By telling

* "Family Life Education in This Scientific Age," *op. cit.*

** "College Youth and Sexual Confusion," by Lester Kirkendall. *Journal of the National Association of Women's Deans and Counselors,* January, 1963.

them, it's like saying, 'See, I'd never do that' and you reassure them, but you don't talk about the less shocking things you *do* do." "I often wonder how my mother ever had children," a Barnard junior said with a sigh of weariness.

Many girls give their parents so little credit for sexual sophistication—and indeed, any kind of sophistication—they are often surprised when Mama comes up with a sexually aware remark. "My mother came up to me with the most shocking thing," a San Diego State coed remarked. "She said, 'Sexually, the times are changing!' Can you imagine?" A very conservative Minnesota coed told of coming in from a date in tears. "My mother said, 'What's the matter, did a boy put a hand on your breast?' I practically screamed, 'Mother!' And Mom said to me, 'Boy, are *you* a prude.' "

The range of parental concern for sexual needs ranged from the dozen parents who suggested to their daughters that they be fitted for diaphragms before leaving for college to the mother who answered a daughter's sex biology query with a firm, "You'll learn all that you need to know from me on your wedding night."

Many college girls spoke wistfully of wishing sex were a subject they could discuss candidly with their parents. Just as many felt parents should be "protected from the truth" or "not made uncomfortable telling you something they don't really want you to know." Some expressed resentment for misinformation. "Parents lie," a San Diego coed said. "Like when they tell you you're going to get pregnant the first time you do it or your life will be ruined." An Oberlin girl seemed delighted with her father's reminder, "After you squeeze the melon in the market, you always insist on a fresh one."

Many college girls suggested it was unwise for parents to be sexually permissive even if they strongly believed in sexual freedom. "If my mother told me about contraception and diaphragms, it would be like handing me a license," a Smith senior said. "I don't think parents should be put in that position." "Kids don't want parents to be modern," said the lovely, flaxen-haired daughter of a couple who were. "Every child needs an excuse to be good," she said. "Giving them some restraints slows them down. Kids need restrictions because they don't really understand reasoning. You need a higher thing to judge by. You don't have to say it's 'morally right' or 'morally wrong'! You can say, it's 'unwise' or 'safer.' Kids understand that. I shall never forgive my parents for never saying 'no' to me about anything. It all happened too fast. It would have been better if I'd been 18 instead of 16, if I'd had something to rebel against. I just never realized my parents loved me until recently. I used to think, if they really loved me, they'd care what happened." She was a very bitter girl and it seemed sadly ironic to me that her parents had failed her in trying to live up to their own college-formed free love principle. There seemed to be repeated communication breakdown regardless of which camp the two generations stood in.

The potential for disagreement—along traditional lines— was underscored in the findings of a recent questionnaire submitted to 217 Temple University coeds and their mothers. "How important do you think it is that a girl be a virgin when she marries?" was the first question. Of the mothers, 88 percent said it was "very wrong" not to be a virgin, 12 percent, "generally wrong" and none circled "right in many situations," compared to 55, 34, and 13 percent for their daughters. Asked, "Do you think sexual intercourse during engagement is: very wrong, generally wrong, right in many situations?" mothers responded "very wrong" 83 percent, "generally wrong" 15 percent, and "right in many situations" 2 percent, compared to 35, 48, and 17 percent for their daughters. "To minimize the conflict inherent in these findings, many girls avoid discussing sex with their mothers," the Temple investigators noted. Only 37 percent of the daughters compared to 83 percent of the mothers felt girls should freely answer Mother's questions about attitudes toward sexual intimacy. *

If my own experience talking to these girls had not already convinced me that parental warnings and actions pale in significance within the college experience, than the comments of

* "Mother and Daughter Attitudes to Premarital Sexual Behavior," by Robert R. Bell and Jack V. Buerkle. *Marriage and Family Living*, November, 1961.

Prof. Kirkendall would: "Youth and adults are ideologically and sociologically separated from each other." This is what Kirkendall told delegates to the 1961 North American Conference on Church and Family: "In the area of sexual standards we are likely to consider the problem as a youth problem . . . The adults are more of a problem so far as doing anything constructive is concerned . . . Nothing can be done until we as adults face facts in a realistic, frank, and objective way. The average adult is so ashamed of sex, and so fearful of the sexual impulse, that he is hampered and inhibited in any effort to be objective about sex . . . The average adult has lost the capacity to acknowledge his own sexuality openly or refer to his own sexual needs and desires . . . in any serious discussion of sex many adults are profoundly ill at ease." *

Students want help. That's what they're seeking when they huddle together until 4 A.M. in the morning asking each other questions, trying out their own ideas to hear how they sound aloud.

But parents and educators will never bridge the chasm between generations until they have the courage to admit there can be good sex outside of marriage. Good: healthy, proper, wholesome, desirable; all possible interpretations of good, including moral. "Anything that promotes successful interpersonal relations is moral," psychiatrist Walter Stokes has suggested.** Such a redefinition of morality should not be advanced as a norm. A girl should not need to feel that she is abnormal or frigid or immature if she has not known such a relationship. But it should no longer be flatly written off. If adults can only manage this formidable hurdle, they may be ready to enter the dialogue that seeks to define a value framework to judge the quality of sexual behavior.

* *Foundations for Christian Family Policy,* by Elizabeth Steel Genne and William Henry. National Council of the Churches of Christ in the U.S.A., 1961.

** At a "Work Conference on Current Sex Mores Among Young People," Sponsored by Columbia University's Teachers College, July 29–August 9, 1963. Conferees agreed the subject of sex must be discussed openly and frankly on college campuses rather than being kept as a forbidden topic mentioned secretly. The conference, needless to say, was held behind locked doors.

And the dialogue is only now beginning, fitfully, with all the alarm and paralyzing fears Kirkendall has seen in action for thirty years of beseeching adults to contemplate such a value system.

We have yet to hear the final word on masculinity and femininity. We have not yet agreed on what is properly woman's role, what we want from education for young women, what kinds of activity provide the most complete and rewarding fulfillment for the female. We are not content with Freud's definition of sexuality as masculine. We are only beginning to find out what sex means to us. And our concept of love is very young and ever changing.

Many churches and religious leaders have moved from the idea of sex as exclusively procreative to the concept of "wholesome sensuality"—wholesome meaning married. But a persuasive number of professional family counselors and teachers are coming to challenge the conflicts and inadequacies of traditional sex ethics. One of the few college textbooks to explore some of the conflicts is Robert Bell's *Marriage and Family Interaction*. The Temple University sociologist presents the claims and counterclaims of both conservative and liberal camps, which I have arranged in a chart:

CONSERVATIVE ARGUMENT	REBUTTAL
1. Premarital coitus is almost exclusively a physical relationship, with little or no affection and tenderness but primarily promiscuous and lustful.	1. True for some relationships, particularly for the male; clearly not true for all. Studies of sexual relations between those in love and/or engaged show relationships are often emotionally strong.
2. When couples have premarital sexual relationships, they become sex-oriented rather than emotionally person-oriented.	2. Argument fails to see that in many premarital relationships the sexual act is only meaningful within the broader emotional relationships.
3. Breakdown of premarital	3. In some cases true; how-

sex mores has damaged group welfare as evidenced by early marriage, premature parenthood, and early termination of education.

4. Sexual release during adolescence is a need that is overestimated and it could be conditioned—at least to a degree.

5. The sex drive can be channeled in the direction of nonsexual gratification.

6. The prime motivation for marriage is removed when there are no controls to premarital intercourse.

ever, the dangers all center around problems resulting from pregnancy—which could be eliminated by more effective contraception.

4. Sociologically naive in terms of today's society where we develop more and more erotic and sexually stimulating influences to titillate the adolescent. There is a vast body of literature pointing out possible dangers of sexual inhibition through social conditioning.

5. The sex drive generally requires a sexual release and it is very doubtful that the young person in an erotic society can inhibit the sex drive through nonsexual forces. It may be set aside, but the drive is not altered.

6. Premarital intercourse shows an increase over the past five years at the same time as marriage rate soars. This argument assumes individuals got married primarily for sexual gratification.

LIBERAL ARGUMENTS

1. In many relationships of sexual involvement there are deep personal and emotional involvements.

2. It is important that young people be taught to think for

REBUTTAL

1. How many relationships meet all the tests of maturity and each-other centeredness?

2. This argument can probably be best applied to the un-

themselves and it is the responsibility of the adult world to provide them with the necessary knowledge and insight.

3. Adults assume they are wise and know what is best for young people but in reality adults have come up with few prescriptions to deal with the changing sex role of the young person.

4. Traditional position is rife with inconsistencies. Punishment for deviation from adult-created norms is often excessive. Adult reaction frequently determined by degree sexual deviation is known to the community. Excessiveness of punishment for the girl, both psychologically and socially, may have long-range personal implications. Righteously indignant often fail to realize the punishment may be more problem-creating than the deviation.

married who have entered early adult years; can hardly apply to adolescents who lack maturity to make decisions on so complex a matter as premarital coitus.

3. Adults *are* wise. (Dr. Bell has offered no rebuttal to this argument, so I have inserted the original assumption as a possible reply.)

4. (No rebuttal offered, but presumably, conservatives could simply deny the truth of each point.)

Although Dr. Bell points out to his student readers that no moral judgments have been drawn in this attempt to study the arguments "factually and logically," it is clear where his sympathies lie. * And it is also clear that many of the conservative arguments become more difficult to defend. "Fear as a motive is a crutch, a sign of weakness and not of strength,"

* *Marriage and Family Interaction,* by Robert R. Bell. Homewood (Ill.): Dorsey Press, 1963.

Kirkendall has written. "These older social controls must be replaced with individual internalized controls which will stabilize family life and promote personal fulfillment even in the midst of conflict and change." Kirkendall is a cautious and patient man. He has been fighting ostriches, blank stares, and black scare headlines for a long time and he softens what he has to say by asking questions. His first objective is to get those concerned with sexual behavior to concede that differences of opinion exist. His questions to the deans and counselors in the January, 1963, issue of their *National Journal* went like this:

"1. Against what value framework shall judgments about sexual behavior for all age and class levels be made?

a) Should we hold to the belief that increasing freedom in sex is a threat to civilization and that its free use should be restricted in every possible way? b) Should all literature or art which might appeal to prurient interests be banned from circulation or does literature afford a kind of sublimation or diversion which is important for some people? c) How should sex be treated in advertising and in mass media? d) Should we accept orderly dissemination of contraceptive information to all groups, or let it be spread underground? What would be the results of a more open policy? e) Should differential standards be developed, taking into account such factors as age, sex, degree of emotional involvement, and maturity? f) How deeply should we seek to embed sexual behavior in a context of love?

"2. What is the function of sex expression? What is a positive approach?

a) Does some childhood and adolescent sexual functioning have a significance which we have failed to recognize? Should some premarital sexual expression be approved? b) In view of the wide chasm between youth and adults, how can sexual values be discussed and passed on from one generation to another? c) If the double standard is to be resolved should the new standard be nearer the present male or female standard?"

In the frightened and suspicious frame of reference with which we approach sex, we often overlook the real immorali-

ties of heterosexual relationships: the exploitation, the manip-
ulation of male seduction and of the female marriage hunt,
the scheming and calculating abuse of another's weaknesses,
none of which need involve deep physical intimacies to be
truly immoral.

"Whenever a decision or a choice is to be made concerning
behavior," Kirkendall writes, "the moral decision will be the
one which works toward the creation of trust, confidence, and
integrity in relationships. It should increase the capacity of individuals to cooperate and enhance the sense of self-respect
in the individual. Acts which create distrust, suspicion and
misunderstanding, which build barriers and destroy integrity,
are immoral."

In terms of sexual behavior, what Kirkendall is saying is
simply that the relationship that is already a lie will not be
improved by sex; and a good relationship probably will be
able to handle the conflicts of premarital sex, perhaps even be
enhanced by it. But how can we prepare a young girl to stand
back from the dizzying excitement of what feels and looks and
tastes like love and expect her to judge if her relationship
measures up to Kirkendall's standards? How do we immunize
her against fooling herself? How old must one be to have a
good interpersonal relationship? How can we hope to siphon
out the immoralities in heterosexual relationships when they
thrive elsewhere throughout daily existence?

These are the questions yet to be answered. But we can be
optimistic about finding answers if we accept the premise of
Ashley Montagu and other anthropologists that man is by
nature a *social animal,* that man's drive may conflict but
his need to be close to others strengthens his altruistic im-
pulses over those of hostility.

When I listen to the tapes of campus interviews and pore
over my notes and think back to the hundreds of hours spent
listening to college girls talk about themselves in terms of love
and sex and gender, I realize there was a pervading sameness
of theme in many of their voices. With only a few exceptions,
they were asking for answers. In all the popular avoidance of
the words "moral" and "morality," they seemed to be seek-

ing a morality that would mean something, that would be logical, that might in many cases help them to stop disliking themselves. And I grow more impressed as I think back to the calm and secure sex ethic that a particular self-respecting Midwestern girl described and explained: "My father is a warm and lovable and passionate man," she began, "and what he has told me over the years has formed my ideas about sex. I remember his telling me, during the summer of my sophomore year, that next to love, sex is the highest kind of ecstasy you can ever know. He said people get too messed up about it —and it's just too precious to mess around with. He said if you hold too much to one side, you are frigid and too much to the other, you're loose. He said he respected my judgment and he hoped I would fall in love, and that I must never think just because I had been in love once and gone to bed was any reason you had to fall into bed with the next boy. He said you couldn't go wrong if you really tried never to hurt anyone, but the most important person not to hurt was yourself."

It was probably not the message of any single summer afternoon. It was undoubtedly a lifetime of stated and unstated messages. But her manner, her confidence, her obvious joy in life and herself, and all that I learned about her sexual behavior was convincing evidence that sex can and must be judged, as Kirkendall believes, "in the context of meaningful living."

If adults have the insight, tolerance, intelligence, and optimism to concede the collapse of fear as a sexual control and the need for a new moral orientation, they will be answering not only the desperate needs of youth but pointing to a new direction for adults themselves. Such an orientation must provide both a convincing argument against exploitive, destructive sex and a respect for the immense potential of fulfillment possible in joyous and responsible sex that builds both a relationship and the self.

BIBLIOGRAPHY

American Social Health Association: "Research in Adolescent Behavior," December, 1959.

Aronowitz, Alfred G. "The Cornell Affair," *The New York Post*, Oct. 16, 1962.

Aronson, Harvey. "The College Student and Sex," *Newsday*, May 27–29, 1963.

Attwood, William, George B. Leonard, Jr., and Robert J. Moskin. "The Decline of the American Male," *Look Magazine*, 1958.

Baumgartner, Dr. Leona. "What Parents Must Know about Teenagers and V.D.," *McCalls Magazine*, January, 1963.

Beauvoir, Simone de. *The Second Sex*. N.Y.: Alfred A. Knopf, Inc., 1953.

Bell, Robert R. *Marriage and Family Interaction*. Hopewell (Ill.): Dorsey Press, 1963.

————, and Leonard Blumberg. "Courtship Intimacy and Religious Background," *Marriage and Family Living*, November, 1959.

————, and Leonard Blumberg. "Courtship Stages and Intimacy Attitudes," *Family Life Coordinator*, March, 1960.

————, and Jack V. Buerkle. "Mother and Daughter Attitudes to Premarital Sexual Behavior," *Marriage and Family Living*, November, 1961.

Bester, Alfred. "The University of Pennsylvania," *Holiday Magazine*, November, 1962.

Bettelheim, Bruno. "Growing Up Female," *Harper's Magazine*, October, 1962.

Binder, Pearl, *Muffs and Morals*. N.Y.: William Morrow & Co., 1955.

Binger, Dr. Carl. "The Pressures on College Girls Today," *Atlantic Monthly*, February, 1961.

Blaine, Graham B., Jr., and Charles C. McArthur (eds.). *Emotional Problems of the Student*. N.Y.: Appleton-Century-Crofts, Inc., 1961.

BIBLIOGRAPHY

Blanding, Sarah Gibson. "The Day I Spoke Off the Cuff to the Girls of Vassar," *McCalls Magazine,* November, 1962.

Blood, Robert O. "Romance and Premarital Intercourse—Incompatibles?," *Marriage and Family Living,* May, 1952.

Bocca, Geoffrey. "Those Student Tours to Europe," *McCalls Magazine,* July, 1963.

Boroff, David. *Campus U.S.A.* N.Y.: Harper & Brothers, 1961.

————. "Sex: The Quiet Revolution," *Esquire Magazine,* July, 1962.

————. "Showdown on Fraternity Row," *The New York Times Magazine,* November 11, 1962.

————. "The Case for the Asphalt Campus," *The New York Times Magazine,* April 21, 1963.

Bromley, Dorothy D., and Florence H. Britten. *Youth and Sex: A Study of 1,300 College Students.* N.Y.: Harper & Brothers, 1938.

Brown, Norman O. *Life Against Death, The Psychoanalytical Meaning of History.* Middletown (Conn.): Wesleyan University Press, 1959.

Burchinal, Lee G. "Adolescent Role Deprivation and High School Age Marriage," *Marriage and Family Living,* November, 1959.

————. "Research on Young Marriage: Implications for Family Life Education," *Family Life Coordinator,* September, 1960.

Burgess, Ernest W., and Paul Wallin. *Courtship, Engagement and Marriage.* Philadelphia: J. B. Lippincott, 1953.

Burt, Jesse C. "Sex and Teen-age Marriage." *American Mercury,* January, 1957.

Butler, Richard. O.P. *God on the Secular Campus.* Garden City (N.Y.): Doubleday & Co., Inc., 1963.

"Case of College Morals or The Snag in the Blue Stocking, The," *Glamour Magazine,* August, 1962.

Christensen, Harold T. "Cultural Relativism and Premarital Sex Norms," *American Sociological Review,* February, 1960.

————, and George R. Carpenter. "Timing Patterns in the Development of Sexual Intimacy: An Attitudinal Report on Three Modern Western Societies," *Marriage and Family Living,* February, 1962.

Cole, William Graham. "Early Marriage," *The Nation Magazine,* February 8, 1958.

Congdon, Tom. "Bermuda—Where the Girls Are," *Saturday Evening Post,* May 26, 1962.

Davis, Kingsley. "Adolescence and the Social Structure," in *Adoles-*

cent: A Book of Readings, edited by Jerome M. Seidman. N.Y.: Holt, Rinehart and Winston, Inc., 1960.

De Ropp, Robert S. *Drugs and the Mind*. N.Y.: St. Martin's Press, 1957.

Didion, Joan. "Berkeley's Giant: The University of California," *Mademoiselle Magazine*, January, 1960.

Didman, Jean. "The Relationship Between Religious Attitude and Attitude Toward Premarital Sex Relations," *Marriage and Family Living*, May, 1959.

Dubbe, Marvin. "What Do Your Adolescents Tell You?," *E. C. Brown Trust Co.*, Portland, Ore.

Duvalls, Evelyn M., and Sylvanus M. (eds.). *Sex Ways—In Fact and Faith*. N.Y.: Association Press, 1961.

Eckman, Fern Marja. "What College Students Think," *The New York Post*, October, 1961. (With Judy Michaelson, Marvin Smilon, Dolores Alexander, Anthony Scaduto, and Sarah Schoenkopf)

Ehrmann, Winston, *Premarital Dating Behavior*. N.Y.: Henry Holt, 1959.

———. "Premarital Sexual Behavior and Sex Codes of Conduct with Acquaintances, Friends and Lovers," *Social Forces*, December, 1959.

———. "Changing Sexual Mores," in *Values and Ideals of American Youth*, E. Ginzberg (ed.). N.Y.: Columbia University Press, 1961.

Ellis, Albert. *The Folklore of Sex*. N.Y.: Charles Boni, 1951.

———. *The American Sexual Tragedy*. N.Y.: Twayne, 1954.

———. *Sex Without Guilt*. N.Y.: Lyle Stuart, 1958.

———. *Sex and the Single Man*. N.Y.: Lyle Stuart, 1963.

Ellison, Jerome. "Troubles of Sun-Tan U," *Saturday Evening Post*, September 16, 1961.

Escalona, Sibylle. "Children and the Threat of Nuclear War," *Child Study Association Publication*, in cooperation with The National Institute of Mental Health, 1962.

Ford, Clellan S., and Frank A. Beach. *Patterns of Sexual Behavior*. N.Y.: Harper & Brothers, 1951.

Friedan, Betty. *The Feminine Mystique*. N.Y.: W. W. Norton & Co., Inc., 1963.

Friedenberg, Edgar Z. *The Vanishing Adolescent*. Boston: Beacon Press, 1959.

Garraty, John A., and Walter Adams. *From Main Street to the Left Bank*. East Lansing (Mich.): Michigan State University Press, 1959.

BIBLIOGRAPHY

Gebhard, Paul H., Wardell B. Pomeroy, Clyde E. Martin, and Cornelia V. Christenson. *Pregnancy, Birth and Abortion.* N.Y.: Harper & Brothers, 1958.

Genne, Elizabeth Steel and Henry (eds.). "Foundations for Christian Family Policy," *The Proceedings of the North American Conference on Church and Family,* April 30–May 5, 1961, National Council of the Churches of Christ in the U.S.A.

Gilmore, Mildred. "Why Can't They Wait to Wed?," *Parents Magazine,* November, 1958.

Gordon, Mrs. Katherine K. and Dr. Richard E. *The Blight on the Ivy.* N.Y.: Prentice-Hall, 1963.

Grafton, Samuel. "Why Teen-Age Marriages Are Falling Apart," *McCalls Magazine,* November, 1959.

Greenwald, Harold, *The Call Girl.* N.Y.: Ballantine Books, 1958.

Guitar, Mary Anne. "College Marriage Courses," *Mademoiselle Magazine,* February, 1961.

Guttmacher, Dr. Alan F. *Babies by Choice or by Chance.* Garden City (N.Y.): Doubleday & Co., Inc., 1959.

———. *The Complete Book of Birth Control.* N.Y.: Ballantine Books, 1961.

Havemann, Ernest, *Men, Women and Marriage.* Garden City (N.Y.): Doubleday & Co., Inc., 1962.

Hechinger, Fred M. "Affluent Delinquency," *New York Times,* September 5, 1963

Hechinger, Grace and Fred M. "125 Years of Holyoke Girls," *The New York Times Magazine,* February 11, 1962.

———. "College Morals Mirror Our Society," *The New York Times Magazine,* April 14, 1963.

Hunt, Morton M. *The Natural History of Love.* N.Y.: Alfred A. Knopf, Inc., 1959.

——— and Rena Corman. "The Tormented Generation," *The Saturday Evening Post,* October 12, 1963.

Johnson, Nora. "Sex and the College Girl," *The Atlantic Monthly,* November, 1959.

Journal of the National Association of Women Deans and Counselors, January, 1963:

Christensen, Harold T. "Premarital Sex Norms in America and Scandinavia."

Christenson, Cornelia V. "Premarital Pregnancies and Their Outcome."

Ehrmann, Winston W. "The Variety and Meaning of Premarital Heterosexual Experiences for the College Student."

Kirkendall, Lester A. "College Youth and Sexual Confusion."

Mueller, Kate Hevner. "The Role of the Counselor in Sex Behavior and Standards."

Rubin, Isadore. "Sex and the College Student: A Bibliography of New Findings and Insights."

Solomon, Edward C. "Educational Needs of College Women for Marriage and Family Planning."

Kanin, Eugene J. "Male, Aggression in Dating-Courtship Relations," *American Journal of Sociology,* September, 1957.

————. "Premarital Sex Adjustments, Social Class and Associated Behaviors," *Marriage and Family Living,* August, 1960.

————, and David H. Howard. "Postmarital Consequences of Premarital Sex Adjustments," *American Sociological Review,* October, 1958.

Karen, Robert L. "Some Variables Affecting Sexual Attitudes, Behavior and Inconsistency," *Marriage and Family Living,* August, 1959.

Kinsey, Alfred C., Wardell B. Pomeroy, Clyde E. Martin, and Paul H. Gebhard. *Sexual Behavior in the Human Female.* Philadelphia: W. B. Saunders Co., 1953.

Kirkendall, Lester A. "Where Should We Go in Sex Education?," *The Coordinator,* December, 1957.

————. "A Suggested Approach to the Teaching of Sexual Morality," *Journal of Family Welfare,* Bombay, India, June, 1959.

————. "Sex Education of Adolescents: An Exchange," *Marriage and Family Living,* November, 1960.

————. "Reply to Mower and Poffenberger," *Marriage and Family Living,* November, 1960.

————. *Premarital Intercourse and Interpersonal Relationships.* N.Y.: The Julian Press, Inc., 1961.

Kirkpatrick, Clifford, and Eugene Kanin. "Male Sex Aggression on a University Campus," *American Sociological Review,* February, 1957.

Klein, Roger (ed.). *Young Americans Abroad.* N.Y.: Harper & Row, 1963.

Krich, A. M. (ed.). *Women, The Variety and Meaning of Their Sexual Experience.* N.Y.: Dell Books, 1953.

————. *Men, The Variety and Meaning of Their Sexual Experience.* N.Y.: Dell Books, 1954.

Kronhausen, Drs. Phyllis and Eberhard. *Sex Histories of American College Men.* N.Y.: Ballantine Books, 1960.

BIBLIOGRAPHY

Langer, Lawrence. *The Importance of Wearing Clothes.* N.Y.: Hastings House, 1959.

Lerner, Max. "Cornell Story," *The New York Post,* October 15, 1962.

———. "Gilded Rebel," *The New York Post,* April 26, 1963.

———. "Return of the Femme Fatale," *The Ladies Home Journal,* June, 1963.

———. "College Morals," *The New York Post,* November 15, 1963.

Levin, Alan, and John Cashman. "Delinquency in Suburbia," *The New York Post,* June 24–28, 1963.

Levine, Milton, and Maya Pines. "Sex: The Problem Colleges Evade," *Harper's Magazine,* October, 1961.

Lewis, Anthony. "Sex . . . and the Supreme Court," *Esquire Magazine,* June, 1963.

"Look What's Going on at Radcliffe," *Life Magazine,* January 4, 1963.

Lovejoy, Clarence E. *Lovejoy's College Guide.* N.Y.: Simon and Schuster, 1962–63.

Lynch, Nancy. "Lady Chatterley Goes to College." *Mademoiselle Magazine,* August, 1963.

Lyons, John O. *The College Novel in America.* Carbondale (Ill.): Southern Illinois University Press, 1962.

Mace, Dr. David R. "Let's Take a Sane Look at the Hysterical Quest for a Husband," *McCalls Magazine,* September, 1962.

Martinson, Floyd M. "Ego Deficiency as a Factor in Marriage," *American Sociological Review,* April, 1955.

———. "Ego Deficiency as a Factor in Marriage—a Male Sample," *Marriage and Family Living,* February, 1959.

Mayer, Martin "Getting Alienated with the Right Crowd at Harvard," *Esquire Magazine,* September, 1963.

McClellan, James E., Jr., and Solon T. Kimball. *Education and the New America.* N.Y.: Random House, 1963.

McIntosh, Millicent. "Out of a Morals Revolution: A Moral Revelation," *Glamour Magazine,* January, 1963.

Mead, Margaret. "Sex on the Campus: The Real Issue," *Redbook Magazine,* October, 1962.

Montagu, Ashley. "Has Chastity a Chance at College?," *McCalls Magazine,* September, 1963.

Morris, Terry. "What Clergymen Tell Young People about Marriage," *Redbook Magazine,* March, 1963.

Moskin, J. Robert. "Morality USA," *Look Magazine,* September 24, 1963.

Moss, Allyn. "Whatever Happened to Courtship?," *Mademoiselle Magazine,* April, 1963.

Moss, J. Joel, and Ruby Gingles. "The Relationship of Personality to the Incidence of Early Marriage," *Marriage and Family Living,* November, 1959.

Newcomb, Theodore M., Eugene L. Hartley, and others. *Readings in Social Psychology,* N.Y.: Henry Holt & Co., 1947.

O'Reilly, Jane. "A Very Attractive Cooky Cutter" (Profile of Trinity College in Washington, D.C.), *Mademoiselle Magazine,* June, 1963.

Parkinson, Margaret B. "Bryn Mawr's Barefoot Intellectuals," *Mademoiselle Magazine,* October, 1962.

Parton, Margaret. "Why Do They Marry So Young?," *The Ladies Home Journal,* November, 1958.

Peck, Joseph H. *Life with Women and How to Survive It.* Englewood Cliffs (N.J.): Prentice-Hall, 1961.

Perenyi, Eleanor. "Maybe," *Esquire Magazine,* July, 1962.

Poffenberger, Thomas. "Family Life Education in This Scientific Age," *Marriage and Family Living,* May, 1959.

———. "Individual Choice in Adolescent Premarital Sex Behavior," *Marriage and Family Living,* November, 1960.

———, et al. "Premarital Sexual Behavior: A Symposium," *Marriage and Family Living,* August, 1962.

Reevy, W. R. "Premarital Petting Behavior and Marital Happiness Prediction," *Marriage and Family Living,* November, 1959.

Reik, Theodore. *Of Love and Lust.* N.Y.: Farrar, Straus and Company, 1949.

———. *Sex in Man and Woman, Its Emotional Variations.* N.Y.: Farrar, Straus and Cudahy, Inc., 1960.

Reiss, Ira L. "The Treatment of Premarital Coitus in 'Marriage and Family' Texts," *Social Problems,* April, 1957.

———. *Premarital Sexual Standards in America.* The Free Press of Glencoe, Illinois, 1960.

Riesman, David. "Permissiveness and Sex Roles," *Marriage and Family Living,* August, 1959.

———, With Nathan Glazer and Reuel Denney. *The Lonely Crowd.* New Haven: Yale University Press, 1950.

Rinehart, Jonathan. "Mothers without Joy," *The Saturday Evening Post,* March 23, 1963.

Sanford, Nevitt (ed.). *The American College.* N.Y.: John Wiley & Sons, 1962.

BIBLIOGRAPHY

Spock, Dr. Benjamin. "America's Spoiled Parents," *The Ladies Home Journal,* June, 1963.

Steinem, Gloria. "The Moral Disarmament of Betty Coed," *Esquire Magazine,* September, 1962.

Stokes, Walter R., and David R. Mace. "Premarital Sexual Behavior," *Marriage and Family Living,* August, 1953.

Stone, W. L. "Sex Ignorance of College Students," *Family Life,* October, 1960.

Susskind, David. "Banned Program: The Sexual Revolution in America," *Mademoiselle Magazine,* October, 1963.

Talese, Gay. "Accommodation—Italian Style," *Esquire Magazine,* February, 1963.

Tebor, Irving B. "Male Virgins: Conflicts and Group Support in American Culture," *Family Life Coordinator,* March–June, 1961.

Vincent, Clark E. *Unmarried Mothers.* The Free Press of Glencoe, Illinois, 1961.

Voss, Virginia. "University of Chicago," *Mademoiselle Magazine,* February, 1956.

————. "Hunter College," *Mademoiselle Magazine,* October, 1957.

————. "Kalamazoo College," *Mademoiselle Magazine,* February, 1959.

Wakefield, Dan. "Dan Wakefield's Sophisticated Lady," *Esquire Magazine,* July, 1962.

"What Every Girl Should Know," *Seventeen Magazine,* July, 1958.

"What Girls Think about Sex," *Seventeen Magazine,* July, 1959.

Whitbread, Jane. "A Report on Current Attitudes Toward Chastity," *Mademoiselle Magazine,* July, 1959.

Willis, Ellen. "The Birth Control Pill," *Mademoiselle Magazine,* January, 1961.

Extensive bibliographies are to be found in the Kinsey volumes, Reiss's *Premarital Sexual Standards in America,* Kirkendall's *Premarital Intercourse and Interpersonal Relationships,"* Vincent's *Unmarried Mothers,* Bell's *Marriage and Family Interaction,* and the Duvalls' *Sex Ways in Fact and Faith.*

RELATED FICTION

Brickner, Richard P. *The Broken Year*. Garden City (N.Y.): Doubleday & Co., Inc., 1962.

Brodky, Harold. "A Sentimental Education," *The New Yorker Magazine*, July 6, 1957, *First Love and Other Sorrows*, The Dial
Press, Inc., N.Y.: 1958.

Deal, Babs H. *The Grail*. N.Y.: David McKay Company, Inc., 1963.

Faulkner, William. *Sanctuary*, J. Cape and H. Smith, 1931. N.Y.:
Modern Library Inc., 1932.

Frede, Richard. *Entry E*. N.Y.: Random House, 1958.

Glassman, Joyce. *Come and Join the Dance*. N.Y.: Atheneum, 1962.

Goodman, Aubrey. *The Golden Youth of Lee Prince*. N.Y.: Simon &
Schuster, 1959.

Gover, Robert. *One Hundred Dollar Misunderstanding*. N.Y.: Grove
Press, 1962.

Gutwillig, Robert. *After Long Silence*. Boston: Little, Brown & Co.,
Co., 1958.

Hall, Oakley. *The Corpus of Joe Bailey*. N.Y.: Viking Press, 1953.

Jackson, Shirley. *Hangsaman*. N.Y.: Farrar, Straus and Young, 1951.

Jarrell, Randall. *Pictures from an Institution*. N.Y.: Alfred A. Knopf,
1954.

Johnson, Nora. *A Step Beyond Innocence*. Boston: Little, Brown &
Co., 1961

Kaufmann, Myron S. *Remember Me to God*. Philadelphia: J. B. Lippincott Co., 1957.

Kozol, Jonathan. *The Fume of Poppies*. Boston: Houghton Mifflin Co.,
1958.

Kubly, Herbert. *The Whistling Zone*. N.Y.: Simon & Schuster, 1963.

Leslie, Warren. *Love or Whatever It Is*. N.Y.: McGraw-Hill, 1960.

Lumbard, Charles G. *Senior Spring*. N.Y.: Simon & Schuster, 1954.

Lurie, Alison. *Love and Friendship*. N.Y.: Macmillan Co., 1962.

Macauley, Robie. *The Disguises of Love.* N.Y.: Random House, 1952.

McCarthy, Mary. *The Groves of Academe.* N.Y.: Harcourt, Brace & Co., 1952.

————. *The Group.* N.Y.: Harcourt, Brace and World, 1963.

Mailer, Norman. "The Time of Her Time," from *Advertisements for Myself.* N.Y.: G. P. Putnam's Sons, 1959.

Malamud, Bernard. *A New Life.* N.Y.: Farrar, Straus & Cudahy, 1961.

Manchester, William R. *The Long Gainer.* Boston: Little, Brown & Co., 1961.

Miller, Nolan. *Why I Am So Beat.* N.Y.: G. P. Putnam's Sons, 1954.

Miller, Warren. *The Bright Young Things.* Boston: Little, Brown & Co., 1958.

Perutz, Kathrin. *The Garden.* N.Y.: Atheneum, 1962.

Roth, Philip. *Goodbye, Columbus.* Boston: Houghton Mifflin Co., 1960.

————. *Letting Go.* N.Y.: Random House, 1962.

St. John, Leonie. (pseud.) *Love with a Harvard Accent.* N.Y.: Ace Books, 1962.

Sherman, Susan. *Give Me Myself.* Cleveland (Ohio): World Publishing Co., 1961.

Solomon, Barbara P. *The Beat of Life.* Philadelphia: J. B. Lippincott Co., 1960.

Sullivan, Scott. *The Shortest, Gladdest Years.* N.Y.: Simon & Schuster, 1962.

Swarthout, Glendon. *Where the Boys Are.* N.Y.: Random House, 1960.

Thompson, Charles. *Halfway Down the Stairs.* N.Y.: Harper & Brothers, 1957.

Wolfe, Bernard. *The Magic of Their Singing.* N.Y.: Charles Scribner's Sons, 1961.

For an extensive list of college novels, beginning with Nathaniel Hawthorne's *Fanshawe* (1828) and including such prim period pieces as *Two College Girls* (1886) by Helen Dawes Brown and *Nelly Brown: or The Trials, Temptations and Pleasures of College Life* by Tim Whippoorwill (pseud.) see:

Lyons, John O. *The College Novel in America.* Carbondale (Ill.): Southern Illinois University Press, 1962.